Mussolini's Empire

The Rise and Fall of the Fascist Vision

Edwin P. Hoyt

John Wiley & Sons, Inc.
New York • Chichester • Brisbane • Toronto • Singapore

Copyright © 1994 by Edwin P. Hoyt
Published by John Wiley & Sons, Inc.

Library of Congress Cataloging-in-Publication Data:
Hoyt, Edwin Palmer.
    Mussolini's empire : the rise and fall of the fascist vision /
Edwin P. Hoyt.
      p. cm.
    Includes bibliographical references and index.
    ISBN 0-471-59151-3
    1. Mussolini, Benito, 1883–1945. 2. Heads of state—Italy–
Biography. 3. Fascism—Italy—History. 4. Italy–
History—1914–1945.   I. Title.
    DG575.M8A63   1994
  945.091'092—dc20
  [B]
                            93–11881

Printed in the United States of America
10 9 8 7 6 5 4 3 2 1

This book is for Merrill and Donna Needham,
who sheltered me in a time of need.

∽

I am indebted to Merrill and Donna Needham for finding many needed books in the shops in the Washington, D.C., area. Archivists at the U.S. National Archives responded faithfully and promptly to my requests and supplied the materials I needed. The libraries of Montgomery County, Maryland, were very helpful and I am indebted to a number of librarians there for information and assistance. I also would like to thank the Italian Embassy in Washington, D.C., and the library of International House, Tokyo.

Contents

Introduction

This is the story of one of the most powerful and interesting men of the twentieth century: Benito Amilcare Andrea Mussolini, son of an Italian peasant blacksmith, radical, womanizer, politician, dictator, and, finally, political philosopher. The mark he left on the century was profound; he was the inventor of a totalitarian political system that brought Italy out of poverty and depression to a position of world leadership. His fascism was a model for Adolf Hitler and General Francisco Franco of Spain. Hitler was in awe of him all his life, even after Mussolini's dreadful error of dragging Italy into a war that the Italian people neither wanted nor were capable of fighting. If fascism was the bête noir of the Western democracies in the late 1930s and 1940s, that fact was ignored in the 1920s when such men as Winston Churchill came to pay their respects to Mussolini. Churchill said that if he had been an Italian in these years, he would have been a Fascist. Even Mahatma Gandhi called him "one of the great statesmen of all time."

From the beginning Mussolini was ruthless in his political life. He began as a rebel against his society, with an overweening hatred of the rich and powerful. He joined the socialist movement and rose high in its ranks. But he then discarded socialism as an Italian nationalist, because the Socialists opposed Italy's entry into World War I, and Mussolini believed the only way Italy could emerge as a power was to fight and help the Western allies win the war. He formed his own political party, which was dedicated to state socialism, through which he hoped to level income and wealth in Italy. He never cared for wealth; power was his God, and when he achieved it, his worst sin was to abuse it and create a dictatorship that developed into the one-man rule over a

1

nation of forty million people. Yet, although he was the son of an atheist, he was deeply religious at times and, on behalf of the people of Italy, healed a long-standing breach between the Church of Rome and the government of Italy. He came to power in a bloodless coup d'état occasioned by the collapse of representative government in Italy. But all during his twenty-one years of leadership of Italy, he ruled within the limits of the Italian Constitution; his extraordinary powers were given to him and repeatedly endorsed by the King, to whom he reported weekly.

∽

Mussolini began his political life with great respect for France and England, Italy's allies of World War I, but he became disillusioned and was driven from them by their failure to respond to the aspirations of Italy, their greed in cutting up Europe and Africa, and their harsh dealing with Germany in the Treaty of Versailles. Italy had been induced to join the war on the side of the Western democracies by promises of an empire, which were forgotten when the peace was made. Britain and France trampled Germany in the dirt and then expressed surprise in the 1930s when Hitler was brought to power by a resentful people. Once Hitler achieved power he set out to right the wrongs of Versailles, but then he went much further. It was Mussolini who singlehandedly stopped him in 1934, when the French and British refused to act to prevent the rape of Austria. At that time, Mussolini proposed an equal alliance of all the major powers of Europe, including Germany, but the plan was torpedoed by the arrogance of France and Britain, and Mussolini was shoved by them into the arms of a Hitler he never liked.

His character was quixotic in the extreme. He could be generous, as when he would give all the money in his pocket to an unfortunate he met on the street. "I have been hungry," he said sometimes. "I know the look of a hungry man when I see one." But he could also send his best friends to prison for failing to honor his fascist principles; it is certain that in the early years of his power (1923–24) he established a *cheka*, "the squadraccia of the Viminale," a small terrorist group of high-level Fascists who operated from the building of the Ministry of Interior to frighten Mussolini's enemies, and to punish them physically. This group administered beatings, dosed its victims with castor oil, and committed acts of vandalism. One of its most publicized adventures was to invade and vandalize the home of former Prime Minister Francesco Nitti. The group was also responsible for the death of Socialist Deputy Giacomo Matteotti, who was kidnapped and killed in

1924, providing the most celebrated case ever publicized against Mussolini's method of ruling. But what is almost never mentioned in judgment is how little of this violence there was in comparison with other dictatorial and oligarchic governments.

Mussolini's twenty-one-year rule was marked infrequently by acts of violence, much less often than the regimes of Stalin, Hitler, or Generalissimo Franco. As dictators went, Mussolini was *very humane,* and there was far less brutality in Italy than in Soviet Russia, Germany, or Spain. This can be attributed in part to the nature of the Italian people, long suffering and willing to live under whatever establishment is in control. Despite his intense radicalism, Mussolini was that way himself, and even at the height of his power he communicated to the Italian people that what he was doing, he was doing for Italy. At the end he sacrificed himself for Italy, knowing full well that his Salò Republic was a charade, but knowing better than anyone else that if he did not conform to Hitler's wishes, the wrath of Germany would descend on his Italian people.

Another reason for his humanness was that for much of his political regime, the majority of the Italian people were solidly behind him: first, because of their disgust with the inanity of their parliamentary democracy, and, second, because his government brought Italy out of the depths and gave her factories that ran, trains that met their schedules, and better living conditions. All of this came to an end when Mussolini forced Italy into World War II. Thereafter, his popularity descended steadily and rapidly, as millions of Italians saw their sons killed or captured by the enemy. One whole Italian army, sent to fight in Russia, simply disappeared, ground up in the battle of Stalingrad; virtually none of the survivors ever reached home again.

As a political figure Mussolini combined great sagacity with acts of complete blindness. His success was due to his early realization that the parliamentary democracy of Italy had run its course and was incapable of governing. His great mistake was to force Italy into World War II when it was totally unnecessary for Italy's survival or prosperity and served only to maintain his own illusion of creating a new Roman Empire. Some called him nothing but a ham actor, and the portrayal of him on the American screen by comedian Jack Oakie in the movie *The Great Dictator* has more than a grain of truth. He was a strutting, vain, and sometimes laughable creature. But even in his playacting as leader there was method. He recognized in his audience, the Italian people, a love for the dramatic. The newsreels were full of him, threshing grain in the field. But, through just such performances, the "Battle of the Wheat" was won, and Italy's production increased enormously.

Personally he was very brave, although many in the end, including his daughter Edda, called him a coward. His abandonment of Count Galeazzo Ciano to the vengeance of the Germans can be put down to cowardice, but his own estimate was that he was serving the greater good of Italy, which at that moment was supine at the feet of Hitler. The German dictator had already threatened to destroy industrial north Italy if Mussolini refused to form the Salò Republic, and Mussolini knew Hitler was capable of turning his V-2 missiles on Milan, Turin, and Genoa, as Hitler intimated he would do.

Mussolini never had any illusions about himself or the Italian people. Although for a time he thought he could make Legionaries out of his soldiers, he was soon convinced that his Italians were not good cannon fodder. He called them "a nation of sheep," but his answer was that one has to drive sheep. In his early years, he was a real leader and never lost his gift for the spectacular oration. He communicated his hope for Roman greatness to his people and had them thinking in the 1930s that Italy was the leader of nations. In a way there was substance to the claim; for example, Italo Balbo, an aviator and Minister of Air, impressed the world with his development of air routes and long-distance flights, paving the way for commercial air operations. The Italian merchant navy was one of the best in the world.

Mussolini's personal characteristics—his forcefulness, and a "little-boy" air—made him enormously attractive to women, and his affairs of the heart were almost countless. Claretta Petacci, the mistress who followed him and died with him before the firing squad of the partisans, complained about his unfaithfulness to her. And his wife Rachele suffered through Clara and a dozen other mistresses of whom she was aware (in the end she pleaded with him to flee and save himself, which he refused to do).

As far as the outer world is concerned, Mussolini's prime claim to greatness occurred in 1933 and 1934 when he saw a Germany emerging from the ashes of World War I. Despite a vengeful and selfish France and a confused Britain, Mussolini attempted to forge a four-power European alliance that would effectively maintain the peace and curb Hitler's ambitions. At the time Hitler welcomed the pact, but it was so mangled and manipulated by the British and French, it became meaningless even before it was signed. This was really a last chance to safeguard the peace by negotiation. That year, Hitler attempted a coup d'état to take over Austria and would have succeeded had not Mussolini sent forty thousand troops to the Brenner Pass to warn Germany. Hitler then pulled back, but two years later he tried his muscles again, this time marching into the demilitarized Rhineland. Italy had no direct stake there and no way of interfering, and the French simply lay down and let the Germans walk in. Hitler later admitted that had they moved a muscle he would have drawn back.

By 1936 Mussolini had assessed the governments of Europe and found no strength in France or England. After their abortive and timid attempts to interfere in Mussolini's conquest of Ethiopia, he had no further affection for them, and little respect. As he saw the countries lining up, he found no more virtue in Western capitalism than he ever had. So he lined up with the other "have not" nations: Japan and Germany.

Mussolini played one other role in the attempt to secure the peace of Europe, in 1938. Hitler was poised to attack Czechoslovakia. France was so morally corrupt she could not act, and Britain was too divided to take strong action, so the British appealed to Mussolini to intervene with Hitler, which he did, stopping the wheels of the war machine, and giving the Western Allies another chance for peace. At Hitler's request, Mussolini managed the Munich Conference. He had no stake in the outcome and he cannot be blamed for the failure of the Western powers to stand up to Hitler. But seeing the performance of Britain and France, and the successes of Germany and Japan, he felt that he was about to be isolated by an unfriendly West; thus, he went into the alliance with Germany in the spring of 1939 that became the Tripartite Pact. The rest is the history of World War II.

At the end, having become a political philosopher, Mussolini knew that fascism had failed and why: His excesses had deprived the movement of its virility and the party's excesses had driven it to corruption, which cost fascism the faith of the people. He saw the new Western Allies, America and Britain, planning to remake the world once again and predicted their clash with Stalin. His only error was one of degree; he expected a third world war, not knowing that the second war had so destroyed Britain's virility that the clash would end up being a stand-off between the Russians and the Americans. He had none of the myopia about a "brave new world" that afflicted most other countries.

Toward the end Mussolini assessed himself in an interview with the wife of the German press attaché at Lake Garda. He told her that he realized that he should have curbed his ambitions after establishing his empire in Africa and strengthening it with the addition of Albania; that he should have foresworn ambition and devoted himself to strengthening his government and bringing about the social changes he wanted to equalize incomes and social status of all Italy. But, he asked in a burst of self-revelation, did anyone ever know of a dictator in history who could practice moderation?

His last two years were spent in full realization that he had failed Italy, and that he had failed in his own attempts to save the Italian people from the wrath of Adolf Hitler. But really, in this, he succeeded as well as any man could have by sacrificing himself and his ego for the Italy that he had tried to make into something she was not and did not want to be. In essence, *Mussolini's Empire* is the story of an intelligent and charismatic leader gone wrong. He deserves a better rating by history than he has yet been given in the West. Perhaps in the twenty-first century, the patina worn from the age of the British Empire and the age of America, he will receive a new consideration for his real attempt to preserve the peace and stability of Europe in the 1930s.

Edwin P. Hoyt
Tokyo, 1993

PART I

The Formative Years

CHAPTER 1

∽

Boy of Predappio

In the summer of 1883 in the hamlet of Varano de Costa, above the village of Dovia in the county of Predappio in Romagna in northeast Italy, stood an old stone palazzo. It was three stories tall and still bore a certain faded elegance with its mossy walls and balustraded staircase. Here, on the afternoon of July 29, a male child was born to Alessandro Mussolini and his wife Rosa. Like everything else about this child, and later this man, the circumstances of the family are surrounded in conflict and nothing is as it appears on the surface.

The Mussolinis were so different from each other in virtually every way that it seems almost unbelievable that their marriage survived. Rosa's life was not an unhappy one. She was a devout Roman Catholic and a primary school teacher. Her father had been the Forlì veterinary surgeon, and so she grew up in more than modest circumstances. She studied at the Forlì schools and was given a diploma qualifying her to teach the first three grades of elementary school. While teaching at Dovia, a nearby village, she met Alessandro and married him in 1882 over the objections of her parents.

Alessandro was a child of a once-prominent Romagna family that had fallen on hard times. Many years later his son, then dictator of Italy, unearthed a family coat of arms—six black figures in a yellow field—symbols of valor, courage, and force, all qualities that Mussolini lived by.

In the thirteenth century Giovanni Mussolini had ruled Bologna, but later the family was exiled to Argelato and afterward scattered over northern Italy. Alessandro's branch of the family became farmers in Predappio and he was trained as a blacksmith, which is how he earned

9

his living in that principally farming community. Rural Romagna was a center of radical republicanism, a political philosophy that was in keeping with the people's rugged individualism and opposition to the established order. "When they start a new town in Romagna they first throw up a monument to Garibaldi and then build a church, because there is no fun in a civil funeral unless it spites the parish priest. The whole history of the province is concerned with spite of this kind." So wrote a nineteenth-century Italian critic about these nonconforming northerners.

Alessandro Mussolini had little education but did have a burning desire to change the world. In the cellar of the palazzo under his blacksmith shop was buried his most cherished possession, a red silk flag of the international socialist revolution. Above the nuptial bed hung a likeness of Giuseppi Garibaldi, the leader in the movement for Italian unification and independence. Next to it Rosa had hung a portrait of the Virgin Mary. Their child was named Benito Amilcare Andrea in honor of his father's hero Benito Juarez, the Mexican revolutionary, and two revolutionary Italian Socialists, Amilcare Cipriani and Andrea Costa. Benito's younger brother was named for Arnaldo de Brescia, a local hero in the revolutionary struggle with the pope.

As small children, the Mussolinis were brought up in the church, a concession of the atheist Alessandro to his religious wife. Once Benito grumbled: "With so many prayers we'll go to heaven, even if we never get on our knees again in our lives." But as Alessandro had hoped, as soon as Benito was able he abandoned religion for socialist politics. In early childhood the boys had been steeped in socialism by their father and his friends. Alessandro's socialism was essentially benign: "Science illuminating the world, reason mastering faith; free thought overthrowing prejudice; free agreement among men to live a truly civilized life; true justice enthroned on earth; a sublime harmony of concept, thought and action." He established a local branch of the Socialist International. He drafted socialist manifestoes, wrote articles in the socialist magazines, attacked the bourgeoisie and the Catholic clergy, and took an active part in local government and politics. His son was brought up to be a Socialist and at an early age said he was. However, that was illusory, for Mussolini was a revolutionary, not a Socialist. He used the Socialists only as long as it benefited him, then abandoned them, founded his own revolutionary movement, and led Italy in his own way.

In later years Mussolini could say, although he never would, that he was born in a palace. But that, too, was illusory, for the Mussolinis were dirt-poor and rented three rooms and the blacksmith shop in the building. The apartment housed the family, which included Benito's brother Arnaldo and sister Edvige and Rosa's mother. The boys shared a straw pallet in the kitchen of the apartment. Their noon meal was bread and vegetable soup, ladled out of the big stoneware tureen, and supper was salad. On Sundays the family ate meat, usually a cheap cut of boiled mutton.

As a baby, Benito was so slow to speak that his parents worried and took him to the local doctor. Looking at the stubborn face of the child, he comforted them by saying, "He will speak when he wants to. Perhaps then you will find that he will talk too much."

Benito's early memories were of playing on the stone steps of the palazzo. In the cold winter weather of the Apennine hill country he ran and skipped to keep warm. As soon as he was able, his mother taught him the alphabet, which he recalled as "my first practice in worldly affairs." He was enrolled in her school, where he often created chaos by pinching the other children and pulling the girls' hair. His own memory is of growing up a restless and unruly child. By the time he was eight years old he was an accomplished sneak thief, preying on the neighbors' gardens and orchards. He was always a loner; sometimes he would retire to the belfry of the church to read for hours. But, even as a boy, he was subject to fits of compassion. One day he saw an old neighbor named Filippino, sweating over his garden with a spade. He took the spade and dug the garden for the old man, who watched as he sat puffing on his pipe.

His one friend was his much gentler brother Arnaldo. They walked to school in Predappio, two miles away. There Benito usually got into fights with the other boys and was often beaten, but never beaten down. Arnaldo would sponge away the mud and try to hide the bruises that so upset their mother. Benito grew up with a fierce independence and hatred for wealth, but would become a lavish spender and lover of opulence. He wrote in his autobiography, "I detest those who live like parasites, sucking away at the edges of social struggles. I hate men who grow rich in politics."

He loved struggle for its own sake. Once, as a small child, an older boy took away his tiny wooden cart and Benito ran crying to his father. Alessandro gave him no sympathy. "Men have to defend themselves—not ask for pity," he said. "Don't come back to me until you've licked him." So Benito sharpened a flint rock, grasped it in his right fist, and attacked his enemy, leaving him bloody and beaten. This love of combat for its own sake never was to leave him, but it was to be the perpetual sorrow of his mother.

When Benito was nine years old he came home from school one day with two black eyes, and his mother decided he needed the discipline of a boarding school. She and Alessandro had already talked over the prospects, and although they were very poor, Alessandro felt that the boy had a future. His mother wanted him to become a priest, so Benito packed his suitcase to leave for the school run by the Salesian priests in Faenza, twenty miles away. Alessandro, who got out the family cart and the old horse and drove his son to school, on the way counseled his son, "Pay attention to what they teach you, especially geography and history, but don't let them stuff your head with nonsense about God and the saints."

"Don't worry, Papa," Benito said. "I know there is no such person as God."

∽

At the school Benito's first shock was to discover the enormous gulf between Italy's rich and poor. The pupils were divided into three sections according to the wealth of their families. The delineation was most evident in the dining hall, where the first section ate very well, the second section ate fairly well, but Benito's section was fed scraps at a board trestle table. This sequestration, combined with what he had learned from his father's evening discussions with the parlor revolutionaries who were his cronies, made Benito Mussolini into a bitter enemy of the upper class and a real revolutionary. He never forgot his days of misery at that school.

"It no longer worries me that the third grade children had ants in their bread," he recalled when he was master of all Italy, "but the fact that we were graded at all still rankles."

His reaction was to declare war on authority. He spent his days in trouble with the class teacher. One day he was hit with a ruler and retaliated by throwing an ink pot, which struck his tormentor and brought down the wrath of all the school authority. The director decided to expel this unruly student, but Rosa's pleas saved him, and Benito was given the choice of twelve days' punishment or of humbling himself and asking the schoolmaster's pardon. He refused to apologize and took the twelve days' punishment, kneeling for four hours a day on a carpet of cracked corn that dug into his knees. After the tenth day his knees were bleeding, but he still refused to give in and suffered the entire punishment in silence.

If the Fathers had expected punishment to correct the boy's ways, they were wrong. Soon he was brought up again for a breach of discipline and was condemned to sleep in the yard. He even antagonized the watchdogs, who chased him over the gate, and bit out the seat of his trousers before he escaped. For fighting with other boys he was sentenced to spend the recreation breaks alone, face to the wall, in a corner of the playground. The rebellion continued, until the summer of 1894 when, in a quarrel with a fellow pupil, he stabbed the other boy in the buttocks with a pocket knife. Then Mussolini was expelled from the school.

But while Mussolini was rebelling he also was learning. By the time he returned from the Salesian Fathers' school, he was proficient enough in French to undertake the reading of Victor Hugo's *Les Misérables*, which was Alessandro's idea of proper reading for a boy of a revolutionary father. The scenes of misery in Louis XVI's France particularly appealed to the boy, and he sometimes was found in the cowshed and marketplace giving readings from the book to all who would listen. In the Italy of the 1890s, a country dominated by the clergy and the nobility, Hugo's celebration of the revolution was much admired and it lost nothing in the translation by this enthusiastic youngster.

At about this time Benito's growing consciousness of the world around him was expanded by a visit to his mother's relatives in Ravenna, a large city on the Adriatic Sea where the poet Dante had lived. He visited Dante's tomb and the basilica of San Apollinare and spent many hours admiring the fishing boats and bustle of the port. For the first time he was conscious of the world. "I went back with something new and undying. My mind and spirit were filled with expanding consciousness."

Benito sometimes worked in the blacksmith shop and the closer contact with his father strengthened his feelings against the Italian establishment. A constant stream of visitors came to the smithy, for Alessandro liked nothing better than to stop his work and talk awhile. Benito heard stories and complaints that convinced him that "a deep and secret grudge was darkening the hearts of the common people. A country gentry of mediocrity in economic usefulness were hanging upon the multitudes a weight of unjustified privileges."

His restlessness and his espousal of revolutionary ideas convinced his mother and father that further education was in order. One day his mother heard noises from his room, and going there she found him making an imaginary speech. When she asked him what he was doing, he replied that he was "preparing for the day when all Italy will tremble at my words."

So Benito Mussolini was sent off to Forlimpopoli Secondary Modern College for higher education, which at one time had been a Franciscan monastery. The pupils were mostly the sons of elementary school teachers in Romagna, so the fees were very modest. Benito went here with a vow to succeed. Because there was no room to board him at the school, for the first three years he stayed with a family in town, an arrangement that gave him a good deal of freedom and allowed him to go home, eleven miles away, on Sunday. The headmaster, Alfredo Carducci, was a gentle man, who showed a greater understanding of Benito's rebellious character than had the Salesian Fathers, although it took all of Carducci's gentility to do so. On one occasion in the school dining room Mussolini led a rebellion against the quality of the bread they were served. He jumped up on the table and shouted, "We're treated worse than in a pauper's hostel." The enthusiastic boys began pelting the teachers with bread and they fled. Mussolini adopted a later characteristic pose, arms folded, and shouted again: "Enough! To throw bread is to insult the food of the poor." The rebellion ended with the mayor sampling the bread and agreeing with the boys that it was terrible.

In his way, and when it interested him, at Forlimpopoli Benito could be a leader. His interest in his studies, although never great (because he had no intention of becoming a teacher), was enough to get him promoted to the senior school and awarded a scholarship. He was sixteen. His contemporaries remembered him as looking like a worker, with the large pale forehead of his father, framed by a shock of unruly black hair. He was always dressed in black clothes that showed their age, and he wore a flowing black necktie, which was much favored by radicals in those days. Even as an adolescent he continued to be a loner, although he did take part in school games and always in discussion, debates, and arguments. He liked to harangue the other boys on the playground, and he had so much prowess as an orator that the headmaster selected him to speak at a public commemoration of the life of Giuseppi Verdi at the local theater. He made the speech into a protest against the social conditions of Verdi's time. For the first time he got his name in the press, when a Milan socialist newspaper wrote up the speech and called him "Comrade Student Mussolini."

Blossoming adolescence brought him attraction to girls, and despite his first unhappy sexual experience in a brothel—"it made me feel dirty"—he soon became known as the terror of the girls of the countryside, with a furious lust that drove him to undressing every girl he saw with his eyes. He took his pleasures where they were available, against trees, on staircases, and by the bank of the River Rabi. For evermore he would be pursued by lust, which he seemed to find reciprocated in hundreds of women.

∽

On July 8, 1901, Benito went home to Predappio with an elementary school teacher's certificate in his pocket. When his mother urged him to apply for a job opening up in Forlì as Communal Scrivener, he did, but his father's radical writings and speeches stood against him, and the city government refused him the job. Alessandro comforted his son by telling him that his place was out in the world to make the great fight for revolution and reform.

That was all very well, and in keeping with Alessandro's starry-eyed idealism, but it would not support the young teacher. He finally found a teacher's job that summer in the town of Gaultieri, a hundred miles away in the province of Reggio Emilia.

Soon young teacher Mussolini had a reputation in the town as a queer one, who preferred to spend his evenings in a *trattoria* arguing politics to courting the young belles of the town. And his personal habits were alarming the bourgeois shopkeepers. He arose at dawn, bathed naked in the Po River, and then walked to school barefoot along the railroad tracks, his shoes strung over his shoulder on stick, a peasant habit he had learned as child in a family where there were not enough shoes to go around. He also did a lot of drinking and spent many a night bedded down on the floor of a local shop rather than awaken his landlady. Thus, in the summer of 1902, the town decided not to renew his contract. Benito then decided to take Alessandro's advice and become a refugee in Switzerland to begin fighting the war against the "haves." With some small financial support from home and his father's blessing, he bought a train ticket for Switzerland. On July 9, 1902, he set out, carrying his one purchase in the town where he had taught school, a new pair of shoes. As the train left the station, on impulse he picked up the package that contained his shoes and tossed it to his friends on the platform.

"Keep these as a souvenir," he said. "The luck of Mussolini won't depend on a pair of shoes."

Soon enough he was to regret his impulsive action. His own shoes were worn to shreds. He could find work only as a common laborer at Orbe near Yverdon, working eleven hours a day, carrying bricks on a barrow to build a two-story building. The job lasted ten days and then he quit. With the twenty francs he earned he bought a pair of stout mountain boots and moved on to Lausanne. But his fortunes were no better there, and soon he was starving. He saw the rich dining on the terrace of the Beau Rivage Hotel and he hated them, with a growing sharp hatred for the wealthy that never died in him. He took to stealing bread to survive, and he slept in a wooden packing case beneath a bridge. He who had started out to conquer the world was reduced to asking for money from home. He began to receive it, in small amounts, but it was enough to keep him going. Of this period he was to write in his autobiography, "I knew hunger—stark hunger—in those days. But I never bent myself to ask for loans, and I never tried to inspire the pity of those around me."

Brave words these, but unfortunately they were not true. When he wrote to his friend Santo Bedeschi in Italy, Benito told an entirely different story. After he arrived in Lausanne he was able to live for the first week on his earnings from the hod carrier's job. But on Monday the only piece of metal he had in his pocket was a medallion of Karl Marx. He had eaten a little bread in the morning, but by afternoon he was having cramps in his belly, and he sat down on the pedestal of the statue of William Tell in Montbenon Park. The people who came by looked at him suspiciously, a wild and unkempt young man, with a fierce look in his eye, and they avoided him sedulously, which made him even angrier.

In the evening he left Montbenon and went down along the quay, the road on the shore of the lake. Evening came, and in the last light of the sun, the sound of the town's evening bells took him out of himself as he admired the beauty. But then he passed the Beau Rivage Hotel again, where an orchestra was playing on the terrace and the rich were dining and the wine was sparkling. He leaned against the railings of the garden and listened to the music. But the cramp was stabbing his entrails. He looked at the crowd of holidaymakers, and he heard languages he did not understand. An elderly couple passed him. The lady glittered with gold and jewels. As he wrote later in his autobiography, he wanted to ask them for money to get himself a bed for the night, but the words died on his lips.

> I have not a solda, I have no bed, I have no bread. I make off cursing.
> Ah, that blessed idea of anarchy of thought and action. Is it not the
> right of the man lying on the ground to murder him who crushes
> him?

From then until eleven I stay in the public lavatory, from eleven to twelve under an old barge. The wind blows from Savoy and it is cold I return to the town and spend the rest of the night under the Grand Pont. In the morning I look at myself out of curiosity in the windows of a shop. I am unrecognizable. I meet a man from Romagna. I tell him briefly of my affairs. He laughs at me. I curse him. He puts his hand in his pocket and gives me sixty centesimi. I thank him. I hasten to the shop of a baker and buy a piece of bread. Continue walking toward the wood. I feel as though I had a fortune. Having got a long way from the center of the city, I bite into my bread with the ferocity of a cerberus. For twenty-six hours I had not eaten.

Day after day went by like this. Once in a while he secured a task, like running an errand. But he had no work. He was arrested for vagrancy. Money from home got him out of jail, and he had lunch that day at a cafe with a group of Italians. They turned out to be laborers. But more important, they were Socialists. He spoke about his father, who was well known in socialist circles in Romagna, and he had found friends. They got him a job and within four months they had elected him secretary of their Italian Trade Union of Bricklayers and Bricklayers' Assistants. He began signing his letters "Benito Mussolini, Bricklayer."

He began immediately to go to political meetings, and within a week he was a popular speaker. As a speaker he was a rabble-rouser, not really a Socialist, but anarchist, antichurch, antiroyalty, antimilitarist, and antigovernment. There were many like him in the socialist movement in those days. To be bombastic and loud was almost enough to secure attention. Mussolini was both, but he had something else; he captured his audiences with gesture and tone. One afternoon when debating a local minister on the reality of God (the sort of free-for-all that delighted him), he pulled a cheap watch from his pocket.

"It is now 3:30," he said. "If God exists, I give him five minutes to strike me dead."

When nothing happened, Mussolini received a storm of applause and the pastor's argument was drowned out. Within weeks, the Italian-language Lausanne *Tribuna* began referring to Mussolini as "the great Duce" (leader) of the Italian Socialists in the town.

He slept with most of the women he knew. Every new female face aroused a fire in his loins that could only be quenched, and then momentarily, by action. But one woman, Angelica Balabanoff, a plump, blonde Russian, got under his skin. She was thirty-three and he was twenty and they became lovers, but much more. She was a well-known socialist agitator and an intellectual. She got Benito jobs translating

French into Italian. They spent night after night in her lodgings. At first she thought he was a radical Socialist, but she soon learned that he was not a Socialist at all. He did not bleed for the oppression of the masses. Rather, he was indignant about what had happened to him and determined to achieve power.

But translations did not pay enough and so mostly Benito worked as a laborer or an errand boy, anything that would pay him enough money to keep alive. He studied German and French as well. He burned constantly with the fires of anger at his own inability to cope with the world. He was arrested again and escorted to the Italian border, but he returned to Lausanne by way of another canton.

His anger was always intensely personal. When Angelica introduced him to her friend Maria Rygier, a schoolteacher, the teacher took an immediate dislike to Mussolini. She accused him of having no more than personal lusts for wealth and power. He did not deny it. "People eating, drinking and enjoying themselves," he snorted. "And from here I'll travel third class, eating miserable cheap food. How I hate the rich! Why must I suffer this injustice? How long must we wait?" The question, which mixed the welfare of the masses with his own, confused people so that many believed he really had feelings for the poor and was typical of the man. Only a few in those days, like Maria Rygier, spotted the real Mussolini.

Angelica Balabanoff, however, thought better of him, and she persuaded him to attend lectures given by professors at the University of Lausanne. She saw that he knew nothing of history, economics, or socialist theory and that his mind was completely undisciplined. She encouraged him to read Nietzsche, Kant, Hegel, Schopenhauer, and Sorel. He learned something about Buddhism. In the public squares he was often in argument, and his behavior was so unruly that the officials expelled him from the canton. He took refuge then on the French side of the border, where he worked as a laborer and a part-time teacher in a private school. He had an affair with the wife of the sous—prefet, and, although he might have stayed in Annemasse, since she looked favorably on him, he decided to go to Zurich. There he fell under the influence of the German Socialist refugees, for this was the town of Marx and Karl Liebknecht. But although German socialism appealed to him, and he came away talking about the need for discipline in Italy, he never thought to bring himself into the equation.

Finally he was expelled from Zurich after a brawl in a restaurant and he slipped across the border into Germany. He now had something of a trade as a bricklayer, and he followed this in Bern. He also began to write for a socialist newspaper and made a little money. He began speaking at socialist meetings and organized a strike of masons. But always his pugnaciousness went too far. He fought a duel with another professed Socialist. For this he was arrested and expelled from Bern. In October 1903, he went home for a short visit when his mother was ill but when she recovered he went back to Annemasse, to see his French mistress. Although he used a forged passport to get back into Switzerland, he was detected at Geneva and was imprisoned, then expelled again in April 1904. But because his case got a lot of publicity, he was allowed to go to Ticino. He wandered around for some time, always making trouble, and then decided to go home. He had seen something of the world and his mind was full of Marxist ideas, which he had not digested. He was, as ever, indignant in a personal way about the ills of society. As a friend of those days said of him: He was not a Marxist and not a Socialist certainly. He was too much an individual to fit any mold. But he saw in the socialist movement something he thought he could harness to his own yearnings to achieve power.

∽

So Mussolini came back to Italy in December 1904. It was time for him to join the army under the Italian compulsory service program. He did not object. He joined a Bersaglieri regiment in Verona, a famous unit, and he was proud and happy as a soldier, where he accepted the only effective discipline he had ever experienced.

"I liked the life of a soldier," he wrote later. "The sense of willing subordination suited my temperament. I was preceded by a reputation of being restless, a fire-eater, a radical, and a revolutionist. Consider then the astonishment of the captain, the major, and my colonel, who were compelled to speak of me with praise. It was my opportunity to show serenity of spirit and strength of character."

The period of soldiering was perhaps the happiest in Mussolini's life. He had no worries, no fears of tomorrow, and by comporting himself as he did, he had no disciplinary problems. He might have become a professional soldier, he liked the life that much, except for the untimely death of his mother at the age of forty-six, in 1905. His mother was the one person in the world whom he loved with deep and sincere affection and her death shook him to the soul. Worst, for him, it came as a complete surprise. One day he was soldiering, then his captain took him aside and read a telegram, and he hastened back home to arrive just as his mother was expiring. He was not even certain that she recognized him in her last moments. Then, for the first time, he gave way to despair.

CHAPTER 2

✺

The Young Radical

After Mussolini's mother was buried, he returned to his regiment and ended his military service in September 1906. Following his discharge he returned to the family house in Predappio for a few months. While there he had a love affair with the school mistress who had succeeded his mother in the elementary school. Next, he found a job as schoolmaster at the village of Caneva in the commune of Tolmezzo in Friuli, a mountain district, but it was apparent that he was not cut out to be a schoolteacher. For example, his manner of keeping order in the classroom among his forty students was to bribe them with sweets. To him teaching was only necessary to earn his living, because his heart was already deeply immersed in politics. He was threatened with arrest for making subversive speeches, and soon he had renewed his reputation as a vagabond and woman chaser. For the latter he had his comeuppance: He caught syphilis and had to be treated at the local hospital. When his contract expired at the end of the year, it was not renewed.

He returned to Dovia, where he loafed for a while, and then in the fall of 1907 got down to some serious study at home. Early in 1908 he went to Bologna to take an examination in French. He passed the examination and obtained a diploma. This diploma and the friendly intervention of Lucius Serrati, a Socialist leader, got him a job teaching French at a small private school, the Collegio Ulisse Calvi, at Oneglia on the Italian Riviera. Serrati really wanted Mussolini for his editorial services, to run the socialist newspaper *La Lima*, which he had started. Mussolini actually wrote the entire newspaper although he used several pen names, such as *Il Limatore*, *Noi*, and *Vero Erectico*.

Because of an extensive police record kept on Mussolini's activities by the Forlì authorities, he was in trouble with the police in Oneglia. When he arrived there, the Forlì police sent along his dossier.

> Often violent and impulsive, he has an education that is exceptional among the working classes; he enjoys a good reputation. He shows a certain intelligence and cultivation, having attended the Normal School at Forlimpopoli, and secured a teacher's diploma. He mixes with the working classes and obtains some members for his party, but his influence does not extend beyond his own village. He is in relations with the socialist leaders in Romagna and also with the militants in Berne, Zurich, and Lausanne, where he lived from 1901 to October 1903.

His activities in Oneglia brought him to the unfriendly eyes of the local police, who began to make trouble for him. They even went so far as to ask the head of the school to dismiss him, a request that was denied. Mussolini retaliated in the columns of the newspaper, in which he attacked authority and the Roman church. The pressures, exerted by civic leaders and church clergy, built up swiftly, and in June 1908, when the police ordered him to leave Oneglia, he went home. However, home was no longer Predappio, but Forlì. His father had given up the smithy and moved to town, where he ran a wine shop on the Via Mazzini. Alessandro also had taken a common-law wife, Anna Guidi, who came to preside over the wine shop with her teenaged daughter Rachele. Mussolini flirted with Rachele and told her that he would marry her as soon as he got established. She laughed at him.

Benito immediately got involved in local politics and before the month was out was arrested for disturbing the peace and jailed for a few days. The next month he was fined one hundred lire for making a seditious speech. When he was not giving fiery speeches, he was writing fiery articles for socialist journals, advocating violence. In *Il Pensiero Romagnola*, he published a violent attack on a Socialist member of the national Chamber of Deputies, Claudio Treves, for his pacifist views. His reputation as a revolutionary fire-eater spread as far as Trento, 150 miles north in what was at the time Austrian territory, and brought him an offer of a job as secretary with the Chamber of Labor at a small but not unreasonable salary. In addition to his secretarial duties he was to be responsible for the local news weekly, *L'Avvenire del Lavoratore*. This paper was famous; it had been founded in Vienna by Cesare Battisti, who had since come to Trento to establish a much larger newspaper, *Il Popolo*. Battisti had then turned *L'Avvenire* over to the local Socialists. Mussolini's coming was announced in the papers. The Socialists of Trento admired him for the same reasons that authorities detested him. As the Forlì police put it, he attacked Christianity and the Roman church, he called the national flag of Italy "a rag to be planted on a dunghill," and described Italy's government as "cruel and tyrannical."

After Mussolini's arrival in Trento in March 1909, he began in *L'Avvenire* to beat the drums for international socialism and revolution. At the same time he contributed to Battisti's much more important *Il Popolo*, an irredentist newspaper whose policy was dedicated to the return of all of Italian-speaking Austrian territory to Italy. Mussolini wrote nationalistic Italian articles for *Il Popolo* and international revolutionary articles for *L'Avvenire* without a tremor and was so successful at the latter that in August 1909, he became managing editor of *Il Popolo*.

Again, the Forlì police informed the authorities in Trento that Mussolini was a dangerous man. "He needs watching," said the report. So the authorities watched, and in the next few months the paper was banned eleven times, and Mussolini had served six jail terms for inciting violence against authority. By the end of September, he had been expelled and put back across the Italian–Austrian border.

When Mussolini came back to Italy this time he went to find Rachele at her sister's farmhouse and announced that he had come to marry her but that she had to come with him right then. He carried her off that very day and they walked through the rain for a mile and a half to Forlì, where he announced his liaison to Alessandro and Anna at the wine shop. Both tried to dissuade Benito and Rachele. Alessandro observed that his political ambitions ought to cause him to foreswear marriage; Anna was outraged because Benito was a notorious seducer of young women. But Rachele had been in love with him since she was seven years old, and she would not give in. So Alessandro gave them a tumbledown apartment in the Via Merenda and they furnished it with cheap furniture and moved in. There was no marriage; a good Socialist did not believe in bonds created by church or civic authority.

∽

As soon as the couple was settled in at Forlì, Benito began a new career: organizing the socialist clubs of Forlì into a mass movement. He started a newspaper, *La Lotta di Classe* (*The Class Struggle*) and although it never reached a circulation of four hundred copies, it was read by radicals in what was essentially a radical community. He was not only editor but also chief reporter and manager, and principal orator and agitator for the socialist movement in the Romagna district. He was an indefatigable worker and often tramped thirty miles in a day to preach his doctrine to the farmhands of this agricultural district. He and Rachele were very poor and Benito often did odd jobs to earn a little money. When his first child, daughter Edda, was born on September 1, 1910, he had just fifteen lire in his pocket, enough to buy a cheap wooden cradle. He had only one pair of trousers; when they had to be washed he had to stay in bed until they dried. He had few amusements; he liked the theater, but would sit only in the balcony with the workers. He wanted to learn to play the violin, so he bought a cheap fiddle and persuaded Professor Archimede Montanelli to give him lessons. He seldom drank, and after one horrible evening when he came home drunk and smashed up all the family crockery, he promised Rachele he would never drink again, and he lived up to his word.

Mussolini did not need liquor to make him violent. One day the civic authorities announced a rise in the price of milk. Within hours Mussolini had learned this, and he had begun to act. He assembled a mob and led them to the city hall of Forlì where they confronted the mayor. "Either the price of milk is revised," Mussolini told the mayor, "or I'll tell these people to pitch you and all your bigwigs over the balcony." The price of milk immediately went down.

Mussolini succeeded in these enterprises because he was a violent man, in a violent countryside, in violent times. Irredentism, mixed with radicalism, ruled the northern Italian countryside. The unification of Italy was not really complete, and the control of the country still rested firmly with the haves, supported by the Church of Rome.

"I understand now that the Gordian knot of Italian political life could be undone only by an act of violence," Mussolini wrote of these years in his autobiography.

At this time, Mussolini's life became completely wrapped up in politics. His father died. "My father's death marked the end of the family unity for us, the family," he wrote. His inheritance from his father was a new feeling about the sort of revolution that must come to Italy. The elder Mussolini had finally given up on the socialist revolution. "At the end he understood that the old eternal traditional forces such as capitalism could not be permanently overthrown by political revolution. He turned his attention at the end toward bettering the souls of individuals." In his enterprises, Alessandro Mussolini had succeeded in capturing the hearts of many people. His coffin was followed to the grave by three thousand people, a very large funeral procession for Forlì.

If young Mussolini sympathized with his father's gentler view at the time, he concealed it, for he sensed that his future lay in fishing the waters of political strife.

Mussolini's violence was seemingly justified with the socialist-minded people of northern Italy by the unpopular imperialist war against Turkey that began in September 1911 for the conquest of Libya. This conquest was undertaken for national glory—nobody expected Libya to become a valuable colony. But Europe was engaged in the dismemberment of the weakened Turkish Empire. The Austrians had just annexed Bosnia and Herzegovina, and the Italians wanted their piece of the pie.

The Socialists could not make up their minds about colonial expansion, which in their manifestoes they had always criticized, and their desire to support the government in its adventure. Ultimately, doctrine prevailed and they came out against the colonization war. Mussolini, however, had been wavering on different grounds. He was becoming more of a nationalist than a Socialist, and that part of him wanted to support the war. But he knew instinctively that more profit was to be made through violent opposition, which might pave the way to revolution. So at Forlì on September 24, 1911, he advocated in a speech a general strike. "Before conquering Tripoli," he shouted, "let us first conquer Italy. Bring water to parched Puglia, justice to the South, and education everywhere. On to the streets for the General Strike."

He exhorted strikers to set up street barricades, tear up the railway lines, stop the public buses, and organize every sort of resistance to the government. His speech brought on riots at Forlì and troops were called in to restore order. The rioters battled them with stones and fence palings, and women threw themselves in front of the cavalry's horses. Martial law was declared, order was restored, the strike petered out, and Mussolini was arrested for "instigation to delinquency." He chose to act as his own defense counsel and turned the trial into a theatrical performance. "If you acquit me," he told the judges, "you will give me pleasure. If you condemn me, you will do me honor."

The judges condemned him to a year in prison, a sentence that was later shortened to five months. The trial turned out to be the most important event yet, by far, in Mussolini's young life. Before, he had been unknown, except to the police as a troublesome radical and to the people of Forlì. But his impassioned defense, in which he painted himself as a nationalist, aroused some national attention, and still did not disavow his socialist ties, which brought him new attention from

Socialists around the north of Italy. He served his term in Cell 39 of the Forlì jail. And soon he was considered to be the mouthpiece of the intransigent revolutionaries of Italian socialism. In prison at the same time was Pietro Nenni, a Republican who was also jailed for his resistance to the Libyan War. The two developed a friendship in prison that lasted all of Mussolini's life.

While Mussolini was in prison, the pot of radicalism in Italy boiled over. On the morning of March 14, 1912, while the King and Queen of Italy were driving through the Corso on the way to the Pantheon to attend a memorial service for the King's father, the late King Humberto, a man in the crowd fired a revolver twice at the King. He missed the King but wounded one of the guards who was riding beside the carriage. The would-be assassin was a twenty-one-year-old radical named Antonio d'Alba di Cesare.

After Mussolini's release from prison he was lionized by the Socialists, who saw in him the same spark that the Socialists of Switzerland had first noted. They gave him a banquet, and the old Socialist leader Olindo Vernocchi called him "the Duce of all revolutionary Socialists in Italy." Four months later Mussolini traveled to Reggio Emilia to attend the National Congress of the Italian Socialist Party. He was thin and pale from his imprisonment and had several days' growth of thick black beard. He wore a large broad-brimmed hat and a black jacket that was greasy, green with use, and had pockets full of newspapers; a shabby shirt and worn-out flowing necktie; old trousers with crumpled knees; and shoes that had not seen polish for months. The figure he presented complemented his reputation as a dedicated revolutionary and provoked a wave of applause as he began to speak.

As he spoke he knew that for the first time he had a large and attentive audience. He recalled the March 14 attempt to assassinate the king. "Precedent indicated the line of conduct to be followed by Socialists," he said. "What is a king anyway except by definition a useless citizen? There are peoples who have sent their King packing; others even have preferred to take the precaution of sending him to the guillotine, and those peoples are in the vanguard of progress."

This was exactly what this audience of revolutionary Socialists wanted to hear, and they cheered Mussolini on. Having won the acclaim of Socialist leaders, four moderate leaders—Leonida Bissolati, Ivanoe Bonomi, Angiolo Cabrini, and A. Podrecca—were expelled from the party at his request, and Claudio Treves was fired as editor of Avanti!, the party newspaper. Mussolini was elected a member of the party executive committee, along with Angelica Balabanoff. So Mussolini, at the age of twenty-nine, had suddenly become a political force in Italy. As the authoritative *Corriere della Sera* said, the convention had found in Mussolini a man who voiced its own sentiments. Several of the leaders predicted that Mussolini would come to dominate the party. Of the analysts of his character, and there were several at this time, it was Anna Kuliscioff, a prominent Socialist, originally from Lithuania, who was closest to putting her finger on what he was not. "He is nothing of a Marxist, nor is he really a Socialist at all. Nor is he really a politician." But she missed when she tried to define what he was: "a sentimental poetaster who has read Nietzsche." No, that was not Mussolini. He was not an inferior poet, or even a superior one, and Nietzsche was not the source of Mussolini's radicalism, which was personal and fierce. He intended to get ahead in the world, on the backs of the rich. His philosophy was as simple as that, and at the moment, the Socialists served his purpose so he would use them. And as he now knew, he had the capacity to move people's minds.

At the end of the Socialist Party Congress at Reggio Emilia, Mussolini had fulfilled his first ambition in the world. He had become "somebody," and he now had a platform from which he could express his views. His next step was to strengthen that platform and to this task he now set himself with all the ardor and strength of his youth.

CHAPTER 3

∽

"Really, He Was Never a Socialist"

—Angelica Balabanoff

What Mussolini wanted from the Socialists was the editorship of *Avanti!*, the party's official newspaper, published at Milan. He did not get it at the party Congress at Reggio Emilia. That was really too much even for him to expect. But he was in a position, after the Congress, to scheme for the job. It was easy for him to criticize Giovanni Bacci, the nonentity who had been appointed since he, Mussolini, had been responsible for the removal of Claudio Treves from the editorship. What was needed, Mussolini told the other members of the party executive committee, was a man who could arouse the party masses to action and, moreover, could appeal outside the party and make new converts. Who was that man? Benito Mussolini, of course.

It was important that the party broaden its appeal if it was to make political progress in the elections coming up the next year. Mussolini hammered at that theme all summer and fall, because under the new election law of 1912, Italy would for the first time have universal male suffrage, which would bring six million new voters to the polls in 1913.

Mussolini said that the Socialist leadership was not appealing to the youth of the nation. His solution to the problem was to broaden the appeal of the newspaper to attract a larger audience, and, especially the youth. The committee was convinced by his argument and that autumn he was appointed editor of *Avanti!* He realized that from now on he would have to have allies—he could not produce a real newspaper like *Avanti!* by himself—and he insisted that Angelica Balabanoff be appointed as his assistant editor.

On December 1, 1912, Mussolini's first issue of the party newspaper carried a personal message from the new editor: "I embark on my journey carrying intact the burden of my ideas and I hope to reach my goal. That is to say, I hope not to be unworthy of the confidence placed in me by the leadership of the party." The first sentence of that declaration was perfectly true. In his autobiography he boasted that "I did not yield an inch to demagoguery. I have never flattered the crowd, nor wheedled anyone."

His appointment to this important leadership post had been opposed by some, principally by Arturo Vella, a member of the executive committee, who charged that Mussolini would lead the party down devious paths because he was too much of an individualist. But the others saw Mussolini as a new party messiah, and overruled Vella's objections. Angelica Balabanoff, a Socialist through and through, spoke up for Benito. It was true that he lacked political understanding of the history and philosophy of their cause, but he had made up for that in his ability, his adaptability, and his enormous vitality and industry. She rightly saw in him a real revolutionary, but she erred in linking that with the realities of socialism. Always a revolutionary, Mussolini was never a Socialist who would yield to the majority view to obtain consensus. This ability to yield was not a part of the man's character.

At first Mussolini seemed to be the ideal Socialist. He spurned money. Whereas Giovanni Bacci had been paid seven hundred lire a month as editor, Mussolini immediately cut his own pay to five hundred lire a month, to conserve the paper's resources for political development. He and his wife moved into a flat at 19 Castel Morrone, in one of the better districts of Milan, not far from the city hall.

の

He set to work like a whirlwind, spewing forth ideas, changing ways of doing things, bringing new life to the newspaper and to the local Socialist party. His editorial theory was simple: produce a paper that the common people would want to read. He offered constant sensationalism and muckraking to his readers; he attacked the government endlessly. In 1913, when riots in the south of Italy were suppressed ruthlessly by the government, with troops opening fire on the demonstrators, *Avanti!* thundered against the government as murderers of the people.

As Italy prepared for the late October 1913 elections, Mussolini himself stood as the Socialist candidate for Forlì, a Republican stronghold. When the election results were in, the Socialists had gained thirty-seven seats in the Chamber of Deputies, and Mussolini crowed. But the Liberal Constitutional government party gained sixty-two seats and held an absolute majority, three times that of the rest of the parties put together. The only party that did not gain was the Republican. Even the Catholics, sworn enemies of the Socialists, gained twelve seats. Mussolini was not elected, but that did not prevent him and the party from celebrating victory. From the window of the *Avanti!* office, above a roaring crowd, Mussolini smiled his infectious smile, waved, and made a prediction. "Now we can envisage only two blocks of voters, one conservative and the other revolutionary," he said.

Publicly, Mussolini was the total revolutionary; privately it was left to one of his women, Leda Rafanelli, a Muslim anarchist who was his intimate for two years, to recognize that he was volatile and unstable. "During our long conversations I had occasions to note that Mussolini too easily changed his opinions," she said. But he knew his strengths. He could control crowds. He was at his best with an immense emotional crowd, which was at a distance, and whose members were largely unknown to him. He was at his most impressive in a stadium, not at a private gathering.

Mussolini spoke frankly to Leda Rafanelli of his dreams. "I want to rise to the top. In my youth I wanted to be a great musician or a great writer, but I understood that I should have remained mediocre. I shall never be content, I tell you, I must rise. I must make a bound forwards, to the top."

At that time, his vehicle for the rise was *Avanti!*, and day after day he thundered in its columns against the government, against the cowardice of the bourgeoisie, calling always for the revolution, but in such general terms that he managed generally to stay out of jail.

In March 1914 he was tried at Milan for articles published that the prosecution claimed were seditious. That trial lasted two weeks and gave Mussolini a new forum, which he used so effectively that the jury acquitted him on all the charges.

At the Socialist Party Congress in Ancona that spring, Mussolini played a leading role. He managed to put through the Congress a measure outlawing freemasonry in the socialist movement. This move was important largely because it showed his personal strength: There were many Freemasons in the hall that day when the Congress voted overwhelmingly for Mussolini's ban. But his real strength was shown in securing support for public demonstrations for an anarchist soldier and against the formation of penal companies in the army. The Congress agreed to call a general strike if the police tried to repress the movement.

All this was geared to happen on Sunday, June 7, 1914, the day of celebration of the anniversary of the granting of the new constitution to Italy, and the equivalent of the American Fourth of July.

As the American embassy in Rome reported to Washington: "At Ancona, which is so to speak a Socialist center, the Socialists and others strongly opposed to the government decided this year, under the direction of a noted anarchist, to organize for a great meeting to be held on this national holiday, as a protest against the government and a political demonstration."

The government, as the political report said, did ban the meeting. "The meeting, however, was proceeded with, and when the crowd attempted to enter the square a conflict ensued between the mob and the police in which, after a number of policemen had been injured by stones, they fired on the crowd killing two persons and wounding a number of others. Eventually all troops were called out and the town was placed under martial rule." The police did fire into the crowd, and the final count was that they killed three and wounded ten of the demonstrators. The Socialists called for the general strike, and revolutionary fires spread across the country. Mussolini crowed that this would be known as Red Week. But the revolution collapsed on the seventh day when the National Confederation of Labor called off the strike. Mussolini jutted his jaw and laid the blame for the failure on the flabbiness of the Socialist moderates, who had not been willing to go to the barricades. He got away with it, and the blame was diverted from his failure to rouse the crowds to sufficient fury to the less revolutionary.

While all this was happening the circulation of *Avanti!* was increasing. Mussolini ran it up in just over two years from 28,000 to more than 100,000. He, Mussolini, was regarded as the heart and soul of *Avanti!* and *Avanti!* led the party. As one of the other leaders, no admirer of Mussolini's, wrote: "In his hands *Avanti!* has advanced toward a goal which is clear, precise and admitted, namely to infuse a revolutionary spirit into the Italian masses."

The result of all this rhetoric was that in local elections held in June 1914, the extreme wing of the Socialist party prospered. Mussolini was elected to office in Milan and the Socialists gained control of many cities and towns, including Bologna.

The international community took note of the Milan elections. "In Milan" wrote American ambassador Thomas Nelson Page, "the Socialists will have for the first time in Italy an opportunity to try out their programs in a municipal government and I learn that the result of the trial will be watched with a great deal of interest."

∽

On the eve of a leave in the United States, Page sent to Washington an appreciation of the Italian political situation that spring of 1914. He found the people of Italy to be

> kindly, easygoing, lighthearted and friendly; extraordinarily excitable and quick to fall into a passion of excitement over what would scarcely ruffle those of a cooler temperament, and the reports in the press would indicate that they have a tendency to acts of violence.
>
> They have shown, however, on occasions, that under this light demeanor they are capable of great endurance and fortitude, and Italy is, undoubtedly under its present administration, improving gradually in almost every field of enterprise, and rising steadily among the powers of Europe.

While Page was in America on leave, the Europe he knew came unraveled. Austrian Archduke Franz Ferdinand was assassinated on June 28, 1914, at Sarajevo, and central Europe flamed. Hapsburg Austria called on Hohenzollern Germany to honor their treaty of alliance, and the clouds of war gathered. Italy had agreements with Austria that, if honored, would put Italy into the camp of the Hapsburgs and Hohenzollerns. Mussolini and the Italian Socialists took a neutral stand, and so did the Italian government. There was some disarray in the Socialist ranks when the Austrian and German Socialists defected from the Socialist International in a surge of nationalist zeal. For once, Mussolini found himself and the Socialists on the same side of an argument as the government.

"Down With the War" declared *Avanti!* on July 26, 1914.

But Mussolini was uncomfortable being on the side of authority. The very next day he warned: "The members of the proletariat are now on the alert. The moment Italy showed inclination to break neutrality in order to back up the Central Powers, the Italian proletariat would have but one duty, we say it clearly and distinctly: that of rising rebellion." And on July 29 he signed a socialist manifesto appealing to the people to resist involvement in the war. All those opposed, he said, were traitors and renegades.

But the war came, and Benito Mussolini had to observe its consequences even though his Italy remained aloof.

When the Germans failed to take Paris in their first rush, and lost the first battle of the Marne, Mussolini, who like nearly everyone else in Italy had expected the German colossus to triumph easily and quickly, suddenly had doubts about the German ability to win the war. He began to observe the struggle in a new light, and to calculate which side would win. That was the side Mussolini wanted to join.

The war began in August and by the middle of September Mussolini was telling close associates that neutrality was nonsense and that Italy would have to enter the war on the side of England and France. Still, in the pages of *Avanti!* he wrote in defense of neutrality and eventual world revolution. By mid-October *Avanti!* had begun advocating "armed neutrality" and vaguely alluding to the need for Italy to enter the war on the Allied side: "Do you want to be as men and as Socialists inert spectators of this tremendous drama? Or do you not want to be, in some fashion or other, its protagonists? Socialists of Italy, listen, it has happened at times that the letter has killed the spirit. Do not let us keep the letter of the party if that means killing the spirit of socialism."

That article represented Mussolini's final tremors in his personal conflict between ambitions of past and present. The ambition of the past, "to be somebody" had been achieved through the Socialists. Now his ambition turned because he saw the personal advantage of interventionism and how it would bring Italy high in the councils of the West. On October 18, when he was alone in the editorial rooms of *Avanti!* he tore up the front page of the paper and remade it with a leading article advocating Italian support for France, Britain, and Russia in the war. The article stunned the Socialist party leadership and was publicly repudiated by them. And what was to be done with the apostate editor of *Avanti!*? Being Socialists, and committed to discussion and majority rule, the leadership had to debate the issue. While Mussolini's fate was being decided in the party councils, out onto the streets of Milan came a new journal, *Il Popolo d'Italia*, and there on the masthead was the name of the editor, Benito Mussolini. The paper was loud in its advocacy of intervention in the war. Within a few hours it had sold out. The feelings of the Italian people were undergoing marked change to favor joining the Allies.

On the night of November 24, 1914, Mussolini at last was called before a meeting in the Teatro del Popolo by the Milan Socialists to account for his departure from party policy. As he entered the theater and walked down the long aisle to the stage, he was greeted by catcalls and insults. A surge ran through the crowd, *"Chi paga? Chi paga?"*—"Who is paying? Who is paying?"—for the rumor was already abroad that Mussolini had sold out to the capitalists. He came now to explain himself, but the crowd would not let him speak and pelted him with fruit. Someone threw a chair up on the stage, but Mussolini dodged it. The chairman of the meeting, Giacinto Menotti Serrati, tried to quiet the crowd, but the chant continued—*"Chi paga? Chi paga?"*—and Mussolini could not be heard above it. "Sellout, assassin, traitor"—abuse came fast with all the fervor that Ambassador Page had mentioned as characterizing the Italian people.

"Comrades, let him speak," implored Serrati, but the crowd stamped their feet and rose and shrieked at Mussolini and would not let him speak. He opened his mouth, and the crowd responded. "Louder," they shouted. "Louder, louder, speak up!"

Faintly, his voice could be heard. "If You think I am unworthy . . ." Then he was drowned out again, "Yes, yes." He became angry: "I shall have no mercy for those who do not take an open stand in this tragic hour," he said. *"Chi paga?"* they taunted. *"Chi paga? Chi paga? Chi paga?"*

From the podium Mussolini seized a tumbler of water, held it up, and crushed it, and the blood ran down his arm.

"You hate me because you still love me!" he shouted.

"Chi paga? Chi paga? Chi paga?"

"You have not heard the last of me," he thundered.

"Chi paga? Chi paga? Chi paga?"

He gave up and headed for the aisle.

The Milan Socialists voted that night to expel Mussolini. Five days later the Bologna convention of Socialists ratified the vote, expelled him forever, and took away his editorship.

But Mussolini had anticipated all this and had already engaged offices at 35 Via Paolo da Cannobio, in the heart of the red light district, and *Il Popolo d'Italia* was already a going concern.

The question of the Socialists was an apt one. *"Chi paga?"* indeed; although Mussolini was notably indifferent to money, somebody had to be backing the interventionist newspaper. And somebody was. The capitalists of Italy, those power brokers Mussolini hated so much, had put up the capital through Filippo Naldi of Bologna, the publisher of the *Il Resto del Carlino*. They not only put up the capital, they gave Mussolini the idea. The fact was that Mussolini did not care for the money, as he never had. But he did care for the power and prestige that could be attained through the press. He went home to Rachele and warned her that they were going to be poor again.

Il Popolo d'Italia struck the proper note with the people of northern Italy. The circulation began to rise, and soon it spread far beyond northern Italy to give Mussolini a national voice. In 1915 he accepted subsidies from the French to help the paper. He was loudly accused by his old Socialist comrades of "selling out" for money, and an investigation was called. It absolved him of making any personal gain from the subsidies by the French and others who wanted Italy in the war, and he never denied receiving the money. Every time he wrote an article, the circulation of *Il Popolo* seemed to go up. But night after night he would come home to Rachele, with his clothes half torn off, the results of some encounter in the streets with the antiwar activists. On April 12, 1915, he was arrested while leading a pro-war demonstration in Rome and jailed for eight hours. But a month later he was back on the streets urging the people to "shoot a few deputies in the back" and thus persuade the rest to opt for the war.

Later the Fascists were to claim that Mussolini led the way and pushed Italy into the war. This was not true, although he certainly waged an effective campaign and must have convinced many thousands to support the war through his persuasive voice. But the Italian government was moving toward war all this time. Under a secret treaty negotiated at London, the Italians were to receive certain rewards for entering the war on the side of the Allies: South Tirol, Trieste, Gorizia, Gradisca Istria, and the islands of Cherso and Lussino, Dalmatia as far as Cape Planka, Valona, Rhodes, and the Dodecanese group and a loan of fifty million pounds. Thus was to be completed the unification of Italy and begun the colonial philosophy. Italy would suddenly jump at war's end from a badly fragmented country to a modest empire. And on May 24, 1915, Premier Antonio Salandra declared war on Austria.

PART II

The Fight
to the Top

CHAPTER 4

∽

Wars

Mussolini's breach with the Socialist party was one of the sore points of his life and left him with mixed feelings of guilt and relief. He felt guilty at having betrayed the confidence in him (although he did not in the least feel guilty for having advocated the war), and he felt relief because he was rid of the socialist dogma in which he had never really believed.

"I felt lighter, fresher. I was free. I was better prepared to fight my battles than when I was bound by the dogmas of any political organization."

And he now found support from the Syndicalists, the anarchists, and other liberal and radical groups. He formed *Fasci di Azzione Rivoluzionario*, a group of young men who demonstrated for the war. And here he met a future associate, Dino Grandi, a student at Rome University. The name of their organization had no special meaning; *Fasci* was the current title for any political group. They both took part in demonstrations and both were arrested. The demonstrations Mussolini organized were supported editorially by *Il Popolo d'Italia*. Mussolini's articles were moving and powerful, and the English writer Freya Stark was so struck by one she saw by accident that she became a regular reader.

∽

In September 1915, Mussolini followed his talk with action. He joined the 11th Bersaglieri Regiment. As before, he was a model soldier, modest and unassuming, and his regiment served in one of the most difficult sections of the line against Austria in shallow trenches, in the Alps, at three thousand feet. He was the most famous man of all of them and thousands came to shake the hand of the editor of *Il Popolo d'Italia*. But he asked for no privileges and took no advantage of his fame and endured with the rest, mostly in the open weather and often under Austrian shellfire.

Mussolini's was a hard war. At night the temperatures fell below zero sometimes, and the soldiers' boots stuck to the rocks. In November he fell ill with paratyphoid fever and had to be taken to hospital. It was a mark of the prominence that Corporal Mussolini had achieved that he was visited in the hospital by King Victor Emmanuel, who made it a practice to visit soldiers near the front, to raise Italian morale for the war.

When he had recovered sufficiently Benito was given sick leave and used that leave time to straighten out his personal affairs. His second child, a son, had been born in September 1915. He decided to regularize his union with Rachele with a civil marriage and to have the boy named Vittorio, in honor of an Italian victory in the war, and Alessandro, after his father. Meanwhile one of his many love affairs—this one with Ida Dalser, a beauty parlor operator whose advertising had appeared in *Avanti!*—had produced another child. He recognized the child as his own and was ordered by a court to pay support money.

Back at the front Benito and the soldiers were troubled by a chronic shortage of water and seldom wasted it on washing. The lice grew fat on them, and the men grew thin when Austrian shelling prevented the field kitchens from moving up, as they often did. The cold was replaced by spring rains that became torrents; Mussolini grumbled with the rest when Christmas dinner was salt codfish, but he grumbled no more than the rest and endured the cold and the wet and the lice with great fortitude. In one period the rain fell without ending for forty-six days.

During his war service, Mussolini continued to write articles for *Il Popolo* regularly, which were later published as his *Diario di Guerra*, a book that biographer Ivone Kirkpatrick characterized as "a book of remarkable banality." "The entries describe the landscape, the weather, the hardships and the courage of the Italian soldier." Well, what were they supposed to describe? He was an Italian soldier, living in a situation of trench warfare, which meant constant danger, constant boredom, constant banality of existence. It was so hard a life that when home on leave in the Milan apartment, Mussolini found it hard to sleep in the soft bed and slept instead on the marble floor.

His only excitement, if you could call it that, was the writing of his column, which he did with faithful regularity. On one occasion when the company was called out of the line for a few days, he absented himself at the parade, and went to the deserted barracks, where he strewed his papers around four beds, and settled down to write his column.

∽

The dull army life ended on the afternoon of February 23, 1917. Mussolini had just been promoted to Lance Sergeant. He and his unit had been transferred to the Carso, a mountain range north of the Adriatic. The eminence they held was called Hill 144, where the Italians were under constant gunfire from the Austrians.

Benito's platoon was in a pit that day, practice-firing a howitzer. The barrel grew red hot and it blew up. Four men around the gun died instantly, and Mussolini was thrown 15 feet away. His body was hit by forty-four fragments of shrapnel. He was taken to the aid station, and then to a base hospital, where his wounds were so dreadful that the surgeons could put their fists inside some of them. In spite of treatment, the wounds developed gangrene and had to be cut. In one month Sergeant Mussolini underwent twenty-seven operations, only two of them with anesthetic; the rest of the time he was packed with swabs soaked in alcohol to prevent the spread of the infection. His fever went to 103 degrees and remained so high that it was almost as if he were in a coma. It was August before he was discharged from the hospital, and on crutches. Thereafter he always had to wear boots that buttoned or were fastened with a zipper or his left leg would suppurate.

Because of his wounds, and the need for his services at the newspaper, Mussolini petitioned for relief from further military service and the request was granted. So he did not go back to the front but settled in at his desk in Milan.

Indeed, his services were needed at *Il Popolo d'Italia* far more than in the trenches, for in the summer and fall of 1917 Italy was badly divided in opinions about the war. Six million men carried arms and fought on the various fronts against the Austrians, but behind them were hundreds of thousands of Socialists, who clung to pacifism as the symbol of universal humanity and did as much to slander and try to destroy the war effort as Mussolini had ever done to destroy capitalism in the flaming days of his youth.

By now, Mussolini was nearly bald, thin and haggard, and still pained by his wounds. He worked incessantly, to uphold the men at the front. In the last week of October 1917, the Italian Second Army at Caporetto in the Isonzo Valley broke before a combined Austrian-German offensive, and a million men retreated, without firing a shot. A quarter of them were captured. Mussolini redoubled his efforts, calling for a "Stand to the finish" campaign, urging strong measures, such as martial law in northern Italy and the suppression of all Socialist newspapers. And his voice led all others in Italy in support of the war.

The opposition that year was very strong. The neutralists had become pacifists, and they had been joined by Pope Benedict XV, who that year called for a compromise peace. The Allies were very fearful that Italy would drop out of the war altogether and after Caporetto they tried to do something about it. Sir Samuel Hoare, then a staff officer in British Intelligence, came to Rome to find some solutions. He inquired as to who could best help him turn Italian feeling around. Mussolini was recommended. "What is Mussolini?" Hoare asked and was told that he was a gang leader from Milan who had helped bring Italy into the war. Hoare went to Mussolini, put up money for the continuation of *Il Popolo d'Italia*, and Mussolini said, "Leave the matter to me." He was as good as his word. Soon his bullyboys, now called the *Fascio di Combattimento*, were hustling the pacifists off the streets and breaking up their meetings. Pacifism began to decline.

∽

On October 30, 1918, the Italian army under General Armando Diaz smashed the Austrian forces near Vittorio Veneto, forty-three miles from Venice, and brought an end to Italy's war. Throughout the country, soldiers felt that the newspaper *Il Popolo d'Italia*, and the man who ran it, Benito Mussolini, had done the most to support them. It is odd, then, that Mussolini and *Il Popolo d'Italia* received no attention from foreign diplomats in Italy. All during the war the American embassy staff reported regularly on events and their treatment by segments of the Italian press. *Corriere della Sera* was quoted often and *Stella,* and even *Avanti!,* the paper of the Socialists. But *Il Popolo d'Italia* was never mentioned. It was as if to the world of the Americans it did not exist.

The Mussolini who was running *Il Popolo d'Italia* now was a changed man. No longer did he appear in a dirty suit, with cracked shoes and flowing tie. He wore neat dark suits, stiff white collars and clean shirts, neat cravats, and shined shoes. His bald head was neat and clean; but his black protruding eyes remained the unchanged indication of his shrewdness and his ambitions. He was still the revolutionary, but at the moment he was still supporting the mutual efforts of the Allies, and victory was sweet. He led the celebrations at Milan. When

President Wilson visited Italy in January 1919, Mussolini's *Il Popolo d'Italia* greeted him with an article *"Viva Wilson"*—long live Wilson. Mussolini attended the banquet given for the American president at Milan.

And then what? For Mussolini was still the rebel, the revolutionary, and for the moment he was a revolutionary without a cause.

He was not long in finding a cause in postwar Italy. Italy had been cozened into the war by the British with promises of territorial aggrandizement and big loans in the postwar world. Actually she got Trieste and Trento and that was all. President Woodrow Wilson of the United States learned of the secret treaty with Italy and refused to honor it. Italy was shunted aside at Versailles and treated almost as if she was one of the defeated enemy. And after Versailles's disappointments, matters grew worse.

The Italian people suddenly began to believe the Socialists, who had stood strongly all through the war against intervention and then for withdrawal from the conflict. The public debt had become enormous. The returning soldiers could not find jobs because manufacturing industries were moribund in the drying up of their markets.

Italy's best customers before the war had been Germany and Austria, and they were now prostrate. Millions of soldiers came back from the war expecting support from their government and jobs—and got neither. Faced with unemployment, their claims on the government unrecognized, they were often beaten up by civilians. In Milan, a combat veteran who complained when a tram car passenger stepped on his foot was beaten up and his medals stripped off by fellow passengers, who then threw him into the street.

Communism entered the picture, buoyed by the success of the Bolsheviks in Russia. The first Communist demonstration took place in February 1919, and it proved the spur that caused Mussolini to spring into political action.

In this atmosphere the Socialists gained strength, helped by a government amnesty for war deserters. Their party strength rose to 1,200,000. When elections brought them control of two thousand municipalities, they turned the King's picture to the wall, took over the churches and draped the altars with red flags, and ran the red flag up over the Italian tricolor. The Communists, too, with their spectacular success in taking over Russia, began to make a showing in Italy.

In the early months of 1919 Mussolini brooded about these matters, and he decided to found a revolutionary movement of his own. Why not align himself with the other leftists? Because, he said, he was too much of an individual, as his previous experience with the Socialists had taught him. He was too much the anarchist, and by his own admission too intractable and impossible to organize.

So on March 23, 1919, the Fascist party was born in Milan. It was small enough and insignificant enough in the beginning, although advertised in *Il Popolo d'Italia*. Only 145 potential members attended this first meeting, and very few of them were people of any importance. Mussolini had been learning the ropes, and he now recognized the importance of trappings. So he had adopted a new meaning for the *fasces* (a symbol of Roman authority); the newly formed Fascist party was now to be that bundle of slim rods, coupled with an axe, bound by a red cord, which had symbolized a consul's power of life and death in ancient Rome. The meeting was chaired by former officers in the Arditi (shock troops) of the war; they wore black shirts and black sweaters and had stormed the Austrian trenches with daggers held in their teeth and grenades in their hands. The Arditi became another symbol of the new party; with their hands clasped over a dagger blade, they swore to defend Italy, ready to kill or die.

The beginnings were indeed small; only fifty-four members pledged their lives to each other and to Mussolini at this opening meeting. They passed three resolutions: first, to support the rights of former servicemen; second, to oppose imperialism; and third, to oppose the neutralists in all parties. In the afternoon, Mussolini declared political war on the Socialists, declared for the working people, demanded universal suffrage for women, as well as men, and proportional representation in the elections. Mussolini here made his first references to "the Corporate State" without defining it.

For the next few months, Mussolini traveled the country and wrote almost every day in *Il Popolo d'Italia*, refining his ideas, adapting and adopting anything that he had tried out on crowds and had seemed popular, appealing to the left, and attracting the bourgeoisie by appealing to their nationalism. He called himself both a revolutionary and a reactionary.

On June 6, 1919, Mussolini came forth with a document that embodied the announced aims of the Fascist movement. It declared for:

1. Universal suffrage, regional poll lists, proportional representation.
2. Reduction of the right to vote to 18 years, and of members of the Chamber of Deputies to 25.
3. Abolition of the National Senate.

4. Convocation of a national assembly to create the future constitution.
5. Formation of a national council of experts in labor, industry, transport, social hygiene, communications, elected by the trades and professional groups, with legislative powers. This group would elect a commissioner who would have the power of a minister of the government.
6. An eight-hour working day for all.
7. A minimum wage.
8. Participation of workers' representatives in the technical direction of industry.
9. Control of industry and public services by proletarian organizations.
10. Reorganization of railroads and transport.
11. Modification of the draft and insurance laws, reducing the age for old age insurance from 75 to 55.
12. A national militia for defense.
13. Nationalization of the armaments industry.
14. A foreign policy "that would enable Italy to take her proper place in peaceful competition between civilized nations."
15. A heavy progressive tax on capital with the purpose of expropriating wealth.
16. Confiscation of property belonging to religious congregations and abolition of bishops' stipends.
17. The revision of all war contracts and confiscation of 85 percent of war profits.

∽

So, finally, out of all his experiences, Mussolini had devised a program for government that combined his anarchistic will for destruction of the capitalist system with a plan for government. It would have a unicameral legislature, all adults would be able to vote, the emphasis would be on youth. Workers would be protected by a limitation on working hours and a minimum wage. Workers would have a share in management, and proletarian organizations would control industry and public services, the military would be controlled, and all armaments factories would be under government control. A progressive tax on capital wealth would tend to expropriate the holdings of the super rich and equalize wealth. The Church would lose part of its enormous wealth.

Along with the other radical movements, the new Fascist party began to grow, with branches throughout the industrial north, at Turin,

Genoa, Verona, and then Padua and Naples. Fascism crisscrossed the country, coming to Pavia, Trieste, Parma, Bologna, and Perugia. In two years more than twenty-two hundred branches were hailing Mussolini as their leader—*Il Duce.*

The manner of the war's end and the injustices of the peace of Versailles to Italy gave Mussolini his policies. Central to the development of a new Italian nationalism was a resentment against England, which had promised so much and had broken its promises. It was easy for Mussolini, with his personal background of hatred for wealth and power, to bring these sentiments to bear against Britain and France as they cut up Europe to suit themselves. The Austro-Hungarian Empire was dismembered in a fashion that would still have repercussions three-quarters of a century later. Czechs and Slovaks, Bosnians and Serbs were flung together. In the cutting up of the Ottoman Empire the same seeds of discontent were sown as the Italians watched in helpless fury, and the British and French presided over the drawing of a New Europe and a New Middle East, in which their own empires were significantly increased.

Mussolini began speaking of the "have" and "have not" nations, and he put Italy at the top of the "have nots." "In the West," he said, "there are the 'haves'; they are our rivals, our competitors, our enemies, and when they sometimes help us it is not an expression of solidarity but rather something between giving and blackmail." And he spoke vaguely of turning to the East for support. A naval delegation from Japan visited Italy that spring to be greeted enthusiastically with claims of brotherhood, because Japan, too, was seen as one of the "have nots." This was not only the Fascist position but also that of most of the liberals and leftists in Italy, who had come out of the war with a distinct distrust of Britain and France that now extended to the United States.

Industrialists, too, joined in this feeling and talked of recapturing their industrial power by substituting Eastern markets for the lost German and Austrian Empire markets. A new shipping line to run to Istanbul was opened that spring of 1919 with two 3,600-ton vessels, and another steamship line was established to run between Venice and Calcutta.

In the international uncertainties and economic hardship of Italy, strikes were endemic throughout the country. Most of them lasted only a short while but were pursued with such vehemence that they disrupted Italian life. For example, in Rome on April 10, 1919, a twenty-four-hour general strike that began at 6 A.M. completely disrupted trolley lines, general transportation, newspapers, bakeries, and hotel services.

Mussolini could not turn his back on his own past and now agree with the Socialists that intervention in the war had been a dreadful mistake, so he concentrated on the territorial acquisitions, Fiume and Dalmatia, which were promised to Italy by Britain and France in the secret London treaty, as if they were a debt still to be paid by the Allies. Thus was born the concept of Mussolini's Empire, which received excited approval from the disappointed youth who had fought the war only to be told that their contribution had been so minuscule to the Allied victory that they were not entitled to share in the disposition of the wealth of the Hohenzollerns and Hapsburgs.

President Wilson was also called to account for all these excesses, as he was by many other elements in Italy, which had now turned anti-American. Streets in Genoa and elsewhere, which had been named in honor of President Wilson, were renamed. In Genoa, Via Wilson became Via Fiume.

By April 1919, Mussolini felt secure enough to begin going after the Socialists in a new way. To emphasize the breach between the Fascists and the Socialists, he changed the subtitle of *Il Popolo d'Italia* from "The Socialist Daily" to "The Journal of Fighters and Producers" and on April 15, his Fascist action squads in Milan attacked a Socialist demonstration.

As the American embassy reported to Washington, this turned out to be a very important event. It began on Sunday, when the Socialists called a meeting and the Fascists went in to break it up. There was some violence and the police brought order only after several people had been injured. The Socialists then called for a general strike on Tuesday, April 15. This strike shut down Milan very successfully. In the afternoon the Socialists called a meeting at the arena, which was addressed by various Socialist leaders and other "proletariat speakers." When the meeting ended, the Socialists formed a parade, the marchers carrying red banners and singing revolutionary songs as they came back into the city. As the parade approached the city center it was met by a Fascist parade, arranged by Mussolini. The police tried to deflect the Fascists, and at first succeeded in keeping them away from the Socialists, but

a clash ensued in which numerous revolver shots were fired, inflicting a considerable number of casualties. The striker demonstration was routed in this clash, whereupon the counterdemonstration, finding the field free, proceeded to the offices of the Socialist newspaper

Avanti! There they overcame the resistance of the guards and the police stationed there and burned and looted the establishment. Shots were fired from the windows, resulting in further casualties. The total casualties for the day were four killed and twenty-seven wounded before the police secured order by nightfall.

The next day, general strikes were called by the Socialists at Genoa, Turin, and Bologna, and then the unrest spread to Naples. The strikes went on for three days.

Of this the Americans reported: "It is believed that this is not so much of a proletariat revolutionary movement as an organized political movement on the part of a radical element of the Socialist party. Last week was more or less a trial of strength on the part of the official Socialist party."

As a result the authorities at Milan were dismissed and new administrators brought in. Soon the Socialists were retaliating by murdering Fascists.

But the Fascists were not then important enough to be named by the Americans and other foreign observers. The most important political movement forming up was the *Partito Popolare Italiano*, a Catholic party led by a priest named Don Luigi Sturzo. This party was composed of Catholics but not directly affiliated with the Vatican. It was designed specifically as an antidote to the Socialists and other Marxists, and at the same time an antidote to the violent social upheaval demanded by Mussolini's Fascists.

In April 1919, for the first time, the American embassy in Rome *did* take note of *Il Popolo d'Italia* and began quoting some of its comments on the Italian scene. Obviously this was a recognition of the importance of the newspaper following the establishment of Mussolini's Fascist party. On April 22, *Il Popolo* criticized President Wilson, along with nearly every other paper in Italy, but *Il Popolo* drew a sharp distinction between Wilson and the American people, whose contributions to Europe were not forgotten, the paper said.

∽

By the middle of May 1919, Mussolini's dream of an empire was full-fledged. He made a speech one day to the sort of audience he loved, one full of excitement and vigor, one that responded to his calls for Italian greatness. It was at the Verdi Theater in Fiume, the port city on the coast of the new Yugoslavia. He spoke of the inevitability of the annexation of Fiume to Italy, of throwing the Western powers out of the Mediterranean, of freeing Egypt from Britain, and liberating Malta, of cutting up France's Mediterranean and African empire. The crowd cheered him and stamped their feet in enthusiasm and shouted for the leadership of *Il Duce*, to bring all this about.

By the fall of 1919, when national elections were to be held, however, Mussolini's Fascists were still a splinter party and could be grouped alongside the much larger *Fascio di Combattimento* of Gabriele D'Annunzio. At that point international observers grouped the political elements of Italy under three headings:

1. The government of Prime Minister Francesco Nitti;
2. D'Annunzio's militarists, the *Fascio di Combattimento*; and
3. The Socialists, who were now affiliated with the Russian Bolsheviks.

The political campaign had been heating up all summer, and then in September, the Fiume situation boiled over. The prime minister dissolved the Chamber of Deputies, which seemed to relieve the tension caused by the demand for Italian occupation of Fiume, but then, while the government was virtually disbanded, Gabriele D'Annunzio struck with his militarists and occupied Fiume with his Arditi. The Italian government did nothing, which meant the Nitti government's acquiescence, and the move was enormously popular in Italy. Mussolini knew all about it, since he was an ardent supporter of D'Annunzio's plans. In fact, D'Annunzio was the architect of the Fascist movement. Mussolini had borrowed the name *Fascio di Combattimento* from D'Annunzio. And when that leader took Fiume, with his officers and men in their black fezzes and flamboyant uniforms, it was as if Italy was being treated to a wave of the future.

D'Annunzio set up his own government in Fiume, with a government by ten corporations, and declared Fiume to be a province of Italy. He established several new methods of maintaining control. He arrested his opponents and dosed them with castor oil until they confessed to whatever he wanted. He held assemblies almost every day and invented a constant stream of slogans "For the People of Fiume." He held a procession of parades, meetings at which he distributed medals, and other public events designed to appeal to the Italian love for the theatrical. And Mussolini watched all this and took notes.

On September 13, 1919, Mussolini declared to a crowd assembled outside the *Il Popolo* offices that he saluted D'Annunzio and "would obey his every command." He raised funds for Fiume. In October he flew to Fiume and held a long meeting with D'Annunzio. The two of them talked about a march on Rome, to seize power. Mussolini persuaded D'Annunzio to refrain from any acts before the coming elections. But they did sketch out the character of the coming revolution. D'Annunzio was to be chief of state. The Vatican was to be respected. Mussolini warned that conditions for a march would not be proper until the spring of 1921.

But actually Mussolini did all this with tongue in cheek. He was not prepared to play number two to D'Annunzio for long. In spite of his declarations of support for the adventure, he had many reservations and he was sure that the adventure would fail because D'Annunzio did not have the temperament to make it succeed.

Meanwhile the Italian elections were coming up and Mussolini had hopes that his Fascist party would do well in them. Alas for his dreams, the result of the elections was a resounding victory for the Socialist party, which secured 156 seats in the Chamber of Deputies. The Moderate Socialists got 19 seats, the Liberals, 129, and Don Sturzo's Catholics, 101. There were 123 seats divided among splinter parties, but not one single seat for the Fascists. It was a complete and resounding debacle. Even in Milan, the Socialists polled 170,000 votes, and the Fascists 4,795.

The Socialists now crowed that Mussolini was finished and set up a siege of the offices of *Il Popolo,* which were protected by a barricade of barbed wire and guarded by twenty-five armed Arditi. The *Avanti!* published a report that a corpse identified as that of Benito Mussolini had been dragged out of the river. A mock funeral was held with the crowd marching through the streets singing dirty songs and when they reached Mussolini's house, they invited him to attend his own funeral. As they held a mock funeral, Mussolini indulged in his own gallows humor:

"If they break in," he said to associates, "I can always bite half a dozen of them and give them blood poisoning." A few days later, when he learned that the Socialists had paid six men twenty lire apiece to assassinate him, he said, "I thought I was worth more than that," and out of the till of *Il Popolo* gave each of the retired assassins two hundred lire.

Italy was becoming an armed camp and a cesspool of revolution. The Nitti government invoked censorship and cut out of the paper a political attack by *Il Popolo* on the government. Mussolini retaliated by running four pages of blank paper printed only with the masthead and a statement: "Banned by order of that swine Nitti."

∽

Mussolini was not the only one to feel that way. By 1920 Italy was a series of paramilitary forces, barely held together by a central government so insecure that when Prime Minister Nitti had to make a trip to southern Italy he dared not trust himself to the trains; he took an armored limousine to Anzio and boarded a destroyer for the journey.

The left wing Socialists, who were really Bolsheviks, staged a Bolshevik-style coup of metal workers who struck from Milan to Naples in six hundred factories, which they held for a month, flying the red flag of revolution until the industrialists gave in to their demand for a wage hike. Fiat president Giovanni Agnelli was forced to march through a cordon of red flags to his office, and then to kiss a portrait of Lenin that had replaced that of the King.

The communist unions even dominated the farming countryside, and any farmers who would not give in to them found they were boycotted by the barber, the grocer, and the doctor. A line of red flags in a hayfield meant the workers were harvesting their share of the grain, and leaving that employer's share to rot.

In this atmosphere Mussolini promised to bring order and stop the harassment of the people by the reds, and, little by little, his promises were heard.

Mussolini began to distance himself from the tension, which had his nails bitten down to the quick, by taking flying lessons. Although he crashed during a landing attempt on his first solo flight, he continued until he had seventeen thousand flying hours. He learned to drive a sleek Bianchina sports car, although at first he never changed gears and was always boiling the engine over. He learned to fence and challenged all his detractors to duels with rapiers, duels that were fought beneath bridges, in fields, and sometimes in rented rooms. He fixed his rapier to his hand with pitch and was never disarmed; although often bloodied, he never gave in and was always declared, in writing, to be the victor.

∽

In the fall of 1920 Mussolini began to make overtures to Prime Minister Giovanni Giolitti, who privately regarded the Fascist leader as a clown and a person not to be worried about. Giolitti believed he could use Mussolini against the Socialists and then get rid of him. The Rome government began to show a new tolerance for the Fascists and for Fascist bullyboys who carried out violent raids against their political opponents. And so a deal was struck. Mussolini agreed to support the

Italian government's destruction of the D'Annunzio government of Fiume. On Christmas Eve, 1920, an Italian naval squadron bombarded Fiume and after four days D'Annunzio vacated the city. Mussolini did not stir a muscle to assist D'Annunzio, to whom he had promised everything. Mussolini's answer to his critics was that D'Annunzio had fallen out of touch with Italian political reality. He did not mean a word of it. D'Annunzio was his mentor. He had put together the trappings of dictatorship, and Mussolini had decided to displace and copy him. Mussolini would take over the flamboyance and the corporate dictatorship. He would be Il Duce—*The* leader. And he resolved that he would not make what he considered to be D'Annunzio's fatal mistake. He would never set himself up against the army.

That Christmas, as Italy sagged in the face of a new series of strikes and military mutinies, and the government abandoned its occupation of Albania and Valona, Mussolini inveighed against the failures of the government. He saw the French taking over the Middle East, and the British the Mediterranean. Troubles at home and abroad shook all Italy, and in this time of trouble the Fascist promises appeared to offer new hope to hundreds of thousands of people. The Fascists won control of the municipal council of Bologna, and very nearly defeated the Socialists in Milan. Shortly afterward, one of the Fascist members of the Bologna council was killed in an altercation with the Socialists, and Mussolini carried out reprisals against his political enemies. It was the first time that he reacted to violence with violence, and it showed the way of the future. Mussolini was getting ready to act to secure political power over the whole country.

CHAPTER 5

∽

Fascism on the Rise

The tension over Fiume was well illustrated in an incident that occurred in Trieste in November 1920, just before the government sent its bombardment squadron to drive Consul D'Annunzio from the territory and end an unbearable embarrassment to the Italian administration. By that time millions of Italians hated the British and Americans, whom they held responsible for the failure of the Versailles Peace Conference to give Fiume to Italy. The occasion was a gala performance at the Verdi Theater to commemorate the second anniversary of the Italian victory in the Veneto, to which all the consular corps were invited. The American consul, concerned lest there be an incident at the performance, elected not to go but gave his ticket to his secretary, Archie Clifton.

Clifton sat with the other members of the consular corps in the dress circle. At the opening the military band of the Trieste garrison played the Italian national anthem and some patriotic marches. Through the hall could be heard shouts of "Long Live D'Annunzio" and "Fiume." During the interval the British consul, who did not understand Italian, left the performance, and so Clifton and the French consul sat together for the second half. The seats on their right were vacant.

A few moments before the rising of the curtain on the third act came cries of "Down with America, England, and France," followed by more cries for D'Annunzio and Fiume and Dalmatia.

At the end of the third act, a group of young Fascists gathered in the auditorium and tried to force their way into the center, shouting that all Britishers should leave the theater. For some time the Italian police stopped them, but their leader, a lawyer named Giunta, broke through the police line and mounted the director's stand. He then began a fiery speech directed against the British consul and against all Britons in general and against the American consul. The final words of the speech were "It is a good thing that the British consul has already left the theater, otherwise we should have gone to prison or to another world, or he, and we shall beat up every Britisher that we meet in Trieste."

The speech was received with loud applause from the Italian audience. Then the curtain went up for the fourth act, and the theater quieted.

Secretary Clifton then became conscious of an Arditi officer sitting down in the empty seat on his right and concluded that the officer had come to be sure he did not leave the theater. He began to hear whispers, "Is that he?" and the word "American."

But the officer turned out to be with the police, who had been sent by the governor to protect the consular corps. Clifton and the French consul then went down to the vestibule, which they found swarming with police, and the police accompanied them to police headquarters and then home, where they arrived safely.

Such was life for foreigners in this unsettled Italy of 1920. The tension did not end with the bombardment of Fiume and the ejection of D'Annunzio, but what did happen was that the followers of D'Annunzio transferred their allegiance from the fallen one to Mussolini.

Already he had taken over the trappings of the gaudy D'Annunzio, the black shirts and black fezzes, and gray-green trousers and puttees of the military-style uniform. He sat in his offices at 35 Via Paolo da Cannobio, behind a desk, sipping a glass of milk and interviewing visitors, a black skull and bones flag at his back, a machine gun trained on the door. Outside his bullies guarded the offices of *Il Popolo d'Italia*. All over Italy they were now moving freely, ignored or assisted by the authorities who were sick of strikes and Communist and Socialist bullying. At the highest level, Mussolini had an alliance with the cabinet that, although not generally known to the public, was protective of the Fascists. In 1921 Prime Minister Giolitti began to give open support to the Fascists. It was not long before the Socialists split and the Communists split off from their alliance, and the Fascists began to triumph in their encounters. The Fascists grew ever more violent in their assaults. Between January and May of 1921, they destroyed 120 labor union offices and invaded more than 200 Socialist centers, killing 243 people and wounding 1,100. This struggle between the red and the black shirts would continue through all of 1921 and 1922.

To say that Italy was in dire straits in 1920 would be to understate the case. The nation was unraveling. The lira declined steadily in value. International credits were exhausted. And when Italy appealed to Britain for that loan they were supposed to get under the secret treaty, the answer was no. In truth, Britain was suffering, too, from the international inflation and glut of goods produced during the war years; this year, 1920, it afflicted almost all the industrial world. The British ambassador in Rome suggested that Italy might see a revolution similar to that of the Bolsheviks in Russia, and conditions certainly did not seem to deny this. The year 1920 saw nearly two thousand strikes in Italy. The workers in Piedmont and Lombardy took over the factories and set up Workers' Councils in the Bolshevik pattern. Mussolini came out flatfootedly in favor of the move, claiming that the capitalists and industrialists were failing to maintain production and that the workers had the right to take over to maintain their jobs.

But the workers could not manage the technical ends of production and the factories were soon worse off than ever, so the movement collapsed and the industrialists got their factories back. Mussolini was criticized by the industrialists, who were quietly supporting him as a possible answer to Italy's problems. He replied that he had never really believed in the movement, but that his policy was to buy the workers off by improvements in pay and working conditions.

At the same time the military began to rebel against the government. During the war the Italians had taken over Albania and they still held it. But now whole units refused to embark for duty there. The government decided to abandon Albania. Mussolini protested, for he was already deep into his dreams of rejuvenating the Roman Empire in a new Italy. He predicted that Italy would also abandon its hold on Dalmatia and would soon get out of Africa as well.

This was the year that Italy began to turn to Mussolini. His appeal was to the young, to soldiers disillusioned with a government that had not given them anything for their service, to the young voters just coming to grips with public life, who saw in the old political parties nothing but corruption and failure.

In 1921 Prime Minister Giolitti abandoned all hope of reaching accommodation with the Socialists and began to support Mussolini's anti-Socialist campaign openly. Privately Giolitti had no use for Mussolini, but he thought he could use him to destroy the Socialists, and then discard him.

So in April 1921 Giolitti called for new national elections to choose a Chamber of Deputies. Giolitti hoped that a Liberal Democratic bloc, which he led, would win three hundred seats and so make him independent of Socialists and of *Partito Populare* votes. He proposed to Mussolini that the Fascists should form a part of his bloc. His plan was to use the violence of the Fascists to intimidate the Socialists. Mussolini accepted the idea, saying he did not fear the idea of contamination by association with other blocs.

The May 15 elections were held in a relatively calm atmosphere. Genoa, where the election was monitored by American consul John Ball Osborne for the State Department, was more or less on the mark in the returns. The Liberal Democratic bloc led, the Socialists were second, and the *Partito Populare* was third. That is how it was nationally, too, with the Fascists coming in fourth, winning thirty-five seats. But the election was a bitter defeat for Giolitti; his Liberal Democrats won only 159 seats and were worse off than before. In fact, observers got the opinion that the surge of Fascist violence encouraged by Giolitti that spring had been counterproductive and that the general public, having reacted against Socialist violence, was now reacting against Fascist violence.

What was important was that the Fascists now had a place in the Chamber of Deputies, and Mussolini was elected to the Parliament in Milan with 124,000 votes, whereas in 1919 he had received only 4,000.

On June 11, the new parliament assembled to hear the speech of the King, and here Mussolini had the first open challenge to his authority over the party. He wanted to abstain from attendance, because the King would be present, and Benito stood against the monarchy. But he was outvoted in the party caucus.

In the course of the debate on the address by the King, Mussolini made his maiden speech in the Chamber of Deputies. It was a typical attack on the Socialists and on government foreign policy, but it had one extra ingredient. In this speech, Mussolini declared his intention to support the continued existence and position of the Vatican. Since he was unchurched, and his politics had wavered from one side to another, his attitude about the Vatican had never before been clarified. His one caveat was that the Vatican must renounce its dreams of controlling Italy, and he said he thought that was already happening. Otherwise, he had no quarrel. "I say this because the development of Catholicism in the world, an increase in numbers of the four hundred million who in every part of the world look to Rome, is a matter of interest and pride also to us who are Italians."

But these moderate words were belied on the outside by the behavior of the growing Fascist organizations. Fascist enforcers established and enforced rules under which they demanded that localities live. In Adria, south of Venice, they forced liquor dealers to put a pint bottle of castor oil in their windows, a warning to drunks as to what would happen to them if they were found inebriated on the street. In Alessandria, in the Piedmont district, they assembled all the pickpockets, burglars, and con men and told them they had a choice: They could either get jobs and join the community, or they could go to the hospital.

The reaction of the middle class and even the authorities to this takeover of authority had been good at first, but by the middle of 1921 it was beginning to sour. At the end of June, a group of Fascists established a Fascists Club in Valenza, an industrial city in the Alessandria district. The Communists, who were strong there, did not like it. The Fascists paraded with their flags through the city, singing their anthem *"Giovinezza"* (Youth). The Communists responded with *"Banda Rossi Triumfera"* (Red Flag Triumphant), and a scuffle broke out.

When the Fascists left the city in a truck, as they crossed a dark lane a volley of shots broke out, to which the Fascists immediately replied with another. The Fascist shots were ineffective, but the Communist shots killed one and wounded several of the Fascists.

The news spread and brought to the city a large group of other Fascists. They set fire to the Chamber of Labor, and the Communist club. A group of Fascists gathered at city hall and ordered the city authorities to pull down the red flag and place the national flag at half mast.

The Fascists then demanded that the police find and arrest the killers. The police said they had no idea who or where they were. Acts of reprisal went on all day long as the Fascist bands searched the area for the murderers. In the afternoon they discovered a large group of Communists hiding in a wood and attacked. But as darkness fell the Communists escaped without casualties. The Fascists then demanded that the city be put under martial law. They also asked the Socialist city officials to resign and declared a strike in the whole province of Alessandria.

This was duly reported by the American consul in the area, who also noted that the Fascists were carrying out a powerful propaganda campaign in this center of Socialist power, and that their basic appeal seemed to be to students and the young. "During a recent parade," the observer noted, "even small boys of about twelve to fourteen were noticed among those participating."

But these days Mussolini had begun to see that the violence of his people was becoming counterproductive to his dream of becoming the national leader. He, on the other hand, was now a Parliamentarian. When Giolitti suddenly reviewed his options and saw the difficulties of holding a government together, he dissolved the government and called on the King to choose a successor. The King consulted other Parliament leaders, including Mussolini, who recommended one man, but the King chose Ivanoe Bonomi, the reform Socialist. An effort was made to restore order, but by this time the army, police, and provincial administrations had fallen very much under Fascist influence. Mussolini announced that his party would leave the coalition and sit with the opposition from now on.

In June, Mussolini began making overtures for civil peace. In Venice his followers claimed he had gone over to the Republican party, and they began to debate what to do. After some discussion they decided to remain loyal to Mussolini, but the violence against the Socialists and Communists did not cease, and in the middle of that month they set fire to the Socialist Railwaymen's club.

The Fascist leaders in the provinces were beginning to get out of hand. At Ferrara, Italo Balbo captured scores of Socialist red flags and put them down as a carpet for Mussolini when he came to visit. Mussolini angrily refused to walk on them. In Carrara, Fascist leader Renato Ricci organized six thousand Blackshirts to free six Fascists who had been jailed, and they ran a reign of terror until the magistrates gave in and freed the men. In Florence, the Fascists conducted a series of murders of Socialist railroad men.

Mussolini, who had his personal antennae attuned to public opinion, was becoming more and more aware of a public revulsion against these excesses. On June 21, 1921, in a speech in the Chamber of Deputies, he dropped a hint that the Fascists would disarm if their enemies would. The prime minister then called for peace, and Mussolini agreed that it was a good idea. But his followers did not think so. On July 12 the National Fascist Council adopted a resolution saying this was no time for any agreement with their opponents. And as if to emphasize it, the Genoa section of Fascists distributed a manifesto calling on merchants to lower their prices and giving them less than a week to comply. The shopkeepers applied for police protection. But most of the shops did reduce their prices, and so violence was avoided.

An even more strident indication of the Fascist nature occurred when a number of Fascist deputies surrounded a Communist deputy and threw him out of the Chamber. Revolvers were drawn by both sides, although there was no firing.

∽

But Mussolini went ahead with his plans to stop fighting physically and on August 2, 1921, signed an agreement, along with other supporters, with the Socialists to renounce violence. This agreement brought serious dissension within the Fascist movement. At a Congress in Bologna, Fascists from the north condemned the truce. Mussolini replied by resigning from the executive committee of the Fascists and said he would remain a plain member of the Milan Fascist organization. Several leaders, including Dino Grandi and Italo Balbo, challenged Mussolini and were ready to break with him. Mussolini remained in Rome. He was now convinced that to attain power he had to abjure violence.

On August 26 the National Fascist Council met at Florence. Feelings against Mussolini continued to run high, spurred by Balbo and Grandi, who were continuing their terrorist operations against Mussolini, but many of the members, who knew his changeable personality, thought he could be persuaded to reverse his proposition for a peace pact, so they postponed action until the full party Congress, which would come in Rome in November. The decision to remain with Mussolini was furthered by an incident in which eight Fascists were killed at Modena by government forces and Mussolini came to make the funeral address. He said that while he was now opposed to violence, his heart remained with the Fascists. The public yearned for peace, he said, but there could be no peace as long as the Fascists were called thugs, assassins, and mercenaries. This was a left-handed criticism of the continued violence but not an attack on the Balbo–Grandi sector. It was regarded by the moderates as the beginning of a program of reconciliation.

Meanwhile discussions began about Mussolini's idea to create a Fascist political party. The reconciliation was advanced by a new gaudy display of Mussolini's personal bravery. He was challenged to a duel by Francesco Ciccotti, a former friend and Socialist, over an attack on Ciccotti in *Il Popolo D'Italia*. The duel was hard to arrange because the authorities had Mussolini under scrutiny, but it was finally held in a private villa at Leghorn. The fight was long, and after the fourteenth round, Ciccotti's physician intervened and said his heart would not stand more fighting. The fight was called off, but Mussolini regained considerable ground with his militant Fascist comrades because of it.

In October 1921 the Socialists held the National Congress in Milan, and its results, too, furthered the reconciliation. The left wing controlled and they threw out the Social Democrats and and declared themselves to be a revolutionary party. This, Mussolini said, meant that they broke the agreement with him and freed him from it.

So when the Fascists assembled in the Augusteo at Rome, four thousand strong, on November 7, 1921, the ground had already been laid for reunion. At a private meeting Mussolini said that although he could not repudiate the truce with the Socialists, he would do nothing to impede the work of the Fascist squadrons that terrorized the enemy. In the end, the issue was shelved. Mussolini's position was embraced by Grandi and Balbo, and the split was ended. Mussolini had surrendered, rather graciously, but he had also learned a lesson; he determined that he would not again be in a position to be humiliated or deserted by any group. If he attained power, he would take measures to keep his distance from the power of the Fascists.

Over the objections of many of his followers, Mussolini now began the mechanics of creating a political party of what was basically a movement. Supported by Michele Bianchi, secretary of the Milan Fascist unit, he secured passage by the executive committee of a resolution for the organization of the party. This was carried by a large majority against the vote by Grandi and his associates. Mussolini was elected chief of the executive committee and Bianchi secretary general of the party. The new party platform follows:

1. The functions of the state would be limited to those of political nature. The other functions were to be delegated to technical councils elected by professional and economic corporations.
2. The question of monarchy versus republic would be left undecided.
3. Public ownership would be extended to the land where it was suitable but there would be no socialization of the land.
4. The colony would be decentralized and the bureaucracy reformed.
5. The workers would have no right to strike public services.
6. There would be no monopolies and no subsidies. Private industry was to be encouraged.
7. The peace treaties of World War I would be revised based on economic considerations.
8. The army and navy would be maintained and modernized.

The platform, compared to that described in Chapter 4, had switched sharply to the right as Mussolini's experience had broadened. Since his radical beginnings, he had quarreled with socialism. Now he observed in an article in *Il Popolo D'Italia* on November 22, 1921, that the days of democracy were ending. It was probable that the Italian people would turn from government by the masses to government by the few, or look to a dictator. Already, he pointed out, government by the masses had failed in the economic field, and Russia was turning to dictatorship in the factories. That article, old Socialist allies told each other, proclaimed Mussolini's desire to be the savior and dictator of Italy.

As the year came to an end, all the talk about agreement with the Socialists was forgotten. The economic situation in Italy deteriorated further. The important Banca di Sconto failed, ruining thousands of small depositors. New strikes, almost continuous, kept any recovery from possibility. The war between the Fascists and the Socialists grew hotter, not cooler. Italo Balbo led Fascist operations in the north into paramilitary adventures. The extent of their ability to make trouble was well indicated by a visit of a French military mission to the Venezia Giulia area in late September.

The purpose was to honor the French who had been killed on the Italian side in the late war against Austria and Germany. And since the visit was official, the greeting by the Italian authorities was warm and cordial. But from the outset, the Fascists of the area set out to break up the ceremonies. After purely ceremonial matters, the reception continued in Venice and General Diaz, the commander in chief of the Army, arrived to pay his respects for the Italian government.

On the night of his arrival, a noisy group of Fascists arrived to whistle and hoot and curse the *Marseillaise* as it was played. The Fascists came out in force, and although they claimed that the demonstration against the French was a general Italian demonstration, that was not the case. Virtually no groups were seen but the Fascists.

The second day opened with an official reception at the Doge's Palace, and was very successful—inside. But as the parties made their exit from the Palace, the Fascists filled the Piazza San Marco and ignored the pleas of the mayor and other dignitaries to desist from difficulties.

But the worst was the second night when authorities had planned for a musical concert in the Piazza San Marco. So tense was the situation that the prefect and the admiral of Venice suggested that the concert be canceled. The concert broke down almost immediately in a series of fights in the Piazza. The Fascists ordered that the *Giovinezza* be played first and then nothing else. When the band started with the *Marseillaise,* the Fascists began to shout. They threw pepper into the faces of a large choir that had assembled to sing. They surrounded the bandmaster and broke up the band, which never could be gotten together again.

Soldiers began to clear the Piazza as General Diaz came down and tried to speak to the crowd. He was drowned out by the Fascists. Soon the police and soldiers began using clubs and gunbutts, and many people were arrested, all Fascists, from Venice.

In the north, Italo Balbo was given command of the Fascist Squadron, or military unit, in Emilia, Romagna, Mantua, the Marches, Venice, the Trentino, Istria, and Zara. He organized his first paramilitary operation in April and on May 12, 1922, sixty-three thousand Rome Fascists appeared at Ferrara to demand that the authorities initiate local public works to hire the unemployed. From the moment they arrived at the city gate, the life of the whole area was thrown into disruption. Hotels, shops and restaurants had to close down. Public transport stopped. The Fascists closed the city gates and would not let anyone in. The schools were requisitioned as quarters for the Fascists, who seized food from the shops and restaurants. The carabinieri and police were ordered to their barracks and the city was in Fascist hands. Balbo announced that the authorities had forty-eight hours to get permission from Rome to start the public works.

The authorities capitulated and the Fascists withdrew, victorious. Balbo looked for another target and found it in Bologna, where a Blackshirt had been killed by Socialists. On May 22, twenty thousand Fascist militia occupied Bologna. But the prefect of Bologna was tough and he indicated that there would be no capitulation. Balbo was ready for war, but Mussolini forced him to evacuate and suspend his occupation.

The order was tactful, but definite. "Dear Friend, It is necessary to terminate, for a period which will be very short, your magnificent action. The state has resolved to display for the first time and after many indications, its capacity to live and to resist. A pause is necessary. We must not exhaust our superb militia. I am sure you will obey my order with the same discipline as you showed in your mobilization." And Mussolini also sent telegrams of congratulation to Balbo, and Bianchi published a public statement of gratitude and praise for Balbo.

On July 23 the Fascists occupied Ravenna as reprisal for attacks on Fascists there. Two days later the buildings of the *Socialist Cooperatives* were destroyed by fire. Mussolini again ordered Balbo to withdraw, but Balbo moved against Parma, where the local Fascists had complained that the city government was unfriendly. On August 4, Balbo swaggered into the office of the prefect and was received in the presence of the general commanding the local military garrison. Balbo complained that if the Socialist militia was not dissolved, he would take over the authority of the state. The military did enter the Socialist area and took down their barricades but did not try to disarm them. This was not enough and Balbo started his war against the reds. In the midst of it a telephone call came from Bianchi in Rome telling him to avoid conflict with the army at all costs. Balbo said he would ignore the order, but in fact he withdrew and the fighting stopped. But Balbo again met with the authorities and said he would not withdraw from the city until the army had taken over the control of Parma and the Socialists had been disarmed. Ultimately this demand was met. On August 6, the Fascists left the city in parade, and then went through the province, trapping and killing Socialists along the way.

By such means, at the end of the summer of 1922, the power of the Socialists in northern Italy was broken and because of Mussolini's insistence on staying out of trouble with the army, the army tended to look with favor on the Fascists.

CHAPTER 6

∽

Italian Crisis

E ver since the formation of the Fascist party, Mussolini had hesitated between two roads to power. One was the Balbo road advocated by his military lieutenants, who in 1922 were showing what they
could do. But privately Mussolini preferred to take power by following
a constitutional course. In three short years he had become "somebody" in Italy, and although his *Il Popolo D'Italia* was not highly
regarded in diplomatic circles (and was seldom quoted) and many high-
placed authorities regarded him as a "humbug, a poseur, and a charla-
tan," the few foreign journalists who had been to see him were
impressed. George Slocombe, correspondent of the *London Daily Herald*, said he thought Mussolini was destined to play an important role
in Italy. Journalists from such potent papers as *Il Messaggero* and *Corriere della Sera* might sneer at him, but the government no longer did.
And he had also begun to have a taste of internationalism other than
the heavy dose of Swiss socialism he had taken in his youth. He turned
more to serious journalism, less to rabble rousing, and even founded a
review, *Gerarchia*, which was basically a medium for his own message.

In January 1922, he had used his journalistic passport to travel to
Cannes and cover an international conference for *Il Popolo D'Italia*.
There he was received by France's Aristide Briand, the prime minister
of France. He was traveling in rarified circles. A few weeks later he
traveled to Berlin where he met Chancellor Wirth, Gustav Stresemann,
and Walther Rathenau. The attention he received, and the pleasure of
being in such high company, tended to submerge the old revolutionary
hatred for authority and power. Now he was having a taste of that
power and he enjoyed it.

He had a meeting with Pietro Nenni, his old companion of Forlì jail, and they discussed politics and the roads they had taken. The Republican Nenni observed that Mussolini had now become entangled in the trap of his own violent party. Mussolini said that he had fought the civil war with the Socialists to prevent them from taking over Italy, but that he was now ready to make peace. Nenni said that was impossible, he had too far alienated the left wing to ever be able to work with them. Mussolini said then that if war was inevitable, it would be war.

But Mussolini really did not want to fight anymore. When Pope Benedict XV died and Pius XI became the new pope, Mussolini said he hoped that with this new pope, relations between Italy and the Vatican would improve. Here was an indication that as he could not afford to anger the army, so he could not afford to have the enmity of the Vatican. He had come a long way in his search for power.

He had sensed in the last few months of 1921 that Italy was approaching a constitutional crisis. In February 1922 the Bonomi government collapsed in a vote of no confidence by the Chamber of Deputies. The cause was the continuing deterioration of the Italian economy. The fall was accompanied by loud shouts from the crowds denouncing democracy, and calling for military dictatorship. The crisis lasted for about two weeks before a government could be formed, and then it was a very weak government, under Luigi Facta, a politician of very little talent.

∽

Mussolini wrote in *Gerarchia* that it was his belief that the age of democracy had run its short course and that the world was now moving toward the right and totalitarianism. This observation came as a result of his watching the public and its reaction to parliamentary democracy in the past two years. He could hear as well as anyone the unhappy cries of the demonstrators and strikers against a government that could not seem to make the economy run.

As he predicted, the Facta government lasted only a few months, and in the third week of July 1922, it collapsed. But what was the alternative? The King called on Vittorio Orlando, Bonomi, two or three others, and then Orlando again, but nothing could be done to budge the parties from their ironclad positions in opposition to one another. After two weeks of parliamentary crisis, Facta was called again to form a government. That government got into trouble immediately, and the Fascists were the cause. The Socialist Labor alliance proclaimed a general strike on August 1, against the activities of Italo Balbo in Romagna.

Mussolini had already gone on record as being impatient with the parliamentary activities and prepared to use force to attain power. In the first Facta crisis he had spoken up in the chamber of Deputies:

> If from this crisis, a government emerges which resolves the urgent, anxious problem of the hour, that is to say the problem of pacification and of the normalization of relations between the various parties, we'll happily accept it and we shall seek to bring our rank and file to recognize the need, deeply felt by the whole nation, for order, work, and discipline. But if perchance there emerges a reactionary government of violent anti-Fascist complexion, take note, gentlemen, that we shall react with the utmost energy and resolution. To reaction we shall reply by insurrection. I must say that of the two eventualities I prefer the first on patriotic and humane grounds. I prefer that fascism, which is a force that you Socialists can no longer ignore and still less think to destroy, should come to participate in the life of the state by legal means, after preparing for a legal contest of power. But there is also the other contingency to which in good conscience, I must refer. Each of you in the impending crisis and in the discussion between your groups with a view to finding a solution, must take account of my declaration which I entrust to your meditation and to your conscience.

This second Facta crisis was the seventh constitutional crisis suffered by Italy in three years. The public was thoroughly sick of the swings and sways of parliamentary democracy.

The situation came to a head after Facta had been in office for only a few hours. With the general strike call by the Socialists, Mussolini mobilized his Fascist army up north and gave the government forty-eight hours in which to act against public servants on strike. The government did nothing. But the Fascists got some support in taking over, and they ran the public services, the trains for example, without tickets. The strike collapsed on August 2, 1922, and it was a blow to the prestige of Facta and a triumph for Mussolini.

The Reform Socialists—not the militants—recognized the nature of the crisis: "We emerge from this test well beaten. We have played our last card and lost Milan and Genoa, which seemed the strongest card in our defense. In the Lombardy capital the party newspaper has once more gone up in flames, the administration of the town has been snatched from its lawful representatives. It is the same elsewhere. Every important center bears the marks of the Fascist hurricane. We must face facts: the Fascists are masters of the field."

In the north, Balbo's army launched new attacks on the Socialists in Genoa, Leghorn, Parma, and Ancona. As noted, they had burned

Avanti!, the Socialist newspaper, for the second time. To celebrate they needed someone to appear and praise them. Mussolini was called, but Mussolini was off on a dirty journey with a woman, and so Gabriel D'Annunzio was trotted out to do the job. When Mussolini surfaced again in a few days he was chagrined, but he had to congratulate the party and praise them for getting D'Annunzio to do his job.

On August 6, the Italian press was full of speculation (started by *Avanti!*) that the Fascists would now make an attempt to seize power in Italy. But as the days went by the predictors began to feel embarassed because Mussolini did nothing. In an interview with *Mattino* of Naples, Mussolini revealed why. The March on Rome had already begun, he said. The Fascists were ready to take power, but not necessarily by violent means. He wanted new elections.

But the parliamentary crisis continued. One politician after another tried to rig up a government. Mussolini was approached and asked what the Fascists wanted to participate. "Control over the most important offices," Mussolini replied.

He did not need to take these offers seriously. Time was on his side. On August 13, the prefect of Milan reported to the Minister of the Interior that the military could no longer be relied upon to halt emergencies. Too many of them were Fascists. The government calculated then that the Fascist movement had risen to embrace more than a million men, of whom two hundred thousand were armed and uniformed. And every day the public was growing more disgusted with democracy, more prone to accept the Fascists.

On September 20, in a speech at Udine, Mussolini laid out the Fascist plan for all to see. Violence, he said, was not necessarily bad; it could be necessary to cut out a cancer. The cancer now was parliamentary democracy. He did not believe the majority was always right. The task of fascism was to weld the nation into an organized unit—which heaven knew it was not then—and to achieve greatness for Italy.

When somebody asked about his programs, he answered that the Fascists wished to govern Italy. Programs were not important; what was important were men and the resolution to act. He was asked about the monarchy, and he admitted that he did not much like the monarchy but that it would be inexpedient to do anything about that.

The Fascists did not intend to destroy everything in Italy, he assured his audience, but only to demolish the social democratic superstructure that had failed so miserably to govern in behalf of the people. The state the Fascists would create would ignore the miseries of these past four years since the war and it would represent the nation. It would protect all and oppose all who threatened its sovereignty. This was the state that would ignore the ignoble recent past and issue directly from the Italian victory in the war of 1918. This new state would guarantee the greatness of Italy.

These days, even the American embassy was paying attention to what Mussolini said. Following is a part of the embassy's report to Washington on the Udine speech.

> Any utterance by Mussolini commands an extensive audience. Every word he pronounces is carefully reported. Each remark is closely examined. If he vaporizes, his votaries are indulgent. When his language is firm, their praises are unrestrained. And, at all times, he has the constant attention of his opponents. They chafe, they burst into recriminations, they appear pathetic in the light of the Fascist play acting.
>
> In last week's report excerpts from Mussolini's Udine discourse were embodied. At the same time the importance of the speech was indicated. The press, in the following days, allotted considerable space and consideration to his declarations.
>
> The chauvinistic press naturally lined up solidly behind the declarations. The speech of the Fascist dictator was described as the most remarkable document of Mussolini's wisdom, and pleasing because of the recognition that the monarchy represented his stopping point. "Honorable Mussolini," wrote the *Giornale D'Roma* "your firm note in the Udine discourse is the clearest demonstration that Fascism tends to reconstruction rather than destruction."

Il Messaggero applauded the Udine speech for its language, clear and unequivocal. The *Giornale D'Italia* extolled its clarity.

Mussolini took his message not only to Udine but also to Cremona in the valley of the Po, Milan, the industrial heart of Italy, and Naples, the center of southern Italy: "We wish Italy to become fascist for we are tired of seeing her governed by policies which waver between negligence and cowardice, and we are specially tired of seeing her considered abroad as a negligible quantity." "From the banks of the Piave," he added, "we have started our march which will stop only when we have obtained the supreme goal: Rome. No obstacle can stop us."

Afterward he paused.

"I was acclaimed as a conqueror and a savior," he wrote in his autobiography. "This flattered me, but be sure that it did not make me proud. I felt stronger and yet realized the more that I faced mountains of responsibility. In those four cities so different and so far, one from the other, I saw the same light! I had with me the hopes, the good, the pure, the sincere soul of the Italian people."

In Cremona Mussolini was greeted with shouts, "A Roma, A Roma," and as he moved within the Fascist circle, the impatience of his cohort became very apparent. The Fascists wanted action. The people were willing to accept action. Mussolini became infected with the eagerness, and it was well that he did, because the moment of decision was on him, and if he delayed, he could very easily lose the loyalty of his Fascists.

Toward the end of September 1922 the Fascists occupied Balzano and Trent, and on October 6 Mussolini had a conversation with Italo Balbo in which they agreed to make a second attack on Parma and make a march on Rome. But on October 11 he told Balbo to suspend the Parma operation and meet him at Milan on October 16. It was obvious to the leading Fascists that the March on Rome was about to begin.

∽

In October the pace quickened. On October 9 American ambassador Richard Washburn Child wrote Washington that with the approach of the Fascist Congress in the middle of October, Italy was entering a period of danger.

> The essence of this development is that a new and powerful antigovernment force has been evolved. The Fascist movement no longer dedicates itself to support of the government against revolution. To all intents and purposes it now proposes revolution. I have been inclined to weigh the probability that a dictatorship movement wholly new in program and spirit would arise from the whisperings of discontent permeating all classes; I am now convinced that the Fascists, transformed from an antirevolutionary movement to a revolutionary machinery, have the opportunity to submerge for the time all other movements.

On October 7, G. Harlan Miller, Third Secretary of the American embassy in Rome, reported that Mussolini had published in *Il Popolo D'Italia* a long article about the Fascist army that detailed its makeup and regulations. This was the first indication to the public that there really was a Fascist army. Miller's analysis of the reasoning behind this was that it was part of Mussolini's effort to clarify the Fascist position.

"The spectacle of a party that is at the same time an army, with the formal organization of an army, was a factor so real that the press seemed stunned," said Secretary Miller.

That week in *Il Popolo D'Italia*, Mussolini declared, "We cannot go on in this manner. The nation cannot have two governments—it cannot witness a state within a state. The nation can have only one government."

On October 16, Mussolini held a meeting in Milan with Balbo and Generals Fara and Ceccherini in which the plans for military action were laid in great secrecy. The command of the Fascist troops was split among Balbo, General De Vecchi and General De Bono. They all agreed that the moment for action was coming, but Mussolini secured delay until after the Fascist Party Congress of October 24. A Quadrumvirate would be established—Balbo, the other two generals, and Michele Bianchi, secretary of the party. Mussolini would not appear. He was to be above the fray. He produced a draft document:

> Fascists, Italians:
> The hour of decisive battle has struck. Four years ago the national army at about this time launched the supreme offensive which led it to victory. Today the army of the Blackshirts grasps that mutilated victory and moving resolutely on Rome leads her back to the glory of the Capitol. Today leaders and legionaries have been mobilized. The martial law of fascism had been put into force. By order of the duce the military, political, and administrative functions of the party leadership have been vested in a secret quadrumvirate with dictatorial powers. . . ."

Then Mussolini turned to stalling the efforts of the Parliamentarians to bring his Fascists into parliamentary government. He conducted negotiations with Giolitti. He gave an interview to the *Manchester Guardian* saying that Italian fascism wanted only peace and reconstruction. This was to placate foreign opinion. He also went to see American ambassador Child and asked many questions about the American attitude toward fascism.

On October 23, Mussolini arrived at Rome on his way to Naples to the party Congress and stopped off to have a talk with Antonio Salandra. Mussolini demanded the resignation of the Facta government and the award of five ministries in the new government to the Fascists. On October 24 he was in Naples making his speech to the Congress, an aggressive speech in which he said the parliamentary government had rejected his request for five portfolios and so now the only answer was force.

In the afternoon he reviewed forty thousand Fascist troops in the Piazza del Plebescito. That night as Prime Minister Facta telegraphed the King that the danger of a march on Rome was past, Mussolini met with his Quadrumvirate to make final arrangements for the March on Rome. Secret mobilization was fixed for October 27. On the morning of October 28 three columns would advance on the capital. Every effort would be made to avoid conflict with the army. All towns would display the national flag, and all work would be suspended that day.

At last Mussolini closed the meeting and went outside for a look around. The city was illuminated as if for a festival, and although it was the early hours of the morning, the Blackshirts still roamed the streets, singing their fascist songs and shouting "*A Roma, A Roma.*" Before he went to bed he received General Federico Baistrocchi, army commander of the Naples military district, who announced that the army in the south looked with great favor on fascism and Il Duce. Everything was ready for the great day.

CHAPTER 7

∞

The March on Rome

On the morning of October 25, 1922, Mussolini left the Fascist Party Congress at Naples secretly and headed for Milan. Most of the military people went back to prepare for the mobilization, but the Congress continued to sit that day, for the purposes of deception. Dino Grandi announced that he did not approve of military action, but he was nominated nevertheless as chief of staff of the Fascist high command at Perugia.

The Congress sat all night on October 25, and then on the morning of the 26th adjourned and dispersed. On the 27th Prime Minister Facta tried to negotiate with Mussolini and so did Salandra, but the Fascists had started their own wheels to turning and nothing could come of these maneuvers. When word of the Fascist military movement's convergence on Rome got out, Facta called on the King and resigned his government. He also suggested to the King the proclamation of a state of siege of Rome, but the King refused to take such drastic action.

At Perugia the Fascists seized the prefecture government buildings. During that night of October 27-28 Prime Minister Facta held together a caretaker government, and the cabinet decided to issue a proclamation of siege. This was done and the proclamation of siege was posted on the walls of buildings. But when Facta went to get King Victor Emmanuel to sign the proclamation, the King refused. He had learned privately that much of the army was with the Fascists and in the wings stood the Duke of Aosta, who might succeed to the monarchy if the King was overthrown. So the King decided not to do anything to stop the Fascists.

On the night of October 27 the Fascist armed troops assembled. At Tivoli, twenty-two miles from Rome, four thousand Fascists camped in the Villa D'Este's gardens. At Monterotondo fifteen miles to the northeast, thirteen thousand black-shirted Fascists waited to seize the main railroad line that runs north and south down the Italian peninsula. West, at Civitavecchia, the old port of Rome, thousands more Fascists were set to seize the coast railroad. At Naples the Fascists would seize Capua, the junction for the south.

It was an array calculated to frighten, and it did. Yet, the Black-shirts were much less powerful than they pretended to be. They had few arms, and that night they set about stealing and extorting them from all sources. Still, when the morning came they had precious few weapons, especially if they were going to have to face up to the army.

This was precisely what Mussolini wanted to avoid at all costs. So far he had been remarkably successful in avoiding any clashes with the military. His legions, his lieutenants, talked incessantly of fighting, and that was all right when their enemies were the Communists and So-cialists, who were generally no better armed or trained than they. But to go against the armed forces, the trained soldiers, was quite another matter.

Mussolini spent October 28 heading off the parliamentary ad-vances of Antonio Salandra, the legislators' last hope to form a govern-ment that would have to have a lot of Fascists in it but could still be not quite Fascist. Mussolini resisted all offers and quietly announced that he did not intend to leave Milan unless he were called by the King with the specific task for forming a government.

And that day he wrote his last article as editor of *Il Popolo d'Italia:*

> This is the situation. The greater part of northern Italy is in the hands of the Fascists. Central Italy, Tuscany, Umbria, the Marches, Alto Lazio is occupied by the Blackshirts, where the police headquarters and the prefectures have not been taken by assault, the Fascists have occupied stations and post offices, which are the nerve centers of the nation. The political authority—a little surprised and much dis-mayed—has not been able to cope with the movement because a movement of this character cannot be contained and still less broken. A tremendous victory is in sight, with the almost unanimous ap-proval of the nation. But victory is not to be mutilated by eleventh hour combinations. It was not really worth the trouble of mobilizing merely in order to reach a deal with Salandra. The government must have a clearly fascist character.
>
> Fascism will not abuse its victory but is determined it shall not be diminished. Let that be clear to all. Nothing shall disturb the

beauty and the ardor of our offensive. The Fascists have been and are admirable. Their self-sacrifice is great and must be crowned by complete victory. Any other solution is to be rejected. Let the men of Rome understand that the hour has come to finish with the old conventional procedures, which have been on many occasions in less grave circumstances been discarded. Let them understand that up until this present moment a solution to the crisis can be obtained within the framework of the most orthodox constitutionalism. But that tomorrow it will be perhaps too late. Some politicians in Rome show a lack of perception which oscillates between the grotesque and palsied helplessness. Let them decide. Fascism wants power and will have it.

On the night of October 28, to outsiders the victory seemed imminent. The American embassy cabled Washington:

Rome and major part of Italy under martial law, mobilization of Fascisti as prophesied is believed to have resulted in Fascist possession of several large centers and best information indicates general superiority of forces of Fascists outside and north of Rome. Military concentration in Rome, temporary fortifications during the night and cessation of traffic in and out, including railroads. Military authorities indicate that advance of squadrons of Fascisti on Rome is now in progress. The Bourse ordered reported closed this morning until November 6. Ministry presented resignation to King who arrived in Rome yesterday. Fascisti demands have stiffened and attempt to keep them out of Rome indicates real danger of serious conflicts possibility that quick formation of a new Mussolini–Salandra ministry with concessions to Fascisti will avert.

But then the reports from the consulates began to come in. The Fascists had seized Trieste. And half a dozen other centers. And in the early hours of October 29 the Palace called Mussolini, who for several hours was not to be found anywhere in Milan, but who finally checked in, called Rachele to pack his bag, and hurried off to Rome, waiting only for receipt of a telegram confirming the fact that the King was asking him to form a government. It came around noon. Turning to his brother Arnaldo, who was now the business manager of *Il Popolo d'Italia*, Mussolini said: "If only our father were alive."

∽

The afternoon was spent at the newspaper offices. Benito transferred control of the newspaper to Arnaldo. He saw some of his Fascist leaders and gave orders for the destruction of the Socialist *Avanti!* and *Giustizia* newspapers. He said good-bye to Rachele and his now five children. Then he went to the railroad station and specified to the station-master that the 8:30 Milan–Rome train must leave exactly on time and that in future, all trains must leave on time. In these past years of one strike or crisis after another the Italian train system had become notorious for its failures to maintain schedules. One train in northern Italy was four hundred hours late. This was not to happen again, said the new prime minister-designate. Thus was born the myth of Fascist transportation punctuality.

Mussolini waited and spoke to the hundreds of Fascists who had gathered at the station to see him off. Then the magic moment came, the train left, and Mussolini, in a first-class compartment, was off to take over Italy. It had all been done as he had hoped, in a constitutional manner. There had been no conflict with the official government.

The journey was arduous. The express stopped at Piacenza, Pisa, Carrara, Civitavecchia, and at every stop Mussolini had to appear on the platform and greet the shouting, cheering crowds. It was nearing eleven o'clock in the morning when the train reached Rome, and the new prime minister of Italy pulled himself together to get off. He was wearing the black shirt of the Fascists, black trousers, black shoes. At a few minutes before noon he walked into the audience chamber of the Palazzo del Quirinale and strode forth to meet the King.

"Your majesty will forgive my attire," he said. "I have just come from the battlefield."

PART III

The Years
of Power

CHAPTER 8

The Fruits
of Victory

King Victor Emmanuel received his new prime minister graciously. Privately, he had many reservations about this leader of the wild Fascists. He asked Mussolini to put together a government "on a broad basis and with capable men." He was pleased to see that Mussolini apparently understood him and agreed with him, and after a short talk the prime minister went away.

"He is really a man of purpose and I can tell you he will last some time," the King told Vittorio Solaro del Borgo, one of his gentlemen in waiting. "There is in him, if I am not mistaken, the will to act and to act well. I had previously formed quite a different view of him."

Mussolini left this brief interview to go to the Hotel Savoia and take a second floor suite, but there was to be no rest for him, although he had not slept for three nights. His naturally sallow face was whiter than ever, with great black rings beneath his eyes. First he had to arrange for the victory procession of his fascist force, which was descending on Rome by the thousands. A procession was started, to pass along the Roman streets, from the Piazza del Popolo along the Corso Umberto to the Piazza Venezia, up to the Quirinale Palace to salute the King. His loyal Fascists, especially his generals, of whom he was half afraid, had to be greeted by their leader. For Italo Balbo he had a long, silent embrace. For Dino Grandi, his longtime associate, he had a rebuke. "You

didn't believe in my star. I can't put you in the government now." For
departing Premier Facta he had a personal bodyguard and a warning to
his Fascists not to touch a hair of his head.

Giuseppe Mastromattei, one of the early followers of Mussolini
and fascism, remarked that it was a strange sort of revolution, no bloody
daggers.

"No," said Mussolini quietly. "You pay for blood with blood and
I don't want to end up like Cola di Rienzi."*

On the train and now in his suite, Mussolini completed his list of
ministers and undersecretaries. Then at about seven o'clock that evening he borrowed a black frock coat and put on white spats; he was
ready to give his list of ministers to the King.

King Victor Emmanuel was well pleased when he saw the list.
Mussolini would be president of the council and would keep the Ministries of Interior and Foreign Affairs for himself. Otherwise, there were
only three other Fascist ministers, Aldo Oviglio at Justice, Alberto de
Stefani at Finance, and Giovanni Giuriati at the Ministry of Liberated
Colonies. The Minister of War was a general and the Minister of Marine
was an admiral. The others were Nationalists, Catholics, Social Democrats, and Liberals. The undersecretaries also came from a broad base
with nine Fascists and nine non-Fascists. Mussolini's announced reason was to convince the people that he intended to govern from a broad
base, but some cynics suggested also that his Fascists were so green
that he needed the professional skills of the others. If that was true, he
had succeeded in manipulating affairs so that he got the support he
needed, so, in any event, his assumption of power was a success. By
the time he had finished greeting all the faithful who had come to taste
the glory it was nearly midnight. Then he settled down for his first
cabinet meeting.

The whirlwind of change began sweeping through the Italian government offices before eight o'clock the next morning. And by nine
o'clock he was parading through the office of the Palazzo Chigi where
he held forth as foreign minister, significantly dropping his card on the
unoccupied desks. He was on the telephone that morning to thirty ministers and undersecretaries, warning them to hold a daily roll call of
their workers. At eleven o'clock he was at the Interior Ministry, where
a late-arriving bureaucrat was unlucky enough to be seen just coming
in the door.

---

*The reference is to a fourteenth-century Roman tyrant, who seized power and
ruled for a few violent months to be seized in turn by the mob, dragged along the streets,
and hung by his heels outside the church of San Marcello.

"I am sorry you are not in good health, signor," Mussolini said to the offender.

"Your excellency must be mistaken," said the malefactor. "I am perfectly well."

"Then," said Mussolini, between clenched teeth, his fist smiting his palm, "be good enough to explain why you are entering your office at 11 A.M. when the official time is 9." "Take his name," he said to his presidential undersecretary, Giacomo Acerbo, and thus was it made clear that a new broom was sweeping the streets of Rome.

∾

The world now was beating a path to Mussolini's door. That first day, the United States State Department suggested that Ambassador Child "manifest a spirit of somewhat notable friendliness and helpfulness." The Americans had been concerned about the notable anti-American-ism of the Fascists. Now they contented themselves with the obser-vation that "from this angle the Fascisti triumph in Italy appears as a death blow to Bolshevism."

Mussolini's first actions were greeted by the American embassy with guarded approval; the embassy noted that "fascism in power is functioning with vigor and attacking with earnest determination. It is displaying convincing forms. Mussolini himself is setting the pace. His first actions encouragingly have established a firm hand in Italy."

One of Mussolini's first acts was to get the Fascists off the streets. No more bullyboy tactics would suffice, unless they were specifically authorized. In Verona one Fascist group that week seized a newspaper plant and was sternly and immediately repressed. In Taranto, Fascist leaders tried to take over the local government, and Mussolini as Min-ister of the Interior had them arrested. When someone asked him what sort of press restrictions he was going to impose, he announced that he stood for freedom of the press—if the press behaved itself. At the mo-ment that announcement seemed to have a positive ring, for in Rome, when Fascists seized the plant of the *Corriere della Sera*, Mussolini gave an order to them to evacuate or the police would come in shooting.

The immediate reaction to the takeover was almost entirely pos-itive. The opposition had not crystallized, or, rather, the Socialists had been resoundingly beaten and had not recovered, and the other natural enemies of Fascism were quiescent, awaiting developments.

It was apparent in the first week that Mussolini intended to treat labor with kid gloves. The attacks on unions stopped, and the union leaders began to think and act more sympathetically to the Fascists.

Also in that first week, he held a number of cabinet meetings, which were devoted to concrete proposals to reestablish the Italian prestige abroad and restore financial health to the nation. He proposed to have specific plans for the Chamber of Deputies when it would meet in another few days.

At the end of the first week, he had demobilized his Fascist Legion, and there was no bloodshed in the streets on Sunday for the first time in months.

∽

Mussolini drove his government workers hard but he drove himself harder. In the first two months he held thirty-two cabinet meetings. He was at his desk by 8 A.M. and seldom left the office before 9 P.M. He did not know what it was to enjoy a leisurely Roman luncheon; one day when one of his ministers had not returned by 2 P.M., he slammed down the telephone and raged, "What is this bourgeois habit of going to lunch?" he demanded. For himself, he seldom got back to the third-floor apartment he had rented at 156 Via Rasella for something to eat before two or three in the afternoon, and then his servant cooked for him a simple minestrone seasoned with pork cracklings.

For some reason the problems of the railroads attracted his particular attention, and he devoted a lot of time to solving them. An expert was brought in to reform the railroads, and the first thing he did was fire the driver of the Rome Express when he found the train running fourteen minutes late. When robbery of baggage appeared to be a great problem, the administration used special railway police who hid in empty trunks and attacked the robbers who jimmied the locks.

On November 13, Parliament opened and Mussolini presented the Chamber of Deputies to his new government, instead of the traditional other way around. It was significant, a statement that the government was going to rule and not the Chamber. And no one missed the implications. Then, as the American embassy observer noted, "briefly and with sharp firmness," he announced the government's program for national restoration.

On November 16, 1922, Prime Minister Mussolini made his first speech to the Chamber of Deputies. He strode in, in his black shirt and gray jacket, and raised his arm in the unfamiliar Roman salute. Legislators and newsmen gazed around nervously at the public benches, which were packed with Blackshirts, some of them most ostentatiously trimming their fingernails with their daggers.

Mussolini jutted out his jaw. "I could have turned this drab gray hall into a bivouack for my Blackshirts," he said, "and put an end to Parliament."

The legislators winced.

But Mussolini went on.

"It was in my power to do so. But it was not my wish."

The tension dissolved.

"At least not yet," he said. And the flabbergasted legislators did not know what to do, but they were alarmed and warned.

He continued: "The Chamber must understand that I can dissolve it in two days or two years. I claim full powers."

And within a few days the Deputies had granted him those full powers with a handful of Socialists and Communists abstaining in the vote. The score was 275 for full powers and 90 opposed.

At the end of ten days, the Parliament granted Mussolini full power to govern for a year.

That is not to say that the proceedings were always silent. Deputy Turati, a Socialist, rose to express the resolution of the left wing to oppose the Mussolini government "even if revolvers are awaiting us at the door." Fascist leader De Vecchi disputed him and shouted insults. A Catholic member chided De Vecchi as a member of the government. He should not insult the members, he said. De Vecchi spoke insultingly about the Catholics, and a large number of them walked out. Deputy De Nicola, who was presiding, became angry and resigned as chairman. At this point Mussolini intervened.

"If we use the lash" he said, "we use it first against ourselves." And he persuaded De Nicola to withdraw his resignation.

A little later Mussolini showed his ability as a conciliator. Deputy D'Argona, head of the labor confederation, challenged him on labor policy.

"Labor need not fear," said Mussolini. "I, too, was born a worker. I am glad that confederation has declared its independence of all political parties. That is something I have advocated. My government could not go so amiss as to have an antilabor policy. The Italian workers, intuitively feeling the aims of the fascist government, have adopted an attitude of benevolent watchfulness. This government plays no favorites. We shall not be in service to capitalism. We were the first to distinguish between productive and nonproductive bourgeoisie. Both bourgeoisie and workers are doomed to disappointment if they expect special favors from us."

ᔐ

By the end of the year 1922 Mussolini had accomplished a great deal in setting the tone of moderation in his administration. He had been given dictatorial powers by the mixed legislature for one year. He had set in motion the reorganization of the defense forces and was managing to control his Fascist army. It would be organized as The Militia for National Safety, which would be under his direct control. He had presented programs for the economic betterment of the country, and he had served notice on his allies, who had not yet given Italy her share of the spoils of war, that he was going to hold out for them.

He surrounded himself with bodyguards. In November he traveled to Lausanne for a conference with French premier Raymond Poincaré and British Foreign Secretary, Lord Curzon. He did not choose to meet them at their hotel where they had laid on a banquet, but at his hotel, fifteen miles from Lake Geneva. When they arrived, they found him in the foyer of the hotel surrounded by his fascist bodyguards in their black fezzes and black shirts; they stood by with loaded carbines all during the meeting. But there was a reason for this—one attempt to assassinate Mussolini had already been noted by the American embassy and there would be more.

That fear of assassination was also the reason Mussolini's womanizing never allowed him to keep one of his women in his bed overnight. He took up residence in a private apartment and had his women come at all hours. But then it was a quick action, sometimes on the love seat, sometimes on the floor, and the women were sent away. He could not bear the thought of keeping any one of them for long. Only at home, and for months Rachele and the children stayed on in Milan, did he feel comfortable around others. His sexual appetites remained as satyrical as ever, but they had to be satisfied in hurried trips, up the servants' stairway to the Grand Hotel, furtively in his apartment, or in secret missions on which he was driven to private addresses by his chauffeur.

He never relaxed except with Rachele, whom he trusted and held above all women, although he was openly unfaithful to her to such an extent that she paid no more attention. His eating habits were almost savage. He usually ate alone and demolished his food in great gulps. He had absolutely no manners of grace and had to take on the services of a young gentleman to learn how to use his knives and forks at the few banquets he was persuaded to attend.

Mussolini made two trips abroad that year, one to London and one by train to Lausanne to meet with the other members of the entente.

Particularly after that confrontation he was regarded by such a weathered diplomatist as M. Poincaré as "a no good bastard." Most of the polished diplomats looked upon Mussolini as a hayseed. Biographer Richard Collier called him "a baffled peasant, playing premier." If this was true, it was only in matters of protocol. Mussolini had already shown the world that he was anything but the baffled peasant in the management of Italy's national affairs. He had known what was wrong in Italy and when to act. That alone was not an inconsiderable accomplishment. These next months were being used to strengthen the fascist hold on government, and to strengthen Italy.

In the beginning, the acceptance of Mussolini was very general because of the muddle into which Italian affairs had fallen, but as time went on he began to get more unfriendly press coverage. In July 1923, he took the first steps of repression, forbidding the press to publish "untruthful and distorted news." By that time the government controlled much of the press in one way or another. *Il Popolo d'Italia*, of course, was owned by Mussolini and run by his brother. *Giornale de Roma* was a semiofficial paper in Rome. *Idea Nationale* was pro-government because the National Party, whose voice it was, was a part of the government. *Il Messaggero* was an independent paper but at that point was under the influence of the government. *Giornale d'Italia* had just veered away from the government. *L'Epoca* had been pro-fascist but had now lost its influence and most of its readers. *Il Sole* was a commercial paper. *La Stampa* was an organ of former Prime Minister Giolitti. *Corriere della Sera* was an outspoken opposition newspaper that had now started to criticize Mussolini and his government. *Il Mondo* was the organ of former Prime Minister Nitti, and very anti-Mussolini. *Il Secolo*, the oldest Democratic newspaper of Italy, was bought just then by Fascists.

In response to the threat from the government, all the newspapers voiced their intentions to abstain from unnecessary criticism, and the matter was suspended.

Government affairs in the summer of 1923 went along relatively quietly, with the major emphasis on improving the Italian economy. Then on August 27, General Enrico Tellini and several subordinate members of the Italian frontier commission that was marking the border between Greece and Albania were ambushed and murdered on Greek territory. The affair shook Europe worse than anything since the assassination of Archduke Franz Ferdinand and almost brought war between Italy and Greece. Mussolini demanded compensation of 500.000 lire and the arrest and trial of the killers. The Greeks could not find the killers and had no money to pay. So Mussolini took his first new step in the creation of his empire. The Italian fleet bombarded Greek Corfu and seized the island.

This was a violation of the rules of the League of Nations, but Mussolini made it stick and the League passed the case to the Conference of Ambassadors, who decreed that Greece must pay. Greece raised the money and paid, and then the Italian navy relinquished Corfu. Responsibility for the affair was fixed by the Italians on the Greek government, which had been conducting an anti-Italian campaign for months about the Greek–Albanian border, always a sensitive issue between the two countries.

Hardly had the Greek–Italian crisis been weathered, when another internal crisis threatened the fascist unity. The executive council of the party expelled Massimo Rocca, one of Mussolini's most trusted aides. Mussolini did not like it, and said so; in a few days all the members of the executive council were pushed into offering their resignations. The matter would be settled by the Grand Council. Beneath this exterior lay the real crisis, which was a split between the country faction (The Rasses) and the city faction (The Savages). Since the Fascists had come to power, the elite of the party had congregated in Rome. The provincial leaders, back in their home towns, resented the concentration of prestige and power in Rome and occasionally kicked over the traces. Mussolini saw that only he could resolve this issue and that it had to be resolved in favor of the concentration of fascist power. When the council met a few weeks later, Mussolini triumphantly carried the day and emerged with more power than ever. Roberto Farinacci, the Fascist leader of Cremona, who had boasted "Mussolini may rule in Rome, but I rule in Cremona," suddenly went off to America to make a series of addresses to Italian Americans. Cesare de Vecchi, the Turin leader who had challenged Mussolini several times, was sent to Italian Somaliland as the new governor.

So, on October 31, 1923, Mussolini celebrated the first anniversary of the March on Rome. It began with formations of airplanes flying over the city for an hour, beginning at 8 A.M. At nine o'clock the Quadrumvirate of Rome led the Grand Fascist Parade. These were the generals who had actually made the March on Rome. The parade lasted four hours and was reviewed from the Quirinale Palace by the King. Mussolini also participated in the parade and was cheered all along the route. It was apparent that Mussolini had a greater grip on the Fascists and on the people of Italy than he had enjoyed the year before.

John Stambough, the third secretary of the American embassy, chose this occasion to write in his weekly political report to Washington an appraisal of the Mussolini epoch to date:

> The first great reform of Mussolini's administration was to throw out of office the great army of political proteges and incompetent officials which had been created by generations of government by unscrupulous and self-seeking politicians. They have been swept out of the ministries, the local administrative bodies and all the various comfortable sinecures which they considered their lawful perquisites. Mussolini demanded efficiency and work. It was characteristic of his policy that the higher the official the smaller was his chance of being spared in the great cleansing operation. As a result the Italian administration, with greatly reduced staffs, and reduced salaries, is now able to carry out the work of government efficiently and swiftly.
>
> The next step of Mussolini was against the petty political groups, whose noisy squabbles had made parliamentary life in Italy a parody of democracy. Fascism has asserted itself as the heart of a national movement toward an organization of the masses into greater parties with programs established on broad issues. One after the other the old political groups were smashed and obliged to announce themselves for or against, but mostly for, the great Conservative reaction. The Liberals, the popular Party, the Socialists, have all been attacked on questions of principle and their ranks have been broken and scattered.
>
> The electoral reform introduced by Mussolini is an entirely new departure in social organization. He preserves proportional representation but gives to the winning party two thirds of the seats in Parliament. This is in order to assure the governing party of the day the possibility of carrying out the reforms promised in the electoral reform program.
>
> Mussolini has been eminently successful in bringing about social peace and the cessation of class warfare. In the beginning the means were physical, but very soon a tendency to apply more peaceful methods was manifest. The results have been excellent, and during the last twelve months there has not been a single strike in the whole of Italy. This fact even Mussolini's detractors cannot overlook.

Mussolini's financial policies, through Finance Minister de Stefani, had almost done away with the national deficit of many years standing. The railroads, which had been a national disgrace, had been made efficient. They had been bankrupt, and more than fifty thousand workers had been fired. The system had become more efficient and was beginning to pay its way, although fares had gone down.

Mussolini had reversed affairs and established a working relationship with the Vatican. He had strengthened the family as an institution by the abolition of inheritance taxes, and he had shown that Italy was going to have its own foreign policy, and not ride, as it had for years, on Britain's coattails.

This analysis, made by the third secretary of an embassy that had ignored Mussolini almost until the day that he took power, and even then had tended to regard him demeaningly, was a real milestone in Fascist progress. The same views were being revised in most of the embassies in Rome. Mussolini had first been regarded as a joke and then as a wild man; now he was beginning to be considered larger than life.

It was an enormous change for the boy of Predappio and for the people of Italy in one short year.

CHAPTER 9

∽

The Iron Fist
of Fascism

On January 25, 1924, Mussolini dissolved the Parliament and ordered new elections for April 6. Personally he was very displeased with the idea, since he did not like the whole electoral procedure. A number of non-Fascists were included on the Mussolini list, to show national unity. But when the list was finished Mussolini said to one of his aides, "This is the last time. Next time I will nominate them all."

Mussolini promised that the campaign would be conducted fairly, but in fact the Fascists beat up many opponents in Genoa, Milan, Turin, Udine, Savona, and Rome. One Socialist candidate was murdered. The Fascists intimidated voters and falsified ballots. When the polling was finished on April 6, the Mussolini list received 4.5 million votes. The opposition got 3 million votes. Under the electoral law, Mussolini's list got 355 seats in the assembly. That was all very well, he observed, when the votes were counted, but in Piedmont, Lombardy, Liguria, and Venice the opposition outpolled the Fascists, 1,300,000 votes to 1,194,000.

After the election Mussolini went to Milan where he tried to find some answers. There, he met with G. A. Borgese, one of Italy's foremost literary critics and students of politics, and as Mussolini often did, he asked the fellow journalist some questions.

"What do you think of the electoral returns in Lombardy?" he demanded.

"I think that they are a warning. What happens in Lombardy is usually a presage of what will happen in the nation. The electoral returns mean, obviously, a growing discontent."

"What would you do in my place?"

"I would try to put into effect the plan you outlined in a parliamentary speech not long ago. You said that the three large popular parties, the Fascists, the Socialists, and Catholics, should work together for the good of the nation. You said that the factionalism must die if this is the price at which the nation may live. You can do it."

"Too late."

But it was obvious that he did not think so because he went on in the interview to discuss his difficulties. "My opponents do not take into account the fact that a revolutionary movement like this drags with it a wake of criminality. Instead of making my life work difficult they should help me master these forces of darkness."

What to believe? A case in point was the beating of Socialist Deputy Giovanni Amendola. When word of the beating reached Mussolini, administrative secretary Giovanni Marinelli said he went into a fury. He rattled the telephone receiver and made threats against the police, and the instigators of the outrage.

But another of his assistants reported that when Emilio De Bono had telephoned the news of the assault, Mussolini had rubbed his hands, smiled and said, "This morning I am going to lunch with a better appetite."

And on that same visit to Milan he expressed the views of Borgese to another, without quoting Borgese. "There is only one way to save Italy," Mussolini told Socialist journalist Carlo Silvestri, "by collaboration with all parties, above all the Socialist."

Why was Mussolini so concerned, when he had obviously received endorsement from a large sector of the population? Because Mussolini knew that in many areas, half the people did not vote at all, because they were despondent about fascist rule, the continued excesses of the Fascist bands in the streets, and saw no hope of change. He was particularly depressed about the voting in his home territory of northern Italy, in which the Socialist vote and the Socialist abstentions showed the very great strength still of the Socialists.

Borgese also noted that on this visit, no sooner had Mussolini left Milan than the city was plagued with a new outbreak of Fascist violence. Houses of opponents burned in the suburbs, and other opponents were clubbed in the night. It was whispered that Mussolini himself had given the orders for this new series of outrages.

∽

The King opened the new session of the Parliament on May 24, 1924. The only incident was a brief one in which Giacomo Matteotti, a Socialist deputy from Ferrara-Rovigo, questioned the election returns. But this was passed off, and the session ended without any trouble. The first session of the new Parliament was marked by noisy behavior of many new Fascist legislators who knew nothing of parliamentary procedures and were flushed with victory.

On May 30, when the session opened, the president of the Chamber called for a motion confirming the election returns. This was a surprise to everyone and no one was prepared to speak on the subject, but Matteotti got up to speak extemporaneously. He stated that in various constituencies the Fascists had used violence to suppress the voting by others and he named the places.

He said the elections were questionable and demanded that nothing be done to confirm them until investigations had been held. Throughout his speech he was heckled and abused, and even bothered by fighting that broke out on the floor, so his speech took an hour and a half of sustained racket. Thus the day ended, with the Fascists angry, and Matteotti angry and rumored to be preparing another, more damaging speech that would expose financial scandals in the government.

On June 4, Matteotti got into an argument on the floor with Mussolini, who lost his temper. Turning to the members of the left side of the aisle he shouted, "You should receive a charge of lead in the back." Other Fascists spoke up. Roberto Farinacci threatened Matteotti and so did half a dozen other Fascists.

"We are in power and we mean to stay there," shouted one Fascist.

"I am exposing facts," said Matteotti. "Of one hundred Unitarian candidates, sixty were kept by your Fascist muscle men from canvassing their own districts . . . the first fifteen voters at one polling place refused to vote Fascist and were beaten up. . . ." And he went on and on, naming names and places. "Registration cards of people who were afraid to vote had been seized by Fascists and voted ten, twenty times. Youngsters voted the cards of people sixty." He could prove it by the handwriting.

"I am exposing facts which should not provoke noise. Either the facts are true or you must prove them false."

Mussolini was quiet. Others fumed and shouted and fights started on the floor. Finally Matteotti finished.

"For these reasons we ask a total cancellation of the election."

Mussolini sat like stone. He had been planning to merge his Fascist party with the Socialists, whom he knew had the real majority of the left. He wanted to get rid of the bullyboys. But now that had become impossible. He was angry as he left the chamber and headed for the

Palazzo Chigi. He encountered Giovanni Marinelli, the party's administrative secretary, and he let his anger go.

"If you weren't a bunch of cowards," he said, "no man would dare to deliver a speech like that."

And after that events took their course.

On June 11, various legislators remarked on the fact that Matteotti had disappeared. The rumor spread that he had been abducted by the Fascists. The following day Mussolini himself gave assurances that all the resources of the government would be used to discover what had happened. For several days the Chamber of Deputies was in an excited furor, and Fascist deputies promised that if there had been a crime it would be punished. Mussolini rose and appealed for national unity and said that three arrests had been made and that others were expected. What he wanted above all else, he said, was national unity.

G. A. Borgese observed all this from afar:

> He expressed his horror at the mere thought that the disappearance might be final; his worst foe, alone, he averred, could have committed such a crime. But he disbelieved the heartbreaking hypothesis, and his voice fell and rose, to depths of prayer, to heights of mystic faith, as he uttered the hope, nay, the confidence, that Matteotti could suddenly reappear among his colleagues in the Parliament. If ever a man was genuine, this man was Mussolini at that moment. Had he possessed the power of resurrecting the dead, he would not have hesitated an eyewink to resurrect Matteotti. But while voicing in adequately tragic style his pity and terror, his hope and dismay, he knew quite well that the man had been killed and his body dumped somewhere in a remote wasteland of the Roman Campagna.

When Mussolini made his impassioned speech to the Chamber, the opposition was no longer listening. They had resolved not to sit again in the Parliament until the mystery of Matteotti was cleared. They had to wait twenty-three years, until Mussolini was ousted from power, to find out all the facts. So all the opposition left the Parliament and, except for the Communists, never returned.

The investigation was begun, and many high Fascist officials were implicated. The Socialists pointed the finger directly at Mussolini but nothing could be proved.

For days Mussolini was paralyzed and asked no questions. But on June 13, Velia Matteotti came to see him. It was apparent in their interview that she did not believe a word he said about not knowing the fate of her husband. He then began questioning his sycophants, and Giovanni Marinelli broke down and confessed that he had given the orders to seize Matteotti after Mussolini's outburst to him that June day. He was quickly arrested as the main instigator of the crime; he had receipts from the actual murderers for the money he had advanced to them.

Still there was no body, but Mussolini was being accused of murder every day. On June 16, General Emilio de Bono, one of those who had led the March on Rome, resigned as Director of Public Security. A Republican deputy accused Mussolini personally of being an accessory to murder, and Mussolini then resigned his post as Minister of Interior.

That evening Mussolini went to a dinner of state at the Palazzo Quirinale. When the King unfolded his napkin there was a note in it. "Your majesty, Matteotti's murderer sits next to you. Give him up to justice."

The Socialists sent a delegation to call on the King and demand Mussolini's resignation. But there was no body. No proof that Matteotti was dead.

In August the body was found buried in a ditch in the woods on the Via Flaminia, twelve miles from Rome. The Socialists came back to the King.

The Chamber of Deputies had given Mussolini a vote of confidence as of June 26, the King said. He could not go against that vote. Three former prime ministers—Giolitti, Orlando, and Salandra—all backed Mussolini rather than have him align with the Socialists.

The investigation of the murder moved along and mountains of evidence were collected. The investigation implicated a dozen Fascists, but virtually all of them got off with short sentences or none, because they said Matteotti was killed in a struggle, and that the murder was not premeditated.

Whatever the facts, the murder of Matteotti did drive a firm wedge between the Fascists and the rest of the nation and put an end to Mussolini's hope for a government of reconciliation. Much later in life, in 1945, when he was living again in Milan, Mussolini told journalist Carlo Silvestri that the greatest tragedy of his life was that June 10, 1924, murder, which put a stone wall between him and the Socialists. There is no reason to disbelieve it. Mussolini, having gained the power he had sought in 1922, wanted to be loved by the Italian people and to go down in history as a great leader, in the image of the Rome he imagined. After the murder of Matteotti, it was no longer possible.

In fact the murder created a negative climate in Italy for the Fascists, and various organizations that had unwaveringly supported the Fascists began to fall away, such as the Veterans' Association. This summer was the low point of the Fascist movement and Mussolini stated years later that a concerted effort from the opposition would have destroyed his rule.

Mussolini confessed to the British ambassador that autumn that he was much concerned about the mounting violence. At that moment one thousand Fascists were in jail for acts of violence and five thousand more were awaiting prosecution. Italo Balbo had made the mistake of suing a newspaper that accused him of a murder, because in court, the defense had brought out so much proof of acts of violence on Balbo's part that he had resigned in disgrace as commander of the Fascist militia.

From Mussolini's statements of the time and later, it seems that he was really hoping to get rid of the "bullyboy" members of the Fascist party, but there was no way he could do it without destroying the party apparatus, which they largely controlled.

That fall Mussolini made several speeches to the Chamber of Deputies in relationship to matters of confidence, and in all of them he received votes of confidence from the members. But he was losing the confidence of the extremists in the party. Early in December a number of leaders were convoked in a meeting by Balbo, who appointed a committee of five to take over the militia in event of emergency. This showed a growing distrust of Mussolini. At the end of the month some thirty members called on Mussolini to protest his appeasement of the masses. They declared they were tired of procrastinating. Either all the Fascists should be in prison, or all should be free. But the prisons were full of Fascists. Mussolini spoke to the group of the need for discipline, but they sneered at discipline. This was the revolution. Aldo Tarabella, the spokesman for the group, then got sidetracked in argument with the others, and the meeting deteriorated, and Mussolini was saved from a solid front against him, but he was warned. The faithful were becoming very restless.

At the end of December the Matteotti case leaped up again, when Cesare Rossi, one of the principals of the murder of Matteotti, accused Mussolini of ordering the murder. So the die was cast. Mussolini could no longer have it both ways. Either he would support his militia and his "bullyboys" or he would lose their support. That very day he ordered General Gandolfo, the new leader of the Fascist Militia, to swing into action and a campaign of terror against anti-Fascists was put into motion three days later. Mussolini announced in the Chamber of Deputies that in the next forty-eight hours the nation would see what happened when a government was impelled to turn to force. He was going to demand a new electoral law, he said. This announcement caused consternation in the Chamber. Former Prime Minister Salandra resigned as president of the Budget Committee of the House. Rumors began that all the Liberal ministers would resign. Mussolini countered by giving orders that all the opposition press were to be silenced.

On Saturday, January 3, 1925, it was announced that Mussolini would make an important speech and so the galleries of the Chamber of Deputies were jammed hours before the session began.

Mussolini began by attacking the opposition for trying to implicate him in the Matteotti murder and referred to the provisions of the Constitution that covered impeachment of ministers of the crown. He launched into a bitter diatribe against the opposition and the opposition press and said that he accepted the political, moral, and historical responsibility for all that had taken place in the name of fascism. This statement was greeted by roaring applause. When the wild enthusiasm died down, he said that within forty-eight hours all the questions of the opposition would be clarified. The American ambassador found it significant that a Liberal minister was absent from the session and the former prime minister, Salandra, and his followers, did not applaud. After the session Salandra said that he could no longer support Mussolini, and more of the elements of the opposition that had remained in the Chamber after the first walkout decided to leave.

The Giolitti–Orlando opposition had prepared a resolution that would condemn the government for now restricting free speech and demanding the rigorous support of all parties to law and suppression of violence. When the session resumed, Mussolini laid the resolution over for six months, as he was entitled to do under parliamentary practice, thus preventing debate of the issue.

This speech of January 3 marked the end of civil liberties in fascist Italy. Mussolini had hesitated for months, restrained his followers until he nearly lost their loyalty, and held them back from acts of violence. But the Matteotti murder and its aftermath showed him that the fascist movement he had formed was dedicated, as he had been in his youth, to violence and could not bear the rigors of exposure to public debate. He had come to power on a wave of public revulsion against the inadequacies of a democratic system without leadership, Biographer Ivone Kirkpatrick, who knew Mussolini as well as any Westerner, makes much of the point that by 1924 Mussolini wanted nothing more than to make peace with the Socialists he had deserted in 1914 but never forgotten. But as his militants told him with brutal frankness, if he went that route he would lose the support of his Fascist army. So in January 1925, the fascist dictatorship of Italy was born.

CHAPTER 10

Dictatorship

The course of Italian public life from June till December 1924 offered a spectacle absolutely unparalleled in the political struggle of any other country. It was a mark of shame and infamy which would dishonor any political group. The press, the meetings, the subversive and anti-Fascist parties of every sort, the false intellectuals, the defeated candidates, the soft-brained cowards, the rabble, the parasites, threw themselves like ravens on the corpse of Matteotti. The arrest of the guilty was not enough, the discovery of the corpse and the sworn statement of surgeons that death was not due to a crime but had been produced by Trauma was not enough. . . .

At the end of January 1925 I was getting ready to channel the Fascist revolution into institutions and into constitutional reforms.

Mussolini, from his **Autobiography**

In January 1925, Italy reached a crossroads. As Italian critic G. A. Borgese put it, "Of all the great revolutions fascism had been the least bloody with a death toll much inferior to that of the French Terror or the Russian communism." His explanation for that phenomenon was that the fascist revolution was only a coup d'état, and it was true that Mussolini had chosen in 1922 to adopt the parliamentary government system and had so governed for two years. But in January 1925, all that went packing; if there had not been a fascist revolution before, there was one now. Mussolini moved swiftly to make Italy a fascist state, with himself as supreme dictator.

Observing the Italian political scene during the first week of January 1925, the American embassy's Henry P. Fletcher observed: "It would seem that for the present at least, all efforts to conduct the government along normal parliamentary lines have been abandoned and that a fascist dictatorship will be reestablished. It is too early to judge just what lines Mussolini will follow with regard to parliamentary assistance in the government of the country. . . ."

The correspondent of the *London Times* predicted disaster for Mussolini:

> Nothing for the moment remains but a stark contrast between fascism and the rest of the country and Signor Mussolini has bought a temporary continuance of unfettered despotism at the risk of eventual total extinction. For it is possible to renew in the Blackshirts, the cheers of 1922; it is possible to restore the language and the measures of 1922; but it is not possible to recapture the consent of the country which was the real reason for the success of 1922. And when Signor Mussolini says that the people have cried "basta" to his policy of conciliation he is making the old mistake of identifying the people with those of his own household.

Immediately the changes were notable. The moderate Dino Grandi was replaced as Minister of Home Affairs by Roberto Farinacci, who had sometimes been described as "mad dog" Farinacci. In Genoa a campaign was begun against freemasonry, which the Fascists suddenly discovered to be inimical to their rule, and against other opponents of the regime. The Genoa newspaper *Il Secolo XIX* was quoted:

> The political squad of our police department has executed in the last few days numerous searches in places that were politically suspected and in the houses of the most notable representatives of the subversive parties.
>
> In the house of a noted Communist there were found in the double bottom of a large box, numerous documents and lists of those affiliated with the party. All the documents confiscated in the numerous acquisitions have been transported to the office of the Chief of Police for examination. It appears that there is included a list of all those inscribed in the Communist sections of Liguria. It seems that as of the end of October last the Communist party and the Massimalista Socialist party have made an agreement for common political action.

The paper reported that the prefect had also dissolved three political clubs. The Socialist newspaper *Il Lavoro* had its whole editions seized several times and closed its doors for several days, but it then resumed publication. On January 15, *Cittadino*, the organ of the Catholic party, was seized because of its republication of an article the Fascists found objectionable from a Turin newspaper. Both of these newspaper plants were surrounded by the National Militia to prevent destruction of the plants by fascist sympathizers.

It was the same everywhere in Italy. Within three days Minister Farinacci reported on the closure of 95 clubs, 109 groups of Free Italy associations, 150 offices closed, 655 homes searched, and 111 people arrested. Besides this, in various parts of the country a day did not go by that some newspaper did not have its edition seized for printing something the Fascists did not like.

By mid-January the Parliament was enacting a series of restrictive laws to control all secret societies—aimed at freemasonry—because, said the Fascists, the members of Masonic organizations had loyalties within their groups that prevented them from being loyal to the government.

This legislation was criticized by such organs as *Il Messaggero*, a strong Fascist supporter, and *La Tribuna*, which observed that all these laws would accomplish would be to make secret societies more secret than ever and to give a bad impression abroad.

Mussolini then set out on a course to change Italian society and bring it around to acceptance of Fascist control. The reaction to this active program was strong within the opposition, although this did not show in the Parliament because only the Communists of the opposition reappeared there. So ineffectual was their activity that Mussolini derived considerable benefit from just letting them survive.

In February 1925, Farinacci became secretary of the party and proceeded thereafter to destroy the party machinery in the provinces and so establish firmly Mussolini's personal rule of Italy. The success of this enterprise in the eyes of the outside world is attested to by an article by Harold Begbie in the *London Daily Mail* of September 25, 1925, about "Mussolini, the man and his miracle," and an editorial in that same edition:

> In a sense the Italian Prime Minister has indeed done miraculous things for he has poured fresh life into the veins of a great people, and given it a new inspiration, a new belief in itself, a new ideal of discipline, and self sacrifice, and a new path to happiness and content. That is a wonderful event and it puts Signore Mussolini high among the regenerators and nation builders of all time. Only those will belittle his work who forget or did not know how close to the brink of catastrophe Italy stood three years after the Peace.
>
> The Russian revolution had sent a flood of seditious communism surging over the country. The revolutionists were active, blatant, and violent: the orderly elements of society were suffering under a wave of war weariness and depression; governments were hesitating and timid. Terrorism and mob rule were getting one district after another into their grip. Patriotism was denounced, religion

insulted, law and order defied. Bands of red conspirators were setting up Soviets in the cities and seizing factories in the name of the proletariat. Economic paralysis and political chaos were in sight. It seemed that another Bolshevik tragedy was about to wreck a fine culture and an older civilization than that of the Sarmatian steppe.

From this evil fate Mussolini rescued his countrymen. Today Italy is perhaps the most stable, socially, economically, politically of the nations of Europe.

There are no unemployed and hardly any strikes. Class consciousness, sedulously reached and encouraged by the Communists before Mussolini came to power, has been absorbed in the a larger patriotism with which Il Duce has inspired Young Italy and it would seem Middle aged Italy and Old Italy as well. The Fascists are not loved by everybody and it may be that constitutional changes and heated party conflicts are in store. But sedition has been quenched, law, order and loyalty prevail; and the entire peninsula as far as the foreign observer can see is alive with purposeful energy and pervaded by an enthusiastic sense of unity such as Italy has not often known since the Roman legions ceased to guard her frontiers.

How has it all been done?

Mr. Begbie finds the key to the mystery in a great personality, inspired by a noble ideal. Discipline, self-devotion, and industry sum up the doctrine which Mussolini has imposed upon his countrymen and though some rejected the gospel at first, it has in the end filled them with enthusiasm. Hard work and efficient organization have stimulated commerce, manufacture, and agriculture and the government has assisted the movement by ruthlessly repressing administrative extravagance. What strikes Mr. Begbie most is the "profound composure" which underlies the activity of this reborn Italy. It is a great possession for any people and we cannot be surprised that the vast majority of Italians are still ardent in their devotion to the statesman who has infused this spiritual vigor and refreshment into their political, social and industrial existence.

So by the end of 1925 Mussolini had much of world opinion in his pocket, even though his Fascists were cutting a wide swath. In August, Farinacci expelled former Minister of Justice Oviglio from the party on vague charges, which Oviglio denied.

By October, Farinacci could announce that Italy was finishing up the second wave of the Fascist revolution, the passage of that new body of laws that provided the first step toward the creation of a fascist state. The third would begin in 1926 when this legislation would be examined by the Grand Council of Ministers and by the Fascist Grand Council.

Mussolini was riding high, and as the American chargé d' affaires noted in his weekly report on Italy on October 3, the dictator was showing "unusual self-confidence even bordering on insolence." He had just closed down *La Stampa*, an important Turin newspaper, which was the organ of Giolitti's Liberal party. He was crowing about his accomplishments. *La Stampa* had been suspended for taking advantage of army maneuvers in Piedmont to describe actual scenes of real warfare at Borgofranco, where the military had attacked civilians. Signor Ambrosini, the director of the newspaper, pleaded that the editors had been the victims of faulty telephone transmission and were just trying to show what the military would be like in real warfare. But it did not wash with the Fascists, who used this incident to strike down one of their more important enemies in the north.

"For the opponents of fascism," Mussolini said, "if necessary there will be the cudgel and cold steel. Intransigeance is still the order of the day, for if the declining faiths may permit themselves the luxury of being tolerant, the rising faith must necessarily be intolerant and intransigeant. If I believe that mine is the truth, and I am certain that I am marching on my road toward the grand goal, then I cannot tolerate the clandestine murmur, the little ambush, the calumny, the defamation. All these must be suppressed, overturned, buried."

By mid-October *Il Legionario*, the fascist weekly, could predict that the "complete Fascistification" of Italy would be accomplished in the early months of 1926. The authority of the prefects of the districts of the country had already been extended to make them virtually little dictators in their own regions.

Primary among the changes was the establishment of corporations controlling industry, agriculture, and the professions. These corporations would control everyday life in Italy. As for labor, so far had the revolution progressed that the government could now announce its intent to recognize fascist labor unions and no others, and the lockout and the strike would not be permitted. Another major change, completely subverting the old parliamentary system, would be the election of members of the Upper House, the Senate, by the provincial corporations. "The Senate therefore is to be representative of the social forces of the nation."

All of these startling changes were accepted by the majority of Italians without protest, but among those who did protest now, some became violent. On November 4, 1925, Tito Zaniboni, a Socialist and Freemason, decided he had had enough and made an elaborate plan to assassinate Mussolini. Once he had been a Socialist deputy, until the Socialists refused to serve. He rented a room at the Hotel Dragoni in Rome, just across the Piazza from the Palazzo Chigi, on the day that

Mussolini was scheduled to make a speech from the balcony of the Palazzo. Zaniboni was a skilled marksman, a World War I hero, and he had a high-powered Männlicher rifle trained on the balcony only fifty yards away. But he was betrayed by one of his Socialist friends, who succumbed to greed. The Fascists had money ready to reward anyone who revealed a plot against Mussolini, and this was Zaniboni's undoing. He was arrested before Mussolini got to the balcony and tried and sentenced to thirty years in prison. The American embassy in Rome asked the Secretary of State to send a telegram to Rome congratulating Mussolini on his narrow escape, which Secretary of State Kellogg declined to do, but other governments, entranced by Mussolini's successful defiance of the democratic traditions of Italy, expressed their relief at his safety.

The Zaniboni plot played right into the hands of the Fascists, arousing international sympathy for Mussolini and making it possible for them to close down all the Masonic lodges in Italy and to wipe out the Socialist Unitary Party to which Zaniboni belonged without much public complaint. Never averse to trading on victory, Farinacci moved on against other organizations and destroyed the independence of *Corriere della Sera*, which was Italy's leading newspaper, the equivalent to the *New York Times* or *The Times* of London of those days, independent and highly respected throughout the world. The *Corriere della Sera*'s director was dismissed under the fascist policy, the shareholders sold out, and the Fascists acquired the newspaper.

Before the year 1925 was out, Italy had a body of law under which a university professor could be dismissed for defending cultural liberty at an international meeting, and under which newspaper proprietors were held responsible for the editorial policy of their newspapers. An association of journalists was created that excluded anti-Fascists from the profession.

In January 1926, the government passed an even more restrictive law, depriving of Italian citizenship anyone who committed an act abroad calculated to damage public order in the kingdom or to damage Italian prestige. Immediately several writers and journalists were deprived of citizenship for criticism in the Matteotti case.

∞

As 1925 came to an end, the whole nature of the fascist state had changed. Mussolini was no longer president of the council or prime minister. He was now known as Head of State and he had full authority to decree laws without going to Parliament. Moreover, the law prohibited Parliament from even discussing a public question, let alone acting without the assent of Mussolini.

By the end of 1925 the vestiges of representative national government had been abolished and power was in the hands of Mussolini. The next step was to abolish representative local government. This was accomplished in April 1926, when the powers of the prefects were extended and each of them became the highest state authority in his province. By July 7, 1926, the government could announce that all provincial elections had been suspended. Thus, the Corporate State was established, the real purpose of which was to bring labor and employers under the control of the government.

The Corporate State was based on the principle that the monolithic state controlled every activity in the interest of the nation. The various corporations represented every branch of production and every profession. The Minister of Corporations created them and appointed their executive officers, who were charged with the making of contracts, organization of labor, settlement of disputes, and social welfare. The government was the final arbiter in all cases.

The corporate system was extended to the Chamber of Deputies. First, candidates were nominated by the local corporations. Second, from that list were selected about four hundred candidates selected by the Fascist Grand Council. Last, the list was approved by the electorate. There was only one list and the voters accepted it or rejected it.

That was the next to last step in the liquidation of the parliamentary system in Italy. On November 9, 1926, Roberto Farinacci announced that the parliamentary mandates and the parliamentary immunity from prosecution by the government had lapsed for the opposition candidates who had walked out in 1924. So, at the end of 1926, the fascist revolution was complete. Mussolini had swept out all the obstacles to his exercise of dictatorial power. The only link remaining with the past was the King, who could still remove the head of the government. This was inconvenient to Mussolini, and he worried sometimes lest it become a threat, but it kept up the myth that the Italian Constitution was being respected without seriously impeding Mussolini's dictatorship. All Italy was now Mussolini's in a way that had never existed before.

CHAPTER 11

❦

Italy Joins
the Powers

By 1926 the Fascists controlled every aspect of life in Italy. With one hand, Mussolini turned his attention to improving the lives of Italians and, with the other hand, beckoning the world. Fascist Italy wanted to take its place among the Great Powers.

In his first efforts to secure advantageous trade treaties abroad, and in three years, Mussolini made nineteen commercial treaties with other nations, starting with the November 1922 commercial treaty with France and ending with the October 1925 commercial treaty with Germany. But in the diplomatic field Mussolini did not fare so well. In 1925 Britain's Sir Austen Chamberlain was seeking additional guarantees to maintain peace in Europe, which settled on guarantees of the Franco–German frontier, known as the Locarno Pact. Italy participated along with Britain, France, Germany, and Belgium.

Mussolini made his appearance under conditions that he now found strange. He was not lionized by the people of Locarno, who were basically anti-Fascist. When he called a press conference, only two reporters from the international press corps showed up. The others boycotted the conference in protest over Matteotti's murder. At the appointed hour, Il Duce swept down the stairs of the hotel followed by his enormous retinue of Fascists and found two lonely figures. Furious, he made a short statement, turned on his heel, and left the room. Later he went to the Palace Hotel seeking an encounter with foreign press ringleader George Slocombe of the *London Daily Herald*. His first question was "Well, how is communism going?" Slocombe said "I would not know because I am not a Communist."

"Well, perhaps I am wrong," said Mussolini.

"And that often happens to you," said a Dutch journalist.

Stung beyond words by his ill-advised and ill-fated confrontation with the press, Mussolini swept out of the room.

At the conference, Belgian delegation leader Socialist Emile Vandervelde refused Mussolini's outstretched hand. This was obviously as much a result of Mussolini's socialism desertion as his fascism involvement. Il Duce was not satisfied with the results of the conference, which in his eyes simply guaranteed a status quo in Europe that Italy found unbearable. But the conference established Italy as a European power, a role she had not enjoyed since the end of the war. She could no longer be ignored, and Mussolini had what he wanted, to be on a par with Britain and France. At Locarno, Mussolini and Sir Austen Chamberlain became friends, and relations with Britain improved remarkably. France, on the other hand, had gotten all she expected out of Italy at Locarno and became very unfriendly. At Locarno, Philippe Berthelot, Secretary General of the French Ministry for Foreign Affairs, made slighting remarks about the Italian delegation, which prompted Mussolini to launch a strong anti-French propaganda campaign.

The slighting of Mussolini at Locarno in 1925 was to have a lasting effect on the European situation. His ego was so punctured that he vowed not to leave the borders of Italy again, and did not, for many years. Still considering Italy an outcast, he built his policies based on war. He told the Chamber of Deputies that December: "I have said, and I repeat, that the next five or ten years will be decisive for the destiny of our people. They will be decisive because the international struggle has broken out and will continue to extend and we who have arrived a little late on the international scene cannot disperse our energies."

So Mussolini's energies for the next few years were to be concentrated on national affairs. He still had his youthful dream of making Italy an empire to rival England's, an empire to rival ancient Rome. But this would have to wait until he consolidated the gains of the rapidly growing Fascist movement. The uncertainties of power had affected his extremely sensitive nervous state and took a personal toll on Mussolini. He developed ulcers, which became so serious that he was confined to his bed for forty days. But with the help of Italy's best physicians and sheer willpower, he survived, recovered, and was back at his eighteen-hour daily schedule.

There were further assassination attempts. A mad Irish woman named Violet Gibson shot at him on April 7, 1926, from point-blank range when he opened an International Congress of Surgeons. Because he raised his head to look at a pretty girl who had just tossed him a bouquet of flowers, the shot went through the bridge of his nose instead of into his brain. Mussolini rose to the occasion. Blood streaming from his nose, he went into the building. "Gentlemen," he said to the assembled doctors with a sweeping gesture, "I have come to put myself in your professional hands."

His friendship with Sir Austen saved Ms. Gibson, who was quickly deported to Britain. Mussolini basked in the reflection of his generosity, but assassination was a serious threat. In September, Gino Lucetti threw a hand grenade aimed at the window of Mussolini's Lancia coupe, but Mussolini's chauffeur accelerated the car and the grenade bounced off the roof, exploding fifty yards away. Lucetti was given thirty years in prison.

On October 31, a fifteen-year-old boy named Anteo Zamboni shot at Mussolini. He was traveling in a motorcade on Bologna's Via della Indipendenza, seated against the back of an open scarlet Alfa Romeo. The car was moving at a snail's pace so that Il Duce could enjoy the admiration of the crowd lining the street. The bullet passed through Il Duce's tunic and his ceremonial sash. The boy disappeared under a crowd of Fascists, daggers drawn, and was stabbed fourteen times.

"The bullets pass—Mussolini remains," said Il Duce nonchalantly. But the actions that followed did not suit his words. A new chief of the national police, Arturo Bocchini, prefect of Genoa, concentrated on state security. Thereafter, no pedestrian ever got closer than five hundred yards to Mussolini. The route from Mussolini's office to his Via Rasella apartment was guarded and checked by plainclothes police and the streets were closed to traffic twice a day, when Mussolini came and went. When he opened a new building, agents even searched the sewers for time bombs. Fascist security was complete and effective. Every night local police chiefs compared data on the arrests made that day. Identity cards were issued to every citizen and a network of secret agents was established. This Organizzazione di Vigilanza e Repressione dell' Antifascismo (OVRA) was a bureau of seven hundred agents who employed thousands of waiters, taxi drivers, hotel concierges, porters, and caretakers as undercover agents to check on people who received mail from abroad, made too many telephone calls, or did anything even slightly out of the ordinary. Fascism under Chief Bocchini became a very effective police state.

Antifascism in Italy became a crime equal to drug pushing. The jury system was replaced by special tribunals and headed by military judges. There wasn't any right of appeal or calling of defense witnesses. The anti-Fascists began escaping from Italy: Pietro Nenni escaped to France, E. V. Borgese went to America as a visiting professor and did not return, but some like Alcide de Gasperi, among others, were caught while trying to flee and sent into custody. The Pontine and Lipari islands became concentration camps for the dissenters who were caught by OVRA.

∽

The Special Tribunals began their work, and on May 26, 1927, Mussolini announced that 698 political prisoners had been sentenced. Among them was de Gasperi, who got three years for his failed attempt at escape from the country.

But for the mass of people who managed to live within the confines of fascism, life became a little easier. Roberto Farinacci was replaced as secretary of the party by the more moderate and popular Augusto Turati. After Mussolini had secured the trappings of legality, the party controlled everything; even the National Olympic Committee was under the direct control of the secretary of the Fascist party. By 1928 all youth organizations that did not belong to the *Balilla*, the Fascist youth organization, were dissolved by decree. The new electoral law was passed on March 16, 1928, without debate, and Mussolini admitted to the Chamber of Deputies that parliamentary government had come to an end.

The Grand Council of the Fascist party became an organ of the state, and it controlled such constitutional issues as the succession to the throne, its own composition and function, and the replacement of the Head of Government. Thus, Mussolini set up a procedure through which he could be deprived of office. In that sense, he was not an absolute dictator, but ruled at the convenience of the fascist movement. He could expect to remain in power only as long as he could keep the Fascists' allegiance. At the time, it seemed ridiculous to believe that any situation would arise in which Mussolini would lose Fascist support.

∽

As Mussolini put the finishing touches on his own brand of government, he brought about the end of a most difficult sixty-years-long conflict between the Italian government and the Vatican.

Until 1859 the pope had been king of the Papal States, a region that covered 16,000 square miles with a population of three million people. Between 1859 and 1879 the Kingdom of Italy annexed these territories, and in 1870 the pope, losing his capital to Italian troops, retired to the Vatican, a complex of buildings and gardens behind St. Peter's Cathedral covering 500,000 square yards. In 1871 the Italian government guaranteed the pope's inviolability and granted him the use of the Vatican, the Lateran Palace, and the summer villa at Castel Gaddolfo and authorized him to maintain an armed guard. The Vatican was given full diplomatic powers, and the pope was guaranteed the support of his court and diplomatic service. Because this was not a negotiated treaty, but rather a unilateral act by Italy that could be revoked at any time, the Vatican objected. The situation deadlocked and remained that way for years. After World War I conversations between the Orlando government and the Vatican continued, but nothing ever came of them.

One of the marks of Mussolini's character was a dichotomy—a love-hate relationship with the Roman Catholic church. He professed to be an unbeliever, yet in 1925 he insisted on marrying Rachele in a religious ceremony in Milan. He let it be known that this was simply a ploy to gain favor with the Vatican, but it was more than that. He felt that it was proper for the head of the Italian state to conform to the religion practiced by the vast majority of the Italian people. Furthermore, he could not forget his beloved mother and his Catholic upbringing at her insistence. So it somehow eased his conscience to conform to the mores of his people.

The act certainly did help in his relations with the Vatican. Mussolini had begun the conciliation of the Church in his maiden speech in the Chamber of Deputies, before the March on Rome, when he spoke of the need for the Italian government to reach an accommodation with the Church. After he came to power in 1922 the crucifix was restored to the public schools and law courts, divorce was made more difficult, religious instruction was begun in the elementary school, and church schools were assured of equal treatment with state schools. Many other minor changes came too, such as the appointment of chaplains for the armed services and the exemption from military service of clerics.

In 1923 Mussolini made it apparent in a conversation with Cardinal Gaspari, the Papal Secretary of State, that his Italian government sought an accommodation. In 1925 Mussolini appointed a commission to study the revision of the Italian laws covering the Church to become in tune with the wishes of the Vatican. All very well, said Pope Pius

XI, but this did not solve the problem of the Church's relationship with the government. The popes had for nearly a hundred years considered themselves to be prisoners in the Vatican. It would take a strong action by the Italian government to remove the obstacles to real unity. Mussolini chose to regard that letter as a proposal. He made it clear that he had restored to the nation its Catholic character and repudiated the Liberals' separation of church and state.

The major obstacle to the reconciliation was the reluctance of the King and the repugnance of the Fascists for the reunion. To the King it meant giving up sovereignty over a part of his kingdom. The Fascists considered agnosticism a part of their political faith. Beginning in August 1926, talks began, this time instigated by Pope Pius XI.

In October 1926 negotiations began in earnest to arrange a political settlement that would give the Pope the status of a sovereign and assign certain territory to the Vatican. All was going smoothly that autumn until Fascists attacked Catholic establishments in fourteen cities. The Vatican stopped the negotiations and demanded a public apology and assurances that such events would not occur in the future.

This situation posed a serious problem for Mussolini. Anticlericalism was part of the bedrock of fascist policy and Mussolini had at one time encouraged it. He sent word to the prefects around the country to desist from violence but he did not want to move too fast, given his own record.

The situation was made worse in December, when the Italian government introduced a bill under which the state claimed a monopoly on education. It was to be carried out by the Youth Organization, whereas the organizations that dealt with youth were to be abolished. The Vatican insisted that the bill be suspended, and when Mussolini refused to do so, the pope spoke of the danger to education of totalitarianism. This seemed like stalemate, but Mussolini used his power to control the press to keep the fascist newspapers from aggravating the quarrel. This contretemps, however, suspended negotiations for a whole year. In 1928 the negotiations resumed after tempers had cooled. The next several months brought long and tenuous negotiations. The Vatican authorities wanted more territory, outside of the Vatican, but finally gave in on that point. They would not give in on the provisions relating to marriage and education. It was a tribute to Mussolini's patience and will to solve the problem that the parties were able to resolve this sticking point. In the fall of 1928 all the basic points had been settled and in January 1929 Mussolini took over negotiations for the Italian government. He met fifteen times with Cardinal Pacelli.

As these delicate negotiations were going on, opponents in Italy assured the world that there was no chance of the Vatican and the fascist government agreeing. Mussolini saw an article by former Prime Minister Nitti that had appeared in several European papers, saying just this, and Benito sent a copy of it to the King. It was good for a laugh, which they needed. As Mussolini wrote the King that January, the negotiations had proved most difficult: "I do not conceal from Your Majesty that the most difficult obstacle to surmount in the concordat has been the article on marriage. Here the state has retreated a long way and has been virtually excluded in so fundamental a matter as the constitution and the evolution of the family. But it seems that the Holy See regards this as an essential condition of first-class importance on which the whole of the treaty depends."

Finally the two treaties covering the physical and the spiritual were signed on February 11, 1929, and Mussolini celebrated with a forty-minute speech in which he played the role of a loyal son of the Church. Within a matter of hours the news spread through Rome and crowds came out to cheer the pope, the King, and Mussolini. The pope was granting his usual audience that day to the parish priests of Rome and he told them about the signing. The next day, at the St. Peter's celebration of the seventh anniversary of Pius XI's coronation, there were further celebrations by the people in St. Peter's Square.

Under the final agreements, Italy recognized the sovereignty of the pope and the pope recognized the Savoy dynasty of Italy. The pope received title to what is now Vatican City and a large indemnity in bonds. The question of education was resolved by the state recognizing the church education through the secondary schools, and recognizing the Vatican's approval of textbooks. The government agreed that religious marriage would be equal to civil, and that the nullification of a marriage on the grounds of nonconsummation should be left to the ecclesiastical courts to decide.

Characteristically, Mussolini followed this generous performance with an attack on the church in the Chamber of Deputies, belittling its origins and some of its interference with civil affairs in the past. The pope took offense at this and for months the state and the Vatican were at odds, while the Fascists cheered. But all this was a tempest in a teapot, calculated by Mussolini to please his Fascist extremists, and it did not alter the fact that Mussolini had resolved the basic quarrel of the Italian government with the Church of Rome when no one else could do it. In spite of the squabbling that went on, the agreements were ratified by both sides in June 1929, and the Holy See and Italy exchanged ambassadors. For Mussolini, it was a chance to appease one of his problem children—Cesare de Vecchi, who had a tendency to get out of control. By becoming ambassador to the Vatican, De Vecchi had a post in which he was happy while still being under close supervision of Il Duce.

The law concerning the Grand Council passed through both houses of the Parliament, thus burying the Constitution and destroying the last vestiges of Italian liberty. The elections that would take place after 1928 would be nothing like those of the past. In 1922 the Chamber of Deputies was fragmented with no party having more than about 150 seats. In 1926 the Chamber was 85 percent Fascist. The new chamber would be 100 percent Fascist. There was a word for it: totalitarianism.

CHAPTER 12

❦

The New Italy

In the 1920s Mussolini showed unusual prescience for a man who often called himself "just a peasant." If he was just a peasant, as the diplomatic corps and upper-class Europeans were quick to agree, then he was a remarkably intelligent one in spite of his table manners. One reason for his concern over the relationship with the Church of Rome was his realization that the Western world was waiting for him to fail, and he was determined to make a success of his revolution that had already changed Italy. As far as power was concerned, it did not matter, but as far as international prestige was concerned and the feeling that the Italian people were unified, it was very important to have a big turnout of voting in the national elections. He remembered only too well that in the elections of 1924 in many areas of Italy only half the people even bothered to go to the polls. His fascist government demanded participation, not supine behavior, and so it was important that he have a vote of confidence in fascism.

He got precisely what he wanted from the Catholics. The central committee of Catholic Action called on Catholics to cooperate and cited the need to show a united face to secure the enforcement of the treaties with the Vatican. The elections of March 24, 1929, brought 90 percent of the voters out to cast their ballots. Mussolini's list of candidates received 8,500,000 votes, and only 135,000 people voted against the Fascists. Mussolini had wanted a demonstration "to the world that Italy is Fascist and that fascism is Italy."

Privately he was unhappy about those 135,000 negative voters, most of whom were in the northern cities, his own domain. In his own stamping ground of Milan, 23,000 negative votes were cast, and 412,000 votes for the Fascists. Privately Mussolini lamented this to Sir Austen Chamberlain, although the support was as high as anyone might expect. It was apparent in this election that the Italian people were impressed by the accomplishments of the fascist government. In the next few years they would be more impressed with solid accomplishment at home.

The end of parliamentary democracy in Italy meant the end of public political conflict. This could have led to general apathy on the part of the public. Having nothing to argue about, they might not have cared what happened in public affairs. But Mussolini very skillfully presented public questions in a manner that demanded the attention of the citizens. When major world stock markets collapsed in 1929 and 1930 and brought general world depression, Italy was hit as well as America, Britain, and the other industrial countries. The fascist government then embarked on a program openly called "The Battle of the Lira," which was an attempt to defend the value of the national currency. This had to be done by reducing prices and subsidies and the middle class and poor bore the cost of it, but it was presented as a matter of survival, and so successfully that the programs received the support of most people.

The depression also forced the reduction of imports by Italy because of the expense and the need to conserve foreign exchange, so with great fanfare Mussolini began "The Battle of the Wheat." All over the world, motion picture goers watched Mussolini in the newsreels stripped to the waist, wielding a hay fork and helping with a combine at harvest season, to show the solidarity of the Italian people. This war was successful. By the end of 1933 Italy was importing 15,000 tons of grain as compared to 221,500 in the year before.

One reason for the increase in grain production was the Fascist Land Reclamation Plan. By the fall of 1933 more than nine million acres of arable land had been recovered all over the country. The Pontine Marshes were drained, a project begun in the days of parliamentary democracy that had collapsed for want of energy and direction. This was community planning at its best. And 150,000 acres of malarial marshland between Rome and Terracina were transformed into valuable farmland, on which 75,000 poor people from all over the country were settled. On December 19, 1931, Il Duce opened with great ceremony the little town of Littoria in the center of the area. Soon half a dozen towns were established, roads and canals were constructed, public services were established, and malaria was controlled.

These agricultural accomplishments were real and could not be controverted. Critics complained that Mussolini did it all for self-advertisement, but this could not be the case. Too much effort went into the agricultural rebirth for that. Another campaign, which is likely to be regarded with disdain in a world conscious of population pressures, was Mussolini's "Battle of the People," in which he sought to increase Italy's population from 40,000,000 to 60,000,000 people by the middle of the twentieth century. This was a part of Mussolini's dream of recreating the grandeur and power of ancient Rome. To become a first-rate power, he claimed, Italy would have to increase its population by half. The measures chosen were to propagandize childbirth with every means possible. Bachelors were taxed for remaining single. Prizes were awarded all over the country for the most fertile women; the competition was brought to Rome and on December 23, 1933, Mussolini held a reception for the ninety-three most fertile women in Italy, who had produced thirteen hundred children among them. But the birthrate did not rise; instead it fell from 27.5 per thousand to 24.5. Mussolini was facing the same problem as the leaders of other industrial countries. The hard times did not encourage large families, no matter what the state and the church tried to do. But the concern with health and maternity and infant mortality brought a better standard of living to the poor of Italy, whose health needs were more clearly met than they had ever been under the parliamentary democracy. At the same time, Italian emigration continued to all the civilized countries that could take immigrants, some of it for political reasons, but mostly for economic opportunity.

In these years, Italy did attract the attention of the world and of Europe in particular. If Mussolini would not go abroad, which he firmly refused to do after the slights of Locarno, then Europe and America would come to him. In 1920, President Wilson came to advertise his Fourteen Points. In the four years after 1926, in addition to all the commercial agreements that favored Italy, Mussolini signed eight diplomatic treaties. Sir Austen Chamberlain developed a close relationship with Mussolini that kept Il Duce in the British camp for years, although his advisors said it was useless to tie his canoe to the British fleet.

Mussolini developed a huge world following. Mahatma Gandhi called him a superman. The Archbishop of Canterbury saw him as the only giant figure among Europe's leaders. Fascism was new, it seemed to work, and it was exciting to a world grown weary of the endless talk of the politicians. Thomas Edison called him the greatest genius of modern times. The American banker Otto Kahn said the world owed

Mussolini a debt of gratitude for showing how a forlorn nation could be brought out of confusion and poverty. Winston Churchill came to see him. Churchill was taken aback when Mussolini's guards asked him to put out his cigar before entering the grand office of the dictator. He did so. Then, when he entered the huge office, so large that Mussolini's aides used hand signals like semaphores to convey information, Churchill saw that Mussolini did not rise from his desk. Piqued, he lit up another big cigar and then advanced across the seventy-foot-long office. Mussolini leaped to his feet and pumped Churchill's hand. Mollified, Churchill went away with a positive impression of the Italian leader. "If I had been Italian," he said, "I am sure I would have been with you from the beginning to the end of your struggle against the bestial appetites of Leninism."

Yet in the 1920s Mussolini showed little use for the French. And when a young admirer named Adolf Hitler asked through the head of the Italian Chamber of Commerce in Berlin for a signed photograph, Mussolini refused. From the outset of Hitler's rise to power, which aped the methods and philosophy of state socialism of Mussolini, Hitler was one of the Italian dictator's firmest admirers. But the compliment was not returned.

To the world Mussolini was a great meeter and greeter. Between 1922 and 1929 he had granted sixty thousand audiences, and almost no one who wrote to Il Duce failed to get a personal reply. Biographer Richard Collier says Mussolini dealt with two million requests from ordinary citizens. At Christmas he received thirty thousand greeting cards from all over the world. He was, indeed, the world's most popular political figure of the late 1920s, and early 1930s.

His popularity increased with the years. He undertook public works with grand gestures, like the 2.2-mile Ponta della Liberta that linked Venice to the mainland. He followed that with four thousand miles of roads and aqueducts to bring water to the parched lands of Apulia. He built four hundred new bridges and not only made sure the trains ran on time but also that telephone communication was improved with six hundred telephone exchanges. New buildings were put up for fascist headquarters, post offices, government offices, and sports arenas and facilities. They were almost all a triumph of size over good taste, "grandiloquent and gaudy." Within five years Rome must appear as a "marvel to the nations of the world," Mussolini said, "vast, orderly, powerful, as it was in the times of the Augustan empire." Here was a clue to Mussolini's new turn of thought. In the first two decades of the twentieth century he had yearned for power. When he achieved the power, he first sought to rebuild Italy.

He devoted some attention to Rome with less satisfactory results. Like Hitler after him in Berlin, he wanted to leave his mark on the Eternal City. He built an Italian merchant marine whose traditions lasted long after his time; in 1933 the liner *Rex* would cross the Atlantic in four and a half days to set a new record, and the Italian liners were always notable for their food and luxurious service. Fascist firebrand Italo Balbo, who had been an aviator in World War I, was made Minister of Aviation and he built a pioneer air service for Italy, making several transoceanic flights, including one from Rome to Chicago. Mussolini also carried out a brisk and successful crusade against crime in Italy and conquered the Mafia of Sicily, where murders dropped from 278 a year to 25. Dom Vito Cascio Ferro, the master mind of the Mafia, was arrested and brought under control. Not until Mussolini's rule ended did the Mafia raise its head again, and since then no one has controlled it. He built sixteen thousand public elementary schools and set up seventeen hundred summer camps for city children. Millions of lira were given for family support programs and prenatal clinics for women.

By the mid-1930s he had made Italians largely prosperous—on the surface. But beneath, the national debt was soaring and in 1939, it hit 145 billion lire, which compared with the enormous American national debt. As it would be in America later, the national debt began to hamper prosperity, and affairs were worsened by the central control of the economy through the corporate state system. But none of this was readily apparent in the middle 1930s. Italians, who had been poor and self-conscious, became proud of their country and its leadership. Mussolini's immense vigor in the twenties enhanced life in Italy, and, generally, improvements were such that biographer Ivone Kirkpatrick referred to this period as "The Halcyon Years." Mussolini was content to let his foreign policy star follow the British; there were not yet any serious issues springing up from the ashes of World War I, and Mussolini's direct attacks on public problems were admired the world over.

Following the death of parliamentary democracy, violence decreased remarkably. However, one conflict developed in 1931 over Catholic Action, an organization to which Pope Pius XI attached particular importance as the foundation of defense of Christian social principles. In fact, the wedding between the Church and fascism was ill-matched, in the sense that both organizations claimed omnipotence over the souls and lives of their adherents. The Fascists demanded the total loyalty of their members, and, indeed, the people. So did the

Church. Catholic Action developed a new life, after the conciliation between the pope and Mussolini, because it was one of the few organizations tolerated outside the fascist sphere. Thus, Catholic Action began proselytizing and expanding, a process the Fascist leadership, Mussolini excepted, found distasteful at first and infuriating later.

In the spring of 1931 the quarrel became open when the *Lavoro Fascista* launched a violent attack on Catholic Action; shortly afterward, the government banned congresses of Catholic undergraduates at Ferrara and Padua Universities. On April 19 the secretary of the Fascist party, Giovanni Giuriati, made an impassioned attack on Catholic Action in Milan. The pope reacted sharply. The press attacked Catholic Action in a series of articles. Some Catholic Action centers were assaulted in the old fascist bullyboy fashion. The fascist press referred to the pope by his family name, Ratti, and shouted "Death to the traitor Ratti." The police ordered all branches of the Catholic Youth Organization and the University Federation dissolved. The pope replied by an attack on the "first fruit" of an education antithetical to Christian education. Mussolini was dragged in, unwillingly, and he referred to the anti-fascist nature of some Catholic Action groups and said the state would not tolerate it, in spite of its deep respect for the Catholic church. The pope countered with an encyclical attacking fascism. The government said "you must choose between Catholic Action and fascism." And it went on and on.

But then both sides realized how self-defeating the quarrel was, and a tacit truce was declared. Secretly the pope threatened to excommunicate Mussolini, who promised to find some means of settling the dispute. Mussolini was in a most unenviable position, because he did not really believe what the Fascists were doing, but like the man on the back of the tiger, he found it impossible to get off, and the best he could do was try to control the tiger from its most vicious forays. By the end of the summer he had managed to have all the measures taken against the Catholic Action organizations rescinded. The pope accepted a ban on activities in which the Catholic Youth Organization competed with Fascist Youth. And so the Church and Mussolini's state reverted to an uneasy peace, which Mussolini wanted as the proof of legitimacy of his regime. On February 11, 1932, Mussolini paid a visit to the pope, which signaled to Italy and the world that the breach was healed. And life in Italy was again serene.

∽

By 1931 Mussolini was at the pinnacle of his success, as the acknowledged leader of Italy and as a world statesman. He still would not go abroad so leaders from other countries still came to Rome. Italy had signed agreements with half a dozen nations, a process in which Dino Grandi as foreign minister had achieved a considerable reputation for statesmanship, so much, in fact, that Mussolini suddenly shipped him off to London as ambassador and resumed the foreign ministry himself. Italo Balbo had succeeded so well as Minister of Aviation that he suddenly found himself packed off to Africa to be governor of Libya, and a dozen other intimates suddenly disappeared or were abruptly transferred from positions of influence.

"Mussolini doesn't want advice anymore; he only wants applause," said Leandro Arpinati, the under secretary for Home Affairs, on the eve of his banishment to the island of Lipari. Mussolini admitted that this was true. When asked why he had fired Grandi as foreign minister he said, "He came to know me too well."

But it was not that alone. All powerful, Mussolini continued to lust for power and its symbols. His photograph appeared day after day in the press; Mussolini the driver of fast cars; Mussolini, the aviator; Mussolini in uniform, chest out thrust and jaw jutting forth; Mussolini with his pet lion cub; Mussolini skiing; Mussolini taking a horse over the jumps; Mussolini descending into a coal mine; Mussolini on his balcony at the Palazzo Venezia; Mussolini threshing wheat; Mussolini in top hat, cutaway coat, and striped trousers; Mussolini posed on his white stallion *Atlantico*.

He held all-night sessions of the Fascist Grand Council and lorded it over the membership. His portrait hung in every school classroom. School pupils prayed every morning to Mussolini and Jesus Christ, in that order. What had been the Chamber of Deputies was now rechristened the Chamber of Fascists and Corporations. He had come to believe the official propaganda that he was the statesman of the century, and there was truth in the statement, as evidenced by the newfound respect given him by the leaders of other countries. Had his search for international prestige been rewarded early in the 1930s, he might not have embarked on the thrust for an empire and the alliance with Hitler that led him to destruction. In 1931 Mussolini genuinely favored disarmament and guarantees that would maintain world peace. Speaking at Ravenna early in August, he talked about peace and Italy's position:

"I wish to add that the Fascist government, the Fascist regime, the Fascists, wish peace. We wish peace with all states distant, near or very near. We want peace not because we fear the period of war and the anxieties of battle, but because we wish to remove the Italian people as soon as possible from the deprivations and depressions of the present time since we Fascists are working above all for the people and to the people we do not preach rights alone but duty as well."

His own newspaper *Il Popolo d'Italia* amplified his remarks, saying that Mussolini's words meant a guarantee for a Europe "tormented by serious economic uncertainties and profound political difficulties." It was these uncertainties and difficulties of the early 1930s that provided the turning point for Mussolini's energy and ambitions.

Early in October 1931, a meeting of the Fascist Grand Council furthered this theme. It was Mussolini speaking, for he *was* the Fascist Grand Council, and the other members were rubber stamps. In approving preliminary work carried on at Geneva by Minister Grandi, Mussolini said this: "The Fascist Grand Council, having heard the report on the internal and international situation is of the opinion that the timely measures taken by the fascist government together with the program of social assistance already established will permit the country to meet the crisis during the inevitable increase in seasonal employment; and as regards the world situation the Grand Council declares that they cannot proceed to a settlement unless measures are immediately taken affecting in the first place the world disarmament problem and the problem of debts and reparations." In February 1932, Grandi offered a comprehensive plan for abandonment of heavy artillery, tanks, battleships, submarines, and aircraft carriers and bomber aircraft. It might have worked, but it did not come in time. The German government, responding to demands of the growing Nazi party, stalled and, on August 29, demanded the end of the clauses in the Treaty of Versailles that imposed unilateral disarmament on Germany. Even this was not a final rejection of the concept, had Britain and France been willing to treat openly with real disarmament.

Mussolini was convinced by the events of the past few years that the future of Europe lay in fascism. In a speech celebrating the first decade of fascist control of Italy, made in Turin on October 23, 1932, he predicted "the twentieth century will be the century of fascism; it will be the century of Italian power; it will be the century in which Italy will return for the third time to be the leader of civilization, for outside our faith there is no salvation either for individuals or for peoples."

In those days of world depression, millions in Europe and America felt that the old economic and political systems had failed and might be irreparable, and so Mussolini's words fell on receptive ears. What if the Fascists were right, and their system was the wave of the future?

Mussolini was receiving a hearing and a considerable amount of approval throughout the world.

The Turin visit was a supreme triumph for Mussolini. The buildings along the streets through which his motorcade would pass were decked out in flags. A cordon of troops along the streets kept traffic clear. Mussolini arrived by train at the station, dressed in the uniform of a corporal of the militia, with decorations, and went in an open automobile from the railroad station to the prefect's palace, led by two police cars and followed by a detachment of mounted carabinieri. There he took off the uniform and wearing a black shirt with a single medal commemorating the March on Rome, he appeared on the balcony bareheaded and delivered his speech to the thousands who thronged the Piazza Castello.

In the afternoon Mussolini visited hospitals and a children's home where thirty thousand children had assembled to greet him, and the Casa del Fascio, the fascist headquarters, where he received thirty-five thousand letters of gratitude written to him by workers and employed citizens whose lot had been relieved by charities. In the evening he visited the electrical institute to see an experiment in television and then returned to the prefect's palace to accept the salute of thousands of students and workers who paraded in the Piazza below.

The next morning, accompanied by Balbo and De Vecchi, two of his generals in the March on Rome, Mussolini went to the Fiat factory where he addressed twenty-five thousand workers. Later that day he dressed in the corporal's uniform and, wearing the new steel helmet just issued, reviewed twenty thousand troops. In the afternoon he visited the Lancia motor car factory and a chocolate factory. That evening he traveled forty miles to the royal castle of Conigi, where he was guest of honor at a dinner given by the Crown Prince. On the third day he visited more public institutions and public works and attended a requiem mass for the city's thirty-eight hundred war dead of World War I. In the afternoon he opened the new Turin-Milan highway and drove over it to Milan escorted by two thousand motorists and two hundred airplanes flying overhead. The extravaganza of Turin was repeated at Milan, and Mussolini, surrounded by Fascist officials including Balbo and De Vecchi, accepted a large lictor's fasces from a tribune dressed in velvet. Then he delivered a speech to a crowd of five hundred thousand people gathered in the Piazza del Duomo. In Milan he inspected plans for a tower to be erected with a public building and gave orders that it was not to rise above the statue of the Madonna at the Cathedral. As at Turin, everything he did and said was greeted with thunderous applause and cheers, and the crowd laughed uproariously at all his jokes.

Summing up the results of the visit to northern Italy a few days later, chargé d'affaires Alexander Kirk of the American embassy said, "The outstanding feature of the visit was the sincerity of the popular acclaim which greeted him wherever he went and which had created the general impression that fascism and its leader have today a firmer hold on the Italian people than ever before."

The extraordinary warmth of Mussolini's welcome was particularly notable, because Turin, a Socialist center of the past, had also been one of the electoral districts in which he still received the most rejections by the voters.

In his speeches in northern Italy, Mussolini had dealt with the League of Nations, which was proving to be flabby and helpless in the case of the Japanese invasion of Manchuria and the wrenching away of six provinces to form the puppet state of Manchukuo. Mussolini saw the League's weakness but observed that Italy would remain a member of the almost moribund organization and do what it could to strengthen it. He had also discussed Germany and the demands of the Germans for revision of the Versailles Treaty.

In January 1933, Adolf Hitler was called by President Hindenburg of Germany to be the chancellor of the German Reich. At a dinner at the presidential palace, Hitler was paired with Elisabetta Cerruti, wife of the Italian ambassador to Germany and in the table conversation they talked about Mussolini. "I had too much respect for that great man to disturb him before achieving positive results," Hitler said, "but now it is different. I am looking forward to meeting him. It will be the happiest day of my life."

Within a few hours of taking power, Hitler had sent a personal message to Il Duce expressing his admiration and homage and a desire for closer relations. Although their movements were not identical, he said, he was willing to accept Mussolini's view of the world future. He also indicated the belief that without Mussolini's example, his own rise to power would not have succeeded. He hinted at his ambitions for Austria but indicated that if Mussolini would accept them, then he would back Mussolini's hand in the rest of the Danube basin. Hitler felt that Italy and Germany must have a close alliance.

∽

Thus, the way seemed to be paved for Italy to exert a positive influence on the new Germany. Mussolini tried. He devised a plan that would bring Germany into a European association that would recognize the puerility of the League of Nations. The plan received the enthusiastic endorsement of Ramsay MacDonald, the prime minister of Britain and his foreign minister, Sir John Simon. They paid a visit to Mussolini on his invitation and he laid out the program for a four-power pact between Britain, Italy, France, and Germany, designed to keep the peace of Europe. Italy wanted the four powers to recognize the need for revision of the peace treaties to be fair to the Germans. In the field of disarmament Germany should have equal rights with the others, and the four powers should adopt a common foreign policy to guarantee the security of Europe.

This Mussolini plan was the most foresighted of its time, recognizing that unless there was harmony among these four powers, the peace of Europe could not be guaranteed. He stated what no one else would say—that the League of Nations "collective security" was a myth because none of the smaller powers of the League had any military strength.

But the attempt collapsed because the world was not ready to admit the truth. The French opposed the revision of the harsh peace laid down upon Germany and sought the support of the smaller powers, which did not like the idea of being excluded from the councils that would control Europe. The USSR and Turkey objected because they feared that a four-party alliance would be turned against them. Hitler favored the plan, and, in Britain, Prime Minister MacDonald approved and tried to bring the French around. But the French hatred of Germany was so strong that, when the treaty was put together, it was emasculated. Mussolini had a moment of apparent triumph, when the four powers initialed the treaty at a gala ceremony in Rome. But in the end, French intransigence carried the day, and the pact, weak as it was, was ratified only by Germany and Italy; the chance for peace in Europe was thrown away.

In May 1933 Franklin D. Roosevelt, the newly inaugurated president of the United States, called on Europe and the world for disarmament and the immediate abandonment of offensive weapons. Hitler followed that with a speech endorsing the American idea. Germany, he said, was ready to destroy all her offensive weapons if the rest of the world would destroy theirs. "War is madness," Hitler said.

Conventional history would have it that this was all a pose, but it does not seem to have been. Both Italy and Germany were seeking equality among nations, and equality was denied to them again by Britain and France.

Observing the failure of the peace plan, in October Hitler withdrew from the disarmament conference and the League of Nations. He called for a plebiscite on the subject. The German people approved overwhelmingly. Ninety-five percent voted for the withdrawal. The world began marching to World War II. Mussolini knew. He saw that Hitler had established the same sort of control over Germany that he had over Italy. By the end of 1933 Mussolini had assumed personal control of the Foreign Ministry, the Air Ministry, the War Ministry, and the Navy Ministry. He was-embarked on a major rearmament program and getting Italy ready for war. He had made serious overtures for peace and had been rebuffed by England and France. He was preparing to cross his own Rubicon.

CHAPTER 13

∽

Mussolini's Women

Benito Mussolini was not a mother's boy; he grew up with great respect and affection for his father. But he adored his mother (who wanted him to be a priest) and when she died, he was bereft for weeks. In later life he often recalled her attempts to instill religion into his soul, and ultimately, he rejoined the Church of Rome and married his common-law wife, both in civil and religious ceremonies.

But his women, and particularly the two who loved him, his wife Rachele and his last mistress, Claretta Petacci, played no part in Mussolini's political life, even though in the years of power he saw both of them every day. He kept his personal life so compartmentalized that Rachele did not even know of the affair with Claretta Petacci for eleven years, until the last. He strayed even from Claretta, but he was so overwhelmed by her that he even antagonized his son-in-law, Count Galeazzo Ciano. "It is of no consequence to run after a number of women," Ciano once said. "What is grave and scandalous is to devote oneself assiduously to one woman, and that is the case with Mussolini."

From the day that he reached puberty Benito Mussolini was obsessed with women and the need to prove his manhood. There is not much indication that he really enjoyed sex, as much as his satyriasis compelled him to try to possess every woman he saw. As biographer Richard Collier put it: Just after puberty "already the long series of shabby amours" had begun "against trees, on staircases, by the banks of the River Rabi." Usually he did not take off his trousers. As Mussolini told his boyhood friend Rino Alessio, "I've begun undressing every girl I see with my eyes."

125

In his young manhood, as noted, he contracted syphilis from one of these amours but was treated and apparently cured, although forever afterward he worried about it. In middle age when his intense nervous system caused him to suffer from ulcers, for a time he feared it was a new manifestation of the syphilis and it was hard for his doctors to convince him that he was not going to die.

Women played a large role in shaping his intellectual life as well. The first was Angelica Balabanoff, the Russian Socialist he met in Switzerland who persuaded him to read and go to public lectures, although she was never satisfied that he understood the principles and philosophy of socialism. She was important in his life later when he became editor of *Avanti!*, the socialist newspaper, and took her with him as his assistant. She disappeared from his life when he abandoned socialism in 1915.

Another woman, Leda Rafanelli, a Muslim anarchist and successful novelist, became his intimate and exercised a positive force in his life, although they were not lovers. She saw in him the complete rebel he was and doubted if he could ever become a real Socialist, although at the time he professed to be one. Another woman who brought a new aspect to his life was his *Avanti!* art critic, Margherita Sarfatti.

Rachele Guidi was brought into his life when his father took her mother Anna as his mistress and then common-law wife to help him run an inn in Forlì. Mussolini announced then that he would marry her and a year later he did, over her mother's objection (because of his loose ways). But the marriage was a happy one. Rachele bore Mussolini five children and lived a contented life, wherever fate cast her, from a hovel in Forlì when he struggled to make a living from jobs of odds and ends, until the very last, when he settled her in a villa before he went to meet his enemies and death. Rachele knew about several of his affairs, including the one with Margherita Sarfatti, but that did not keep her from assenting to the employment of Sarfatti in the Mussolini household as housekeeper during the years of power. Most of Mussolini's amours could not even be classified as affairs but were more in the nature of sexual encounters. He simply could not help wanting to go to bed with every attractive woman he saw, and his vigor in his youth, and his power in middle age made most women easy prey to his lusts.

He met death with his mistress Claretta Petacci, whom he met in 1932 at age fifty-six, when he was a powerful figure, the master of Italy, and she was a twenty-year-old girl affianced to an air force officer. Clara was smitten by him, and he by her, but he did not lay a hand on her until her marriage had failed and she came back into his life. Then in an oddly old-fashioned way, he asked her mother if he could become her lover. But that did not keep him from more affairs, so many that Clara once said to a woman friend, "I've got more horns than a basket full of snails. He has these women seven at a time." But there can be no doubt that Mussolini really loved Claretta. At the end he tried to persuade her to leave him and go to Spain with her parents to save herself, but she refused. She was with him to the death, she said.

Through all this, Rachele remained the perfect wife, raising the children and providing a haven and moral support for him until the end. When she finally discovered the affair with Claretta, she erupted in fury and confronted the younger woman. In the scene that followed, Mussolini fled, and Claretta collapsed in the face of Rachele's rage, but she refused to give up Mussolini.

Rachele was always outspoken in the manner of the Republican peasants of northern Italy and deeply religious like Benito's mother. She played no role in his political life and visited his splendiferous office in the Palazzo Venezia only once. She lived most of the great years in the family villa near Rome, where she was absolute mistress, and he bent to her will. "You run the country," she once told him, "and let me run this household." He and the other members of the family paid fines if they were late to midday dinner, the family's principal meal of the day. Rachele said she could tell how Mussolini's political life was going by the number of fines he paid in a month, and as the war in Africa worsened, his fines were almost every day. Once, when the children had been listening to their father's fulminations against the bourgeoisie, and one of the boys quoted him at the table as saying that spaghetti and meat sauce was a vile concoction of the bourgeoisie, she exploded. "That is your imbecile father and his political nonsense," she said "Eat your spaghetti!"

PART IV

Mussolini's Empire

In the early years of Mussolini's rise to power, he was concerned primarily with attracting people to his banner; his interest in foreign affairs, as such, was entirely pragmatic. At the end of World War I he complained as bitterly as anyone else about the refusal of Italy's allied partners to honor the territorial concessions indicated in the secret Treaty of London, which had a great deal to do with Italy's entry into the war. As a youth he had spoken sometimes of an empire, but in an inchoate and nebulous fashion. It was not until 1923, when Mussolini contrived a fusion of his Blackshirt Fascists with the Blue Shirt Nationalist party, that he gained from the Nationalists a new appreciation of the need for a strong foreign policy to make a strong nation. He had always intended to make Italy a strong power, but the Nationalists showed him how he might hope to break the power structure in Europe and become a great power. Luigi Federzoni of the Nationalists became the Minister of Colonies, and in that role encouraged Mussolini to acquire more colonies. As far as relationships with other nations were concerned, he had no real enthusiasm for the League of Nations, but neither did he show any messianic zeal for spreading fascism. Personally his foreign adventures as a youth in Switzerland and his early encounters with diplomacy left him with a strong feeling of inferiority that by 1925 had persuaded him not to travel abroad but to meet foreigners on his own turf.

Italy before World War I had a special relationship with the Hapsburg Empire, and many people of Italian language and national aspirations lived on Austrian soil. The area around the top of the Adriatic Sea was particularly confused. Italy got Trieste, but not Fiume. Mussolini had ambitions to control Albania, and actually to control the Balkans. He did gain control of Fiume, which cut that port off from its Yugoslavia hinterland and condemned it to poverty, but the territorial acquisition meant more to the Fascists.

In 1923, apparently in retaliation for the murder of an Italian general in Greece who was serving on a boundary commission, Mussolini ordered the naval bombardment and occupation of the Greek island of Corfu. But all was not as it seemed, for the Italian navy had been instructed a month earlier to prepare for this action. It may have been at the instigation of the Nationalist party. The reaction of the world was so strong, particularly that of the British, that Mussolini backed down and withdrew the occupation force, but the whole gesture had made him a hero in Italian eyes, and he did not forget that fact.

130

In the late 1920s Dino Grandi, a younger Fascist, became the spokesman on foreign policy, but, except for a short interval from 1929 until 1932, Mussolini retained the Foreign Ministry portfolio. His comportment was satisfactory to the professionals in the Foreign Ministry; by and large there were no mass resignations in protest against the fascist takeover. Here, as in every other avenue of Italian life, people were thoroughly sick of the indecisive policies of the fragmented Italian political scene. The Italian foreign service was moldy with tradition, and nearly all of its members had independent means. It had always been a gentleman's occupation. But Mussolini changed this, bringing in young men who had to depend on their pay and allowances to subsist.

Mussolini's first encounter with European diplomacy came in October 1925, when he managed the Italian signing of the Treaty of Locarno, along with France, Britain, Belgium, and Germany. This treaty guaranteed the Franco–German border as it had been stipulated in the Treaty of Versailles.

After Mussolini came to power he was fond of saying that fascism was not an exportable commodity, that it suited Italy and no attempt would be made to convert other countries. This was, of course, in answer to bolshevism's ambitions for a world revolution and socialism's less blatant hopes. It was true, he was no evangelist, but he did maintain a special office of propaganda to work on industrialists and politicians. He also created the Stampa Estera, on Rome's Via della Mercede, which had been a ramshackle office building. It was remodeled and decorated with plaster of paris pillars, stucco walls, and an imitation dome. Under the dome a bar was set up for foreign journalists, where drinks were cheaper than at any public bar. A telephone service was maintained as well as a library with newspapers and magazines from all over Europe. There were gamerooms and work rooms and part of the building was rented out to various news organizations that kept their offices there. It was all made very convenient for the news correspondents. It was very convenient for the government, too, for here the Fascists could keep tabs on the reporters, know what they were doing, and what they were sending out by cable and by telephone to their media around the world.

All this was supervised by the Ministry of Popular Culture and in the mid-1920s there were fascist movements in many countries abroad, including Britain. But the only countries in which fascism made any lasting impression, so great as to involve government, were Spain, Portugal, and Argentina. The Japanese also developed a peculiar offshoot of their own. Occasionally Il Duce spoke about the fascist revolution as greater than the bolshevik, but this was mostly hyperbole. What he was really interested in was having fascism be peculiarly Italian and dominating every facet of Italian life. The propaganda abroad was steered to create the illusion that Europe looked to Italy with envy and approval, which was not a hard line to sell, because it was mostly true in the first few years of the 1930s.

After Mussolini came to power in a parliamentary coup that some called a coup d'état, he appointed General Armando Diaz as Minister of War. But Diaz took the job seriously and quit when Mussolini refused to reform the army. He was succeeded by General Antonio Di Georgio who quit a few months later for the same reasons. Mussolini then assumed personal control of the army, navy, and air force for the next four years and laid the groundwork for the incompetence of the army in World War II by making Fascist party membership obligatory for promotion to high rank. Thus Marshal Pietro Badoglio became chief of the general staff, although the best generals knew he was incompetent and the principal architect of the dreadful Italian defeat by the Austrians at Caporetto in World War I. General Giuseppi Ferrari, one of the older generals, urged the revamping of the military, the mechanization of the army, and the development of a competent arms industry. The real problem was that the Fascists were not interested in war games and serious discussion of tactics and strategy. They cared more for the cut of their uniforms, and whether beans or cabbage should be the backbone of military rations. By the time that Ferrari ended his career, the military was in the hands of the Fascists, and, as he suggested, they were setting out to paralyze the whole high command. Mussolini, who did not know the first thing about military strategy, was head of the army, the navy, the air force, and the national militia.

∽

The peace settlement of Versailles really shortchanged Italy, which should have received a share of the German colonies. Instead, the French and British greedily took them all, leaving Italy out in the cold. They did not even give her as much as they gave Japan, although Italy's participation in the war was far greater than Japan's. The basic failure was that of the parliamentary negotiators for Italy at Versailles, who could not agree among themselves over their demands; thus, they were left out. Mussolini went through cycles in considering the plight of Italy, but ultimately, he placed the blame where it belonged, on the greed of Britain and France. By the end of the 1920s, revision of the

Peace of Versailles became a cornerstone of Italian policy. One might make a case that Britain and France caused the attack and annexation of Ethiopia and Mussolini's desire to secure an empire by conquest. It is almost certain that had Italy been treated fairly at the conference table, her yen for colonies would have been satisfied quite easily, and Mussolini's military adventure with Germany need never have happened.

CHAPTER 14

∽

Defender of the Peace

Of the European nations, Italy came last on the list of empires and became an imperialist nation for the same reasons as did Japan, on the other side of the world—for reasons of national prestige. Portugal, Spain, France, and England had led the way to empire, and by the nineteenth century the world accepted the concept of empire as the equivalent of power. Even the United States became an imperial nation, all the while denying that this was so. Before Mussolini's time, the Italian government had amassed a small empire, including Libya, Somalia, Eritrea, and the Dodecanese Islands.

Libya had been seized from the Turks in the twilight of the Ottoman Empire before 1914, but having no experience in governing colonies, the Italian Parliament made one mistake after another. The result was an uprising in Libya in 1914 that lasted for three years. By 1918 Italian rule was confined to four towns on the coast. At the end of World War I, agreement was finally reached with the leader, Muhammed Idris, in the coastal area of Cyrenaica, under which the Arab leader was regarded as the civil as well as religious leader of the Senussis. In return for promises of fealty to Rome, the Italian government paid subsidies and stated that the local population were not colonial but had a special relationship to Rome. Real freedom of speech and assembly, education, and right of property were granted to this area. It was a model for colonialism everywhere. Parliaments were set up in Libya for the provinces of Tripolitania and Cyrenaica, and the people enjoyed almost complete self-government. But to the parliamentary rulers of postwar Italy, this situation was only temporary and acceptable until a more tried and true colonial formula, such as the highly restrictive colonial systems of Britain and France in Africa, could be adapted.

The Italians did not know a good thing once they had established it, and Libya Governor Giuseppi Volpi renounced the agreements of the past and decided to conquer the territory by force of arms. Later the liberal parliamentarians of Rome claimed that it was all done without their knowledge, but this was an unbelievable story. Between 1920 and 1925 Volpi used mercenary troops, mostly from independent Ethiopia, to subject the tribes of Tripolitania. The same story applied to Cyrenaica, and by 1929 that colony as well had ceased to be a model for anyone, and harsh European colonial policies were in force. Libya erupted in guerrilla warfare that tied up a large Italian army for ten years. In 1929 General Badoglio was sent to Africa to pacify Cyrenaica and Tripolitania. In June 1930, Badoglio and General Rodolfo Graziani began a reign of terror in Libya that involved moving all the population of Cyrenaica into five concentration camps, closing the Senussi shrines, executing rebels, burning villages, and, in 1931, building a barb wire fence four meters thick from the port of Bardia to the oasis of Jarabub to cut off supplies from Egypt to the rebels. Crowded into the concentration areas, thousands of Berbers died and so did their flocks.

In September 1931 the leader of the rebels, Sheikh Umar al Mukhtar, was captured, put on trial, and then executed. The rebellion was forced to an end, and Rome announced victory. But half the Berber population had been destroyed. Later Rome extended social benefits and education to Libya, but the colonial policy remained harsh and uncompromising.

చ∽

As a young radical before World War I, Mussolini had lamented and sometimes opposed imperialism. He was to remain quizzical about it until 1930. The cases of Fiume and Corfu, where he was involved in an imperial role, were quite different and approached from the viewpoint of Italian nationalism. Even the first stirrings of fascist imperial ambition were tentative.

In 1923 Italy began sending arms and money to the Yemen with conflicting views as to the result. Some Italians thought the British could be unseated here and this Muslim center added to Italy's Empire; others wanted to pursue the course simply to embarrass Britain. In any event, the venture failed and Italy had nothing to show for all the money invested.

Attempts were also made by Mussolini (notwithstanding his claims that fascism was suitable for Italy and he did not give a hang about exporting it) to persuade Egypt to adopt a fascist system. At the same time in 1925, an attempt was made to secure a new agreement with an independent Egypt under British protection to redetermine the boundary between Egypt and Cyrenaica. This developed into a long contest and did not increase Italy's standing with the Egyptians. The effort to deal with Egypt was perhaps prompted by a hope that Italy could take over Egypt and thus make it a cornerstone of the empire for which Mussolini longed in the Mediterranean. But in this too he failed, as well as in attempts to secure a special position for Italy in Palestine because of the relationship of the Holy See with the historic sites of the Holy Land. In these efforts, he was strongly resisted by the British, who were determined to keep their empire intact. While Italy made claims for the empire promised her by England in the secret Treaty of London at the end of the war, the British and French were too busy feathering their own colonial nests to pay attention to the promissory note they had written to draw Italy into the war on the side of the Triple Entente.

Mussolini could not decide whether Italy's role in the world should be to copy the imperial powers or to oppose them, and for a time in 1929 and 1930, he toyed with the idea of standing for equality of peoples and against colonialism altogether. But as fascist Italy became an object of international respect for its accomplishments at home, Mussolini's radicalism was subdued, and he followed the accepted European path to power and embraced colonialism wholeheartedly.

He gave conflicting instructions to the colonial governments of Libya and Cyrenaica. He told the Italian authorities to continue their military efforts at subjugation, but also to use fewer troops and cut their expenditures. A handful of Blackshirts ought to be sufficient to teach the Berbers respect for fascism. In addition to pursuing this farce, the Minister of Colonies, Luigi Federzoni, followed his Nationalist policy and wrecked all the positive institutions that had been established in the east. He also destroyed the two local parliaments on the theory that self-government was not acceptable under fascism.

The first actual fascist contact with colonialism occurred in 1923 when Cesare De Vecchi's sometimes irritating presence in Rome had impelled Mussolini to send him to Somalia as governor. At that time only the southern one-third of the colony was actually under Italian control. The remainder was ruled under a vague protectorate in which the sultans held actual power but paid fealty to Rome. De Vecchi decided that he would indeed govern all of Somalia and embarked on a campaign of pacification of the entire colony. Military campaigns between 1925 and 1927 did reduce the sultans and established Italy's central government, but in so doing De Vecchi made a name throughout North Africa for violence and cruelty that was deplored publicly by Mussolini.

One of the avowed interests of the fascist government was to relieve the population pressure on Italy that had accounted for the enormous emigration, particularly to the United States, of the early twentieth century. Therefore, Rome decreed that lands not actively cultivated in the colony of Libya could be allocated to Italian settlers. This decree was extended to Somalia in 1929. It did encourage some Italian farmers to go to North Africa and establish a working Italian community, but what actually happened as the fascist regime grew more corrupt was that the best lands fell into the hands of party and military officials. Thus during World War II, when General Erwin Rommel arrived to take charge of Axis operations in North Africa, he found the Luftwaffe holding back on bombing of British forces in Italian territory. The Italian high command had asked that Italian properties be spared, the Luftwaffe command told Rommel.

The Italian agricultural colonization of Somalia was not very successful, not nearly so happy as was French colonization of nearby Algeria. In 1935 Rome tried to come to the rescue by a new series of decrees. For example, after that, none but the bananas of Somalia could be sold in Italy, although they were inferior in quality and more expensive than those of the Mediterranean areas.

With the rejection of Mussolini's effort to guarantee the peace of Europe by a four-power pact, he gave up on the Western powers. France's policy was totally self-serving and her government so morally bankrupt by 1934 that the sole purpose of her foreign policy seemed to be to keep Germany down, and she did not even have the will to take action to do that. As for Germany, Mussolini regarded Hitler as a competitor and was particularly concerned about German designs on Austria, where a Nazi party as noisy and violent as that of Germany had sprung up and was prospering.

In the spring of 1933, Hitler asked for advice from Mussolini, still enrapt in his admiration for the Italian dictator and his accomplishments. But when Mussolini counseled Hitler, through Ambassador Vittorio Cerruti, to go slow on anti-Semitism, Hitler erupted and angrily said Mussolini did not know what he was talking about. He, Hitler, was determined to rid the world of the "Jewish menace." This rejection of advice annoyed Mussolini and deepened his distrust. More concern followed in the summer of 1933, when Chancellor Dollfuss of Austria and his wife spent a few days as Mussolini's guests at the family villa at Riccione. The two men had swum and gone boating together and had many talks about European affairs. Dollfuss had confided that the Nazis in Austria were causing him a great deal of trouble and that their moves were part of a Hitler plan to take over Austria. Since the protection of the Austria–Italian border in the Alps was a cornerstone of Mussolini's foreign policy, he had sympathized and given two million schillings to help Dollfuss counter the Nazis.

In May 1933, Hitler had demanded equal treatment with the Western powers as the price of disarmament, and Britain and France had declined the overture. In October, then, Hitler had withdrawn Germany from the League of Nations. At his call 96 percent of the German voters went to the polls in November 1933 to test his leadership and vote on the abandonment of the League. Ninety-five percent approved his action. The way was cleared then for Hitler to lead the German people in any direction he wanted. What he wanted was the immediate establishment of Germany as a world power. What the Western world did not realize, but Mussolini did, was that Hitler was eager to go to war to get it.

On April 1, 1934, Hitler made his plans to take over the military, which was still wary of him. On a voyage aboard the cruiser *Deutschland*, to the site of spring maneuvers in East Prussia, he suborned the senior officers of the army and navy to support him personally. In exchange he would rid himself of the Nazi private army, the Sturmabteilung, which Hermann Goering had built up to have enough power to challenge the army before he turned it over to Ernst Roehm. This was the beginning of Hitler's challenge to the West for power. First he must have the military solidly behind him.

While Hitler was entertaining the military the leader of the Nationalist party that had allied itself with Hitler, Franz von Papen (who also was to become his ambassador to Austria), was making a trip to Italy to test the sentiment there about a German takeover. He got a sharp response, for that spring Dollfuss had appealed again to Mussolini for help against the Austrian Nazis and had gotten it. The real purpose of the von Papen visit was camouflaged: He suggested a visit by Hitler to Italy to discuss the problem of disarmament, on which both Hitler and Mussolini had come out publicly with similar views. Then they should discuss economic policies. Hitler was concerned because Mussolini had signed another of his economic agreements with Austria and Hungary, which the Germans felt might be aimed at Germany. The Germans wanted in. They also wanted the coordination of the two governments on a single policy in central Europe. And finally, von Papen argued, they should also discuss the Austrian problem, a delicate issue.

The last item brought Mussolini to accept a meeting he did not particularly want. He was still annoyed with Hitler for his intemperate language to Ambassador Cerruti and rejection of advice on the Jewish problem. It was time, Mussolini decided, for Hitler to be put in his proper place. He was further encouraged to accept the visit by the German ambassador, Ulrich von Hassell, who suggested that the two leaders could make an agreement that the independence of Austria was to be respected. Hitler had been known earlier to talk about bringing all German-speaking peoples under one German roof, but at the end of 1933, he had also disclaimed any ambitions to take over Austria. So Mussolini accepted the visit and it finally took place on June 14, 1934.

Mussolini greeted Hitler in German at the Venice airport, patted him on the shoulder condescendingly, and lorded it over him. Mussolini was dressed in his fascist uniform, Hitler in a civilian suit and a trenchcoat. The band struck up the *Horst Wessel Song*—one of the symbols of the Nazis—and Hitler squirmed because he was not in uniform. Mussolini brought him to lunch at the Villa Pisani near Venice, which he had taken over for the occasion. After lunch the interpreters were dismissed because Mussolini spoke German, and the two heads of state were closeted for a two-hour talk. When they emerged they said nothing, but Hitler looked angry and observers had heard angry voices raised in the meeting room and the name *Österreich* (Austria) invoked several times. Afterward Hitler went sightseeing in Venice.

The two met again the next day at Fort Alberoni on the Venice Lido, which was really the clubhouse of the local golf club. The pair had another talk and later in the afternoon Mussolini addressed a huge crowd that filled the Piazza San Marco in Venice. Hitler watched from the balcony of a neighboring palace. A parade was held to honor Hitler, but Mussolini kept him waiting on the reviewing stand for half an hour before he showed up and the spectacle could begin. Hitler was thoroughly discomfited by the visit, which was just what Mussolini wanted. He found it difficult to be civil to his German visitor, whom he had disliked at first sight. In private he referred to Hitler as "the new-style Genghiz Khan." They parted then, and Hitler returned to

Germany, awed most by the Italian crowd's obvious loyalty and enthusiasm for their flamboyant leader. But Mussolini regarded Hitler as a dangerous buffoon. Hitler had promised to keep his hands off Austria during those meetings with Mussolini, but the Italian dictator took the opportunity in the next few months to secure statements of support for Austrian independence from Britain and France.

Mussolini's feelings for the German were not improved that summer when the Nazis in Vienna made an attempt to take over and shot Dollfuss. The tragedy was personal as well as political to Mussolini, because Alwine Dollfuss, the Chancellor's wife, was staying up the beach in a villa Mussolini had rented for the family, and the chancellor was scheduled to arrive on the Adriatic shore the next day.

It was late afternoon before Mussolini had the details. Nine Nazis had battered down the door in the Chancellery in Vienna and shot Dollfuss in the throat. They left him without medical care for three hours while he bled to death.

Mussolini acted quickly that day as soon as he knew what had happened. He had no use for Hitler. He had heard the details of the "Night of the Long Knives," when, scarcely two weeks after Hitler's visit to him in Venice, the Nazi dictator had destroyed his own private army, the SA, ordering the killings of the men who had brought him to power.

Now Mussolini knew that the Germans, despite all assurances to the contrary, were determined to have Austria. He was equally determined that they should not, so that day he mobilized forty thousand troops and moved them to the Brenner Pass, which divides Italy from Austria. If the Germans moved, so would the Italians. If Hitler wanted Austria, he would get war.

In Vienna the Nazis had bungled their coup. They had seized the radio station and broadcast that Dollfuss had resigned, but they had been surrounded by loyal Austrian troops in their seized buildings. When they pleaded with Berlin for assistance, Hitler heard, counted the Italian troops on the Austria–Italy border, and backed down. The German press, which had been crowing about the fall of the Dollfuss government, suddenly changed its tune and called the Dollfuss affair an "internal Austrian problem."

Mussolini called on Britain and France to back up their pledges in Austria with action, but nothing happened. In fact, their troops were not needed. Mussolini's were quite enough to frighten Hitler. He had no such force at hand, and so he backed down completely, told the Austrian Legion, poised in Bavaria to attack, that it must stop, fired the

Nazi party inspector for Austria, and let it be known that the murderers of Dollfuss must be arrested and stand trial. Hitler publicly condemned the shooting. Franz von Papen was appointed minister to Austria with orders to repair Austrian–German relations.

Mussolini was not fooled. He had heard the original German reaction to the attempt: "The people have risen in judgment on the government of Dollfuss. The inevitable has happened. The German people in Austria have risen to judgment against their oppressors, jailers, and torturers." So it was apparent that the Austrian affair was anything but ended.

That night he drove to the Dollfuss villa on the Adriatic, broke the news of her husband's death to Dollfuss's wife, and then went home to his own villa for a late dinner. As he sat at the table, twirling tagliatelle, and the children watched him, he spoke up:

"I think we've seen the end of peace in Europe," he said. "Fine speeches won't mean anything any more. We shall need fine guns."

In the failure of the Western Allies to back up fine words with fine deeds, the incident put the final seal on Mussolini's contempt for the Western powers and his final decision that he would not again rely on them for any pledges of security. Earlier he had told Prince Starhemberg that the day that Germany swallowed Austria would mark the beginning of European chaos. That August of 1934 he spoke again to Prince Starhemberg. All he had done in the Brenner Pass incident, he said, had been done in the interest of Italy. The man who had murdered Dollfuss was Hitler. National socialism in Germany represented savage barbarism and it would mean the end of European civilization if Germany were allowed to overrun Europe. It behooved the great powers to organize a coalition against Hitler. "I cannot always be the only one to march to the Brenner," Mussolini said.

But Britain and France were not listening.

Then it was that Mussolini decided he must play his lone role all the way.

CHAPTER 15

༄

Southward the Course of Empire

In 1922, shortly before the March on Rome, the fascist program was outlined for the first time. Since then, fascist principles have been developed into a social philosophy and from it there has issued a kind of religion with all the accompaniments of an established cult, such as rites, altars, creeds and a decalogue to which has been added a touch of mysticism. Over all this the figure of Mussolini looms, all powerful and as the source of all inspiration.

> *From a U.S. Embassy Information Report on Italy to the*
> *State Department, February 4, 1935.*

By 1934 Mussolini had accomplished everything in Italy that counted. In the spring he held new elections, testing the political climate, and was pleased to see that 95 percent of the people came to the polls and that more than ten million voted for the official list, and only fifteen thousand voted against. Once more the biggest protest vote was in Milan, Mussolini's home ground, but also the home ground of the dissident Socialists. Their political power in Italy was long gone, but five thousand of them braved official displeasure and cast negative ballots. Much has always been made of the coercion of the system: Voters were given two papers, one in green, white, and red—the national colors—with the word *Si* written on it, and the other on uncolored paper with the word *No*. The voter placed the ballot he wanted to cast in the box and returned the other to the officials. Obviously, the return of the official ballot would be noted by the officials. But if Mussolini was unpopular, it would have been a simple matter to stay away from the polls altogether. Together with the enormous crowds that came out to demonstrate at Mussolini's speeches and parades, the election was convincing proof that the vast majority of Italians supported him and fascism.

What more could he want?

He had two ambitions. One was to preserve for Italy the peace of Europe, and the other was to bring Italy into the first rank of nations. The first ambition, it was apparent in 1934, demanded the control of German expansion. The second, Mussolini decided, in the time-honored manner of Europe, was to build an important empire to stand with the French and British. He had tried placating and discovered that the French and British still did not realize that in the Versailles Treaty they had created a monster. In so doing they had thrust Mussolini toward Germany, a direction in which he did not want to go. In 1934 the French and British had their last chance. Mussolini viewed the resurgence of German power with serious misgiving, and as his first meeting with Hitler had proved, he did not like that man; and such was Mussolini's nature that personal antipathy was a big factor in national policy.

∽

After the assassination of Chancellor Dollfuss of Austria, Mussolini's warning dispatch of troops to the Tirol had caused Hitler to back off on his first attempt to seize Austria, but it had not damped his ambitions in the least. Thwarted in Austria, he turned to strengthening his armed forces, building U-boats secretly, using the ten-thousand-ton limitation for warships to build pocket battleships, getting around the strictures against maintaining a German air force by training "glider pilots." By the middle of 1934, a quarter of a million factories in Germany were building war materials. Early in 1935, Hitler leaked the word through a British newspaper that he had violated the Versailles Treaty by creating a German air force. The world had an indication of things to come that winter, too, when a plebiscite fomented by the Germans in the Saar industrial basin, which had been given to France for safekeeping, voted ten to one for return to Germany.

The reaction of the British to all this was fumbling. The reaction of the French was to try to rebuild their relationships with Italy. The new French foreign minister, Pierre Laval, came to Italy. Having emasculated Mussolini's four-power treaty at the time that it might have worked, France now wanted to strengthen the old allied front against Germany. On Germany's part there was no interest in treaties. On Mussolini's part, he had now turned to playing a lone hand. He had already decided to take over Ethiopia for his empire, and what he wanted from France was assurance that she would not interfere. At this point he did not want war or even outright colonization but the sort of influence through which Britain and France controlled North Africa. The British and the French had bullied their way to empire by this tactic. Why should he not use the same?

In January 1935, Mussolini thought he had those assurances, through a series of agreements signed with France. For one thing the French finally recognized their promises to Italy in the secret Treaty of London of 1915 and ceded to Italy a strip of desert on the Libyan border, another strip of territory in French Somaliland, and an island in the Red Sea. These were the tangible results. Intangible were the mutual promises of goodwill and promises to consult one another if Austria should be threatened, and that, of course, meant threatened by the Germans.

In early February, French and British leaders met in London and agreed to oppose any changes in the Peace of Versailles. Germany's answer was for Hermann Goering to announce the creation of the Luftwaffe and Hitler to announce the beginning of compulsory military service and a plan for a thirty-six division German army. Stirred by this defiance, now that it was too late, the British began talking about that which they had turned down: a treaty to assure a peaceful Europe. If there was one attribute that Mussolini and Hitler shared, it was a realization that in world affairs, one led from strength, not weakness. Hitler fobbed off the British importunations he would have been glad to accept a year earlier. Mussolini watched the British floundering from Rome with unconcealed disgust. "The best way to stop the Germans is to mobilize the class of 1911," he said. "There is no other way of convincing them."

With this in mind, Mussolini traveled to Stresa on April 11, 1935, to meet with the French and British. Ascendant on Mussolini's mind was the German problem. He hoped to contain Hitler and that meant active support from France and Britain if Hitler threatened Austria. He also wanted a green light from these old allies for his economic penetration of Ethiopia. He expected to get it. After all, he was planning to do nothing in Africa that Britain had not already done in Egypt and France in Algeria and Morocco.

The British at Stresa were divided among themselves. Several members of the delegation saw the overriding need for a common front against a pugnacious Germany. They knew what Mussolini wanted, but they gave no indications of opposing it. As far as Austria was concerned, the British were not prepared to make any commitments. So at the end of the Stresa conference, Mussolini knew that the French and British would not back him to save Austria, which, with the growing strength of Germany, he could no longer do by himself. Since the British had not brought up Ethiopia (and when he had brought up the subject, they had refused to discuss it), he felt that they did not care what happened in Ethiopia. More than ever, Mussolini saw the dangers of war in Europe now, and to strengthen Italy's hand he felt he needed empire.

His biographers have made much of Mussolini's yearning to wipe out the stain of a defeat inflicted on the Italians in Africa in 1896. But it seems totally irrelevant to the world of 1935. The incident came about following Italy's hesitant entry into the field of colonial powers, urged by the British, to serve as a counterbalance for their empire against the French. Toward the end of the nineteenth century the opening of the Suez Canal by France had made the Red Sea important as a gateway to Europe through the Mediterranean. To prevent the French from taking over the territories bordering the Red Sea in Africa, Britain encouraged the fledgling Italian government to go into the colonial business by suggesting that they take over the port of Massawa. The Italians responded positively and sent a small force to Africa. They captured Asmara in 1889 and six months later established the colony of Eritrea. Their colonial appetite whetted, they moved in 1895 into the Tigri-province of Ethiopia, expecting the same sort of easy pickings. But they had not reckoned with the fierce independence and fighting spirit of the Ethiopians. When they reached Lake Ashanga, after a long trek of two hundred miles from their base, they were attacked by the far superior forces of King Menelik, and in a series of battles were resoundingly defeated.

For propaganda purposes, perhaps, Mussolini could have used this ancient defeat as an excuse for vengeance, but that was not his real reason for yearning to take over Ethiopia. He wanted an African base similar to the French Tunisia, Algeria, and Morocco, and the British colonies of Uganda and Tanganyika. Had Britain not been so greedy at Versailles, he might have had the old German East Africa, and all that came later would have been unnecessary. But as it was, the British and French, Portuguese, and Belgians had usurped most of Africa, and by 1935, only independent Ethiopia remained.

Ethiopia was independent but antediluvian. Slavery was still the bedrock of its social system, and when the king applied for admission to the League of Nations after World War I, the British opposed the move. But Italy led the forces favoring it and had its way. Italy's reason was to secure a favored position in Ethiopia, something like that of the British in Egypt. A treaty of amity was signed in 1928, but the Ethiopians did not live up to it, and so Italy, having invested a great deal, found itself no better off there than France and Britain.

In 1932 Mussolini had first addressed the problems of empire seriously, with a campaign of public works to build up Eritrea. The railway from Massawa to Asmara was rebuilt. Roads, hospitals, and airfields were constructed, and a good water supply was assured. A native army was recruited, eventually to number sixty thousand troops. Minister De Bono was put to work planning for a military expedition if this became necessary, and he applied for a commission to lead the military forces.

The Ethiopians provided the excuse for the militarization of the Italian movement in the area by attacking the Italian oasis at Wal Wal, at the junction of Ethiopia, Italian Somaliland, and British Somaliland. The attack occurred on December 5, 1934. The Italians defeated the Ethiopians and then demanded an apology for the attack and an indemnity plus a settlement of the frontier, which was at that point indefinite.

Emperor Haile Selassie claimed that the incident should be settled under terms of the treaty of 1928, which called for arbitration of difficulties. Mussolini prepared to go either way. If Ethiopia proved acquiescent, he would follow the British precedent of moving in diplomatically to make the Ethiopians virtual colonials of Italy. If Ethiopia proved difficult, he would use force. He faced the same situation, no more nor any less justified than the British had been in Egypt in the middle of the nineteenth century. His methods were almost the same.

On December 30, 1934, he issued an Order of Battle secretly; only five copies were made. His plan was that if it was necessary to use force, he would strike in the following autumn as soon as the African rainy season ended. He told De Bono to lay in three years of supply, just in case the British should close the Suez Canal to him. He said he would send ten divisions by October.

In January 1935, De Bono was dispatched to Africa to become High Commissioner for East Africa, and two months later two divisions of troops were sent to Africa. De Bono was encharged with using diplomacy to get Italy's way, but if he could not, Il Duce was ready to fight.

In May two more divisions of regular troops and four Fascist Militia divisions were getting ready to move out for Africa. By the first of June, nearly a million Italians were in the military service and there was no secret about it. Mussolini was prepared to take his empire and also prepared, if necessary, to assist in the put-down of Hitler, although he had cautioned France and Britain that he could not do this alone.

In the late spring of 1935, the British were warned by the Italian chargé d'affaires in London that Mussolini was getting ready to act in Ethiopia; they showed no concern or even any interest. The Italians had placed agents in the British embassy in Rome, so the Italians knew everything London was doing in British–Italian affairs.

Mussolini had a sense of urgency in the question of dealing with Ethiopia. Hitler had declared his universal conscription campaign in June, and the British had responded by signing a naval agreement with the Germans that was supposed to keep the Germans from trying to match the British fleet. In Rome this was generally accepted as presaging Britain's knuckling under to Hitler. This also gave Mussolini the feeling that he must finish with Ethiopia before Hitler was ready to take on Europe, which he now saw as inevitable. His onetime reluctant admiration for Britain was swiftly turning to contempt and antagonism.

Because Mussolini did not like Hitler, he underestimated the regard and respect the German dictator had for him. Hitler knew what was going on in Ethiopia, and he told the Polish ambassador that Mussolini was taking a grave risk in bearding the League of Nations but that he wished the Italian well because of their common ideology.

Britain's decision to play games with Hitler caused Mussolini to alter his anti-Nazi course and to send a new friendly ambassador to Berlin. Thus London was increasingly pushing Italy into Germany's arms. France was shocked by the naval treaty, and her confidence in Britain was badly shaken. Thus, Britain had destroyed the old alliance of 1918, and it could never be repaired.

Too late, again, the British government called Mussolini to step back in his actions and not destroy the League of Nations. They sent a special mission to Rome for that purpose, because of a sudden change in British public opinion, which erupted in a fever of war worry when Mussolini began openly shipping divisions to Africa. Late in May the British had asked Italy to find some formula that would save the prestige of the League of Nations. On the face of it, the League was dying; Japan had withdrawn in 1932 and Germany in 1933. But the British people still believed in the League and the government had to respond. Therefore the government sent Anthony Eden, the Minister without Portfolio for League of Nations Affairs to Rome to seek compromise.

The meeting began at the Palazzo Venezia on June 24, 1935. Eden opened by saying that Britain was concerned about the Ethiopian problem and its repercussions on the League of Nations. If the Italians took an anti-League stand, it would strain relations between Britain and Italy. Mussolini said nothing to this. Eden went on, Britain would cede the bay of Zeila to Ethiopia, thus giving that landlocked country access to the sea. The Italians could take over the Ethiopian province at Ogaden and would receive economic concessions.

Mussolini rejected this idea. He insisted on solving the Ethiopian problem immediately. Italy could not delay because (and this was a thinly veiled reference to Britain's failure to make the joint guarantee of the Austrian border) she could not remain under threat of another attack by Ethiopia when she was perhaps engaged elsewhere. The only compromise acceptable would be the cession of all territories to Italy that were not racially Ethiopian, and the same sort of control over Ethiopia that Britain had over Egypt. France had shown herself willing to stand by in the Ethiopian matter, why could not England? Eden replied by telling Mussolini that the apparent assurances he had from France's Laval were illusory. They did not extend to Italian military action. Mussolini was astonished and did not believe it.

Eden ended the deadlocked meeting by urging Mussolini to reconsider and meet again. They met at 5 P.M. on June 25 and went over the same ground again. Mussolini insisted on having the same sort of control over Ethiopia that Britain had over Egypt. Eden did not respond to that directly. The meetings ended in impasse. They were followed by an anti-Italian campaign in the press in Britain and an anti-British campaign in Italy. Both sides were still hoping for compromise, but neither side was willing to give in. What did not seem apparent at the time was that the British–Italian alliance was very dead. It had been dying since Britain's refusal to support the four-power pact to preserve the peace of Europe. Neither France nor Britain could see any reason for them to change their colonial or foreign policies. In the world, nations were now separating into the "have" and "have nots," a factor that had aroused Mussolini's attention and disapproval years earlier. The haves were determined to keep what they had, while denying the have nots the same use of force majeure colonization that they had used. It was apparent that there could be no agreement in such an atmosphere.

On September 10, 1935, French Foreign Minister Laval had a conversation with Sir Samuel Hoare and Eden, and they agreed that their efforts at conciliation had failed. On the next day, Sir Samuel made a speech to the Assembly of the League of Nations indicating that collective security demanded that the League take action against Italian aggression. He was followed by a stream of speakers saying the same. The world seemed united in its opposition to the Italians' designs on

Ethiopia. The American embassy sent a long report to Washington about a strong revival of anti-Fascist sentiment in Italy and the possibility of the overthrow of Mussolini. The presence of the British fleet, which had been ostentatiously strengthened in the Mediterranean, was said to give the anti-Fascists new hope.

On September 26, Haile Selassie said that Italian aggression was imminent and asked the League of Nations to send observers to see. Two days later he announced general mobilization of his troops; on October 2 it was reported that Italian troops had violated the Ethiopian frontier. From his balcony in the Palazzo Venezia, Mussolini addressed the Italians.

"A solemn hour is about to strike in this story of the fatherland. With Ethiopia we have been patient for forty years. Now enough! To sanctions of an economic character we will reply with discipline, with our sobriety and with our spirit of sacrifice. To sanctions of a military character we will reply with acts of war."

A week later, the American embassy in Rome had to notify the State Department to discount all those reports they had been sending in the recent past attesting to unrest in Italy and the possibility of anti-Fascist action. They had been duped by the British, they admitted.

On the eve of the war, then, the former alliance of World War I was in shards. Britain was moving its Mediterranean fleet around, but, privately, Mussolini knew from his spies inside the British embassy that the fleet was in no condition to fight. Besides, Britain was so badly divided on the issue that nothing could be done. The majority of the nation wanted League of Nations sanctions, for it had been hyped by the strong speeches in Geneva. But a few hard heads like Lord Vansittart, the British foreign minister, argued that Europe was moving toward its real confrontation with Hitler and that nothing must be done to weaken the Stresa front. He did not realize that Britain's failure to provide real assurances at Stresa had cost them the respect and belief of Mussolini. A spokesman for strong action by the League of Nations was Winston Churchill. But France was determined not to take any action against Italy. As biographer Ivone Kirkpatrick put it, neither a strong course against Hitler nor one against Mussolini was adopted. "It is against the background of sloth in Paris, confusion in London and a general fear of a mad-dog act by Mussolini" that the last months of 1935 must be viewed.

Under the vigorous leadership of Anthony Eden, the Council of the League of Nations looked like a powerful body preparing to take strong action. On October 3, 1935, Mussolini invaded Ethiopia with three army corps, about one hundred thousand men. By October 11, sanctions against Mussolini for aggression against Ethiopia had been invoked and a committee appointed to deal with that action. And at that point the League of Nations fell apart. All the committee could do was recommend an arms embargo against Italy, that all business be suspended with Italy, that embargos be placed on goods going to Italy and coming from Italy, and that the states adversely affected thus should have been compensated. Even these weak actions were not taken by some countries.

The real effect of the sanctions was to unify the Italian people in antagonism to the League of Nations. A vigorous propaganda campaign by Mussolini's government found the people good listeners to claims that Italy was once again being victimized by the "have" powers. Even some of the political exiles from fascism rallied to the support of the Italian cause.

The one economic sanction that would have hurt Italy badly would have been an oil embargo. If the League had imposed an oil embargo, Mussolini later said, he would have had to abandon his attempt to conquer Ethiopia. But this bogged down in committee, and nothing ever came of it.

The Italian troops moved swiftly through Ethiopia. By November 8, General De Bono occupied Makale, some eighty miles from the border. He stopped there and Mussolini, who was in a hurry, sent Marshal Badoglio to take over and prosecute the war more strongly. A compromise plan in the League of Nations failed, the question of oil sanctions was shelved, and the League of Nations' activity took on the look of a tempest in a teapot. After Ethiopia, the world no longer believed in the League.

Marshal Badoglio launched an offensive on January 12, 1936, and in four months brought about the flight of the Emperor from Addis Ababa, and the capture of that city on May 5, 1936. On May 9, Mussolini proclaimed the annexation of Ethiopia from the balcony of the Palazzo Venezia and the assumption by the King of the new title: Emperor of Ethiopia.

Mussolini had run great risks. He had defied the League of Nations and the power of the British fleet. He had conquered his empire, and the people of Italy in the square below chanted *"Duce, Duce."* It was a moment of grandeur.

"Italy at last has her empire," he said.

"It is an empire of peace because Italy wants peace for herself and for everyone and decided on war only when she was driven to it by the imperious necessities of life.

"The Italian people have created with their blood an empire. They will render it fertile and fruitful with their work. They will defend it against anyone with their weapons."

And all Italy agreed and cheered. It seemed that the millennium had arrived.

CHAPTER 16

∽

The End of the Triple Entente

The colonial war with Ethiopia was expensive and left Italy with an enormous debt. In some quarters, especially with the rich, the war was unpopular. In 1935 a member of the Italian aristocracy told the American embassy's Breckenridge Long that he had received two letters the day earlier. One was from his banker, asking him to sell his foreign holdings to the government to help the war effort. The other was from the air corps calling him up under his reserve officer's commission. "They not only want my life, they want my money too," he observed.

Italian bankers told the American embassy that they had expected difficulties from the beginning of the war because the area involved was so great. But, they said the expense had not been as serious as expected, because Mussolini employed only about three hundred thousand men in the war, and the Italian economy, having gone on a war footing, was geared for a force of nine million men.

The war had another major development. One could see the change in attitudes toward Italy, largely on the part of those countries and people who believed in the League of Nations. Before, the praise for Italy's accomplishments under Mussolini had drowned out most of the criticism for his methods and the suppression of human rights. The world in the 1930s was more concerned over human survival in the depression economies than human rights. So the beatings, tortures, and, sometimes, killings in Italy had gone largely unremarked upon except by the far left wing parties of the world. In 1935, however, condemned as an aggressor nation, Mussolini's Italy came under sharper criticism. This was quite apparent in the political reporting of the American embassy. All through the 1920s and early 1930s, the reporting had been equable, and often enthusiastic, about Mussolini's accomplishments. But in 1935 the tone changed.

About the war, the Americans in Italy found a great deal of propaganda and a great deal of disbelief. A call for volunteers was put out. The result was, said the American embassy's Long, negative. The universities refused to encourage their students to enlist. The unemployed were told that if they did not enlist, they would not be eligible for further aid. The popular enthusiasm for the war evidenced by the noisy sailings of troopships for Africa was largely manufactured.

When the government issued a special communiqué in March 1935, attesting to the enormous success of the industrial mobilization of the country, there was mumbling, to which Ambassador Long listened carefully. He concluded that Mussolini was about to face a crisis of confidence. In September, when the British fleet began making threatening gestures in the Mediterranean, Long observed that the time seemed more nearly ripe for revolution against Mussolini than at any time in the past. More than anything else, this conclusion indicated a change on the part of the American attitude toward Italy. By May 21, 1937, in spite of the enormous involvement in the Spanish Civil War, the American embassy had to conclude "that there have been certain disturbances, and although criticism of the regime particularly relating to the Spanish policy appears to be more outspoken than has hitherto been customary, these reports cannot be said to indicate any lessening in power of the regime or slackening of its discipline."

So the embassy had been indulging in some wishful thinking.

During the war with Ethiopia, Mussolini learned that Hitler was secretly supplying guns and other weapons to Haile Selassie's forces, and he knew exactly why: Hitler was hoping that Mussolini would get bogged down in Ethiopia and be in no position to oppose his takeover of Austria. For that *Anschluss* with Austria was a vital part of Hitler's plan to bring all ethnic Germans in Europe under the Third Reich, and by early 1936, he was preparing and impatient that he had only half the thirty-six divisions he wanted. He was so impatient that by March he was ready for a gamble. He would invade the Rhineland, in total violation of the Versailles Treaty, knowing full well that Britain and France could mobilize forces so far superior to the German that if they moved, he would have to turn tail and retreat ignominiously. When he informed his generals they were aghast, but on March 7, 1936, the Germans marched. As Hitler had guessed, neither France nor Britain moved to stop him. He was then convinced of the moral decadence of both nations and willing to take more chances.

Mussolini had no stake in the Rhineland, but he watched the performances and came to much the same conclusion as Hitler, although he hoped that Britain could be used to counterbalance Hitler. Consequently, in April Mussolini ordered an end to the cold war he had been waging against England since Anthony Eden had led the League of Nations movement for economic sanctions against Italy. However, there was no real resumption of amity.

Mussolini had nurtured a respect for England, and a feeling of affection spurred by his friendship with Sir Austen Chamberlain. It was now gone. His overtures to Britain the spring of 1936 were strictly political. At the end of April Italian Ambassador Grandi, on instructions from Rome, assured King Edward VIII that Italy wanted complete resumption of the World War I political collaboration. Mussolini talked about treaties to secure the peace of Europe and indicated that the problem was to isolate and frustrate Hitler. One might say it was a final attempt at pulling the Triple Entente of World War I back together again, but it failed because Britain did not respond. Britain still had not recognized the colonization of Ethiopia. Not understanding Mussolini and his limited ambitions, the British threw away the chance for an alliance that might have contained Hitler.

Mussolini had several meetings with Prince Starhemberg, the Austrian chancellor, and expressed his concern over the growing Nazi presence and press of events on Austria. How right he was. Within the month, Starhemberg was forced to resign to appease the Germans, and his successor, Chancellor Kurt von Schuschnigg signed a special treaty with Germany. Schuschnigg understood Mussolini's interest in protecting the independence of Austria, and so he gave advance warning to Mussolini of what he must do to keep the Germans out of the door. Mussolini acquiesced, because there was no way out. As he had foreseen, he was no longer strong enough to hold Germany at bay alone, and he saw that a confused Britain and a rotten France were of no use.

Mixed with this peasant shrewdness now, however, was another element. Mussolini had created an image of a god-leader, omnipotent and omniscient, and had been so successful that he began to believe his own propaganda. This had been a gradual process encouraged by the adulation offered him by the Italian people. He made it a habit to be approachable by the masses and they answered with extravagance: One man walked for two months to present him with a barrel of water from the site of a World War I battle on the River Pave. A twelve-year-old boy walked 450 miles just to meet him. By 1935, Pope Pius XI sardonically referred to him as "halfway between heaven and earth" and warned the Italian ambassador to the Vatican that Mussolini should not think of himself as a god.

But it was hard for a man whose every word was treated as an order to keep humility, and although he remained a shrewd judge of character, generally speaking, often Mussolini failed in this regard. Humility was made no easier by his palace guard, who inflated every positive aspect of fascist leadership and ignored the negative. In the spring of 1936 Count Ciano, his son-in-law and newly appointed foreign minister, told the British ambassador with a straight face that Italy was now the military equal of any power in Europe. If this was true, it was only conditionally so. Such an estimate had to be based on Hitler's as yet incomplete preparations, on the knowledge that France was so morally bankrupt it could not act, and on the knowledge that Britain was too divided in its views on European security to move.

And then, in the summer of 1936, came an event that put Mussolini on a different path altogether. It was the beginning of the Spanish Army rebellion against the Spanish Republic, which was so successful that it immediately developed a more grandiloquent title, the Spanish Civil War.

To understand Mussolini's role in this conflict, one must realize that he was not a democrat, and he had no use for democracy. His whole political career was an example of the triumph of strength over fumbling, and he considered all parliamentary democracy to be fumbling. He had, in the early 1930s, developed a respect for American President Franklin D. Roosevelt, but only because he thought Roosevelt exhibited the strength of an absolute ruler, and he believed that Roosevelt's power was much greater than it really was. He praised "the intensive cult of dictatorship to which President Roosevelt is dedicating himself."

∽

After the conquest of Addis Ababa, although resistance in the land he called Ethiopia continued for many months, Mussolini began now to think always in terms of empire. Four large marble relief maps were built into the wall of the basilica of Maxentius, showing the successive stages of conquest of the ancient Roman Empire. The new watchword among Mussolini's courtiers (no other word so adequately describes these people) was *Roma Doma*—Rome Dominates. In his hour of triumph Mussolini had learned that the Italians glorified the concept of "Empire," and now he was persuaded to pursue it. He had become convinced that Europe and the world faced an ultimate conflict between two philosophies: fascism and communism. What role he assigned to Hitler in these days was not clear; sometimes he said that Hitler was essentially a Fascist, sometimes he said Hitler was irrelevant. He hoped that fascism would take hold in Latin America and prepare it for the conflict he saw coming with North America. He supported fascism in France, and Ireland and England with subsidies.

At this time, Mussolini began adjusting himself to the ultimate German conquest of Austria, since he could see no way of avoiding it, given the flaccidity of Britain and France. In January 1936, he informed Hitler that he was ready to recognize Austria as a satellite of Germany, although he was not yet ready to countenance *Anschluss*. This was a major flopover and represented an essential change in his attitude toward Germany. He also told Hitler that Germany and Italy had a partnership dictated by destiny—a *Schicksalsgemeinschaft*—and that the old alliance with France and England was dead forever. When the German ambassador to Rome hinted that Mussolini seemed to be keeping a foot in both camps, Mussolini said he was just pretending to have friendly feelings for England and France. By 1936, this was true. He had given up any hope that the Western allies would stand with him against Germany, and the right wing of the fascist movement was urging him to a close alliance with Germany, whom they declared to be a winner.

For all these reasons, when civil war broke out in Spain, Mussolini went to the assistance of General Francisco Franco. Earlier he had given money to Antonio Primo de Rivera, the founder of the Falange movement, which was a copy of fascism. But when Primo de Rivera died, that movement seemed to peter out, to be revived in the military rebellion and to become the philosophical base of the revolution.

In the middle of July 1936, representatives of Franco came to Rome. Mussolini met with Foreign Minister Ciano, who recommended strongly that Italy support the rebellion. The Spanish asked for heavy artillery and fifty thousand rifles. Mussolini said he would do better, he would send soldiers. General Badoglio opposed the idea of sending troops to Spain, because he feared that it might precipitate a general European war. So they compromised and called for sixty thousand "volunteers." To get the volunteers, they combed the unemployment rolls, gave the men a basic training in military tactics, and prepared to send them to Spain, with a handful of Blackshirts and officers and noncoms.

In Genoa, the call for volunteers was made by a group of Black-shirts; when the men were gotten together, a proclamation was read asking for those who wanted to go to Spain to fight for Franco to raise their hands. The announcement was greeted by total silence. The names of those present were then put in a hat and "selective draft" conducted. The unlucky ones whose names were drawn presumably were shipped to Spain, according to a report from the American consul.

The first assistance given to Franco was the dozen aircraft he requested, although in the beginning, Mussolini made it conditional that their activity be confined to escorting troop transports from Franco's army in Africa to fight in Spain. But on July 29, 1936, two of the aircraft made forced landings in French Morocco and the jig was up. Mussolini then threw off all pretense and increased the Italian participation in the Spanish Civil War so that it could be said Italy was Franco's principal supporter.

If there was any shred of hope for a reconciliation with Britain, it was eliminated in 1936 and 1937. The Italian agents inside the British embassy had a stream of information from London that indicated the British contempt for Mussolini and Italy. Negative British views about the fighting quality of the Italian soldier persuaded Mussolini to send infantry troops to fight in Spain and get tough. The Italian soldiers did not do so well in Spain. A column advancing on the Guadalajara front was virtually wiped out when it was attacked from the air by Republican aircraft. But the Italian artillery, tanks, and air force did distinguish themselves in Spain, just as did the German Luftwaffe pilots who came to get war experience. Most of these pilots stayed only a few months and were then rotated, so that as many as possible could get combat experience.

The Spanish Civil War did much to draw Hitler and Mussolini together. In the late weeks of 1936 the German ambassador to Rome noted that Italy and France were knocking heads in Spain, and that Britain was checking Mussolini's power in the Mediterranean. Since Mussolini had begun calling the Mediterranean *Mare Nostrum*, and dreaming of extension of his empire like Rome's had been, this friction did tend to ally him with Hitler. Count Ciano was forthright in his feeling that Mussolini should befriend Hitler now. Ciano went to Berlin to pave the way. Hitler told Ciano that in three years he would be ready for war against the democracies, and that he was interested only in northern Europe. He offered Mussolini the Mediterranean. And that is what Mussolini really wanted. One of his primary reasons for aiding Franco was to secure a position of influence for fascism in the Mediterranean. But he got more deeply involved than he had expected. Franco had talked loftily of winning the war in a matter of weeks. It did not happen. The Loyalists fought hard. They were aided by the Russians who wanted to test their weapons in the firepot too. So the struggle went on and on. By the end of 1936 Mussolini had sent seventy thousand troops to Spain plus equipment, tanks, planes, and artillery. It was much more than Mussolini had bargained for, particularly after the enormous expense of the Ethiopian campaign he had just waged.

During this period, Mussolini's breach with the Western powers became complete, largely because Britain and France could not make up their minds to stand with Mussolini against Hitler on the matter of Austria. France was supplying the Republican government of Spain with arms. Britain was playing both sides of the street. To prevent the Spanish conflict from becoming general war, twenty-six nations formed the Non-Intervention Committee, which represented all the nations that were deeply involved—France, Britain, Italy, Germany, Russia, and others involved in one way or another. Italy did all it could to further the Franco cause, even going so far as to send submarines out to sink neutral ships under the pretense that they were Spanish submarines.

All these efforts combined to drive a wedge between Mussolini and the Western powers, but it was not a matter of concern now, because the Western powers had not given Mussolini any hope at all that they would stand for Austria, and to Mussolini, Austria was the key to Hitler's success or failure. It was so obvious now that he could not possibly face Hitler down by himself, and the West was moribund. And so reluctantly he turned to embrace the man he did not love, Adolf Hitler, assessing the situation as a coming struggle between the haves and the have nots. The haves had proved that they had no intention of moving from their comfortable superiority. Mussolini knew exactly what Hitler was up to, and until 1937 there seemed to be some chance, at least in his mind, that Britain and France could be aroused. But it did not happen.

Meanwhile Hitler was courting Mussolini. In the summer of 1936 he sent word that he was ready to recognize the Mussolini empire whenever Mussolini wanted. In September one of the visiting Germans brought an invitation for Mussolini to visit Germany. Ciano went to Germany in October to visit Hitler at Berchtesgaden and was flattered beyond what should have been belief. Hitler spoke of Mussolini as *the* leading statesman of the world. He spoke of Mussolini's bringing of Italy to the status of world power in a few years. He offered a friendship between the Teutons and the Latins and painted a picture of a world they would dominate. Westerners have since painted this as games-manship; but a cold examination of Hitler's relations with Mussolini all through the years shows that the German dictator had a feeling of hero worship for Mussolini that lasted until the end. He was not playing games. He was willing to split the Western world with the man he considered to be his mentor and the developer of totalitarianism.

Ciano came away from the meetings with Hitler entranced with the thought of a partnership with the Germans and ultimate rulership of the civilized world of the West.

During Ciano's German visit, he signed a secret treaty with Germany that promised friendship and cooperation. He pledged Italy to cooperate with Germany regarding Austria. Germany pledged to accept Mussolini's empire. They both pledged to recognize Manchukuo, the Japanese puppet state, for the plans were already afoot to broaden their partnership to control the world to include a militant Japan.

The Western countries, and this included America, began looking for reasons to back up their growing distrust of Italy. In the spring of 1937, the American ambassador to Italy requested reports from the cities of northern Italy on unrest under fascism. The response was almost a set piece, for as anyone familiar with Italy knew, the areas of Lombardy, Turin, Milan, and Genoa had always been socialist strongholds, and if you wanted to find criticism of Mussolini, this was where to go.

The consuls responded nobly with tales of fascist wickedness. From the consul at Milan came stories of communist literature being distributed. From Turin came reports of an auto running around, bearing Milan license plates, distributing anti-Fascist propaganda in Sandigliano Micca, a nearby town. The carabinieri were sent out and gathered up some leaflets, but the conspirators all escaped. And then there was the story of a plane flying overhead at night and dropping leaflets in the area. This was given some cogency because for several nights around May 1 military planes flew around the area every night.

But the consul at Genoa was able to come up with just what the embassy wanted. Early in May a number of workers were arrested at the Ansealdo factory, which was making munitions, when a flood of anti-Fascist leaflets was found in the plant. Because of the arrests, three hundred workers staged a four-hour work stoppage. A Fascist general named Montana was sent to the plant. He gave a conciliatory lecture, reminding the workers how much better their working conditions were than those of nearby countries. Finally the workers went back to work, and the people arrested were released. But while they had been held, the story was, some of them were beaten.

"The appearance of anti-Fascist symbols and phrases was reported in several factories in Savona and Ilva. There were arrests but as in the previously cited instance, most of the prisoners later were released."

The consul also reported that a crowd, demonstrating against the forced loan imposed on workers by the government to support the military, had hurled missiles at the tax officer and broken several windows before it was dispersed and that similar demonstrations occurred in nearby towns. In Genoa there were reports of attacks by Blackshirts on local citizens, and some of these were actually confirmed.

A broker named Enrico Pozzi was attacked in the street by four Fascists after he had been heard making some derogatory statements about Mussolini on the floor of the stock exchange. The attack occurred at noon when he was on his way home for lunch. Three ribs were cracked. The Blackshirts commented as they let him go that this should teach him a lesson.

On May 11, six streetcar workers were seized as they finished the night shift and taken to a fascist headquarters, beaten, and given doses of castor oil. They were accused of making hostile remarks. The Fascists retained their numbered caps and presented them the next day to the tram company with a request that the men be fired. The request was not honored because the company was afraid of employee demonstrations if it paid attention.

A newspaper man name Sacheri, employed by the former socialist daily *Lavoro*, was beaten while coming home from work at night. The excuse was that he was wearing a red tie. Another newspaper man employed by the same journal reported that two shots were fired at him while he was walking along a dark street.

"It is estimated that one thousand persons have been arrested recently in a police campaign against workers' groups that assembled in bars and *bottiglieri* to listen to radio broadcasts from Barcelona (the Spanish Republic). Some 110 such places have been closed."

Why was all this happening? According to the consular report, worsening economic conditions were the reason for discontent in the north. The cost of living had been going up. The import of goods had shrunk by 30 percent. The Genoa stock exchange was virtually inactive, because most of the stocks were owned by the government. "Businessmen feel the bureaucracy interferes with efficient transaction of their affairs and the program is viewed with bitterness and alarm."

Most observers, the consul said, felt that economic conditions would affect the attitude of the public toward the government. But as to speaking out, a strict censorship was imposed on newspapers and even foreign correspondents.

Also, police controls had increased. The consul, returning to the city from a trip at about midnight on April 30, had been stopped three times and asked to display his papers. Once the car was searched.

At Como, near the Swiss frontier, the radio sets in the small restaurants and cafés bore placards that warned the public against tuning in on foreign broadcasts.

There was nothing new about this; such behavior by the fascist Blackshirts had been common since the 1920s. But the American State Department had never been interested in the details of repression before. This new interest indicated a new mind-set in Washington opposed to fascism. No longer were Americans talking about fascist accomplishments, such as making the trains run on time. Now they talked about violation of civil liberties, as if it were a development of the last few months. Mussolini now became linked in the Western eye with Hitler.

∽

In September 1937, Mussolini visited Berlin and Bavaria and was given the full diplomatic treatment; special trains brought out hundreds of thousands of cheering Germans, and there were pledges of amity and banquet after banquet. He visited the Krupp factories and was awed by the German war production. He was impressed by the German troops and their discipline. He left Germany with a definitely more favorable impression of the country and the leadership than he had previously shown.

On Mussolini's return to Italy, he pondered long and hard. His distrust and dislike of Hitler never changed, even though he had seen so much strength in Berlin that he was impressed. When he looked to France and Britain, he saw nothing positive. They were still fumbling with the future while Hitler was showing the future he envisaged. And, in a sense, the Italian intelligence service's infiltration of the British embassy was a disservice. Mussolini was reading the embassy's private mail, and much of what he read was antipathetic to himself and fascism. It certainly showed that Britain could not be counted on to stand by Italy in any confrontation with Hitler, and this was the crux. By the end of the year, Mussolini was burning his bridges to the West. He withdrew Italy from the League of Nations. It was a matter so unimportant that it was considered for two minutes by the Supreme Council of Fascists.

On November 6, 1937, Mussolini signed a tripartite Anti-Comintern Pact that linked him with Japan and Germany, both of which were considering war with Russia. That day, in conversation with Germany's special ambassador, Von Ribbentrop, Mussolini listened as the German remarked that in the grand strategy of Germany and Italy now, Austria represented a small problem that must be settled. Mussolini did not blink an eye. He observed that Austria was a German country, and that he was tired of guaranteeing its independence. The best course was to let events take their course, as long as the Germans abided by their agreement not to take any action before Italy had been informed.

Mussolini's previous disapproval of the seizure of Austria had kept Hitler's hands tied for three years, but now the German dictator had the green light to go ahead, and the movement began. On February 4, Von Ribbentrop was appointed foreign minister. A week later Chancellor Schuschnigg was invited to Berchtesgaden to discuss Austrian–German affairs and was bullied into signing a seven-point agreement that virtually ended Austria's independence. And Hitler said at that time, "With Mussolini I am in the clear, my ties of friendship are very close." He knew as well as Mussolini that England would not lift a finger to save Austria. As for France, she had been tested when Hitler marched into the Rhineland and she did nothing. Hitler was not worried about the Western powers. He knew they did not have the will to stop him, although they still had the might. If they had allied themselves with Mussolini, Hitler would never have dared to move.

And so, in 1937, Mussolini had allied himself with Hitler, and war in Europe was inevitable. The war in Spain dragged on. Mussolini would continue to support it until the end in March 1939, at a monetary cost to Italy of more than twelve billion lire or twice as much as Italy's entire military budget. Did this expenditure achieve what Mussolini wanted? It brought one more fascist government into Europe, but that government was so impoverished by the war that Franco wisely adopted a strict policy of neutrality in the European quarrels; so, in the sense of being an ally, Spain was of no use whatsoever to Italy in the years to come.

But events in Europe moved so rapidly in the next two years after Mussolini acceded to the German annexation of Austria that the events in Spain seemed totally unimportant. In those years, all Europe caught

fire. By the end of 1937, Italy's position and direction were set. She had
been pushed from alliance with the Western powers to a new alliance
with Germany that would soon include alliance with Japan in a struggle
between the "have and have not nations." The Triple Entente was finished forever.

CHAPTER 17

∽

Europe in Chaos

1938. It was all written down in *Mein Kampf* for the world to see; Hitler would go as far as he could to destroy the legacy of Versailles and bring Germany back to the power and glory she had known under the Hohenzollern Empire, and more, to bring all the ethnic Germans together under one flag, which had never happened before.

Who would stop him?

Mussolini had stopped him in 1934 and held him in check ever since, but Mussolini was tired of playing the game alone; instead, he was getting nothing but abuse from England and from France for doing in Ethiopia precisely what they had done all around the world in an earlier century.

Looking around the world he had half-decided that the Western democracies were moribund and that the real contest would ultimately be between fascism and communism. As far as the United States was concerned, he had decided nothing at all. The United States had placed itself outside the pale at the end of World War I and remained there, an unknown and seldom-considered factor. It was to the competition between the dynamic forces of fascism and communism that he now set his mind.

Hitler wanted an empire; Mussolini already had his empire, although it wanted some enlarging. And the two dictators were agreed that they would go the course together. If there was any chance that this would not be so, the impetus would have to come from the democratic powers. Mussolini had given up on them and so, reluctantly, after the assassination of his friend Dollfuss, had set his course for war.

Given the green light by Mussolini, Hitler began to set the stage for the annexation of Austria to the Third Reich. On return from Berchtesgaden early in February 1938, Chancellor Schuschnigg found himself beset by the Austrian Nazis and a stream of demands from Germany for one concession after another. By the end of the month Schuschnigg decided to hold a plebiscite to ascertain the wishes of Austria's voters, certain that they would vote to remain free. He told Mussolini what he was going to do. Mussolini counseled against a plebiscite. If Schuschnigg remained steadfast, he said, the German pressure would relax. Schuschnigg did not believe him and announced the plebiscite for March 13.

Hitler decided he would move before the plebiscite, which might bring him some unwelcome news. So he conjured up the vision of a predatory Schuschnigg government, bent on restoring the glory of the Hapsburg Empire and preparing to fight Germany by fortifying its frontiers. This predatory Austria, said Hitler, was getting ready to bring the weight of twenty million people against Germany. Hitler assembled his army on the Austrian border, ready to march, and then he told Mussolini what he intended to do, still not quite sure that Mussolini's announced approval would be followed in the end. He assured Mussolini that he would never challenge him in the south.

"I have drawn a definite boundary between Germany and France and now draw one just as definite between Italy and us. It is the Brenner. This decision will never be questioned or changed."

Hitler then sent this message by the hand of Prince Philip of Hesse. Mussolini listened and said quietly that he understood and there was no objection. He sent his regards to Hitler. When Hitler had that message he became almost overcome with relief and gratitude. "Tell Mussolini I will never forget him for this. Never, never. Whatever happens. As soon as this Austrian affair is settled I shall be ready to go with him through thick and thin no matter what happens. . . . If he should need any help or be in any danger he can be convinced that I shall stick to him whatever may happen, even if the whole world were against him."

But Mussolini was not as trustful of his German ally as he let the world believe. Immediately after the *Anschluss* he began to test the British water again, dealing with the new prime minister, Neville Chamberlain, the son of his old friend Austen Chamberlain. One reason for his hope that Britain might be different was that Anthony Eden, whom Mussolini did not like, had resigned from the government. But once again he was disappointed. Britain was thoroughly confused in her attitudes and the general population had decided that the evils of fascism, as shown in Mussolini's support of Franco, were more numerous than its virtues of producing and maintaining an orderly Italy. So it was apparent that nothing was to be gained in England to counterbalance Germany. Mussolini could now see that his commitment to the cause of totalitarian entente was complete. The real reason for the agreement sought with England, however, was to secure the British approval of the Ethiopian addition to the empire; the pact that was signed in April 1938 stipulated that the agreement would not go into force until Britain recognized the Ethiopian colony. By the time the agreement did go into force, seven months later, it was meaningless, left behind in the debris of a collapsing Europe.

On May 3 Hitler came to Rome for a weeklong visit, where he stayed at the Quirinale Palace with the King. He was entertained nobly with his entourage, which included Ribbentrop, Goebbels, Rudolf Hess, Heinrich Himmler, Sepp Dietrich, General Keitel, and a small army of journalists from the Ministry of Propaganda.

Hitler did not like the King and the feeling was reciprocated. More important, Hitler did not like or appreciate the difference between the government of Italy and his own Third Reich, of which he was absolute master. Mussolini, Hitler learned, was still a constitutional ruler. He dictated the course of Italy, but only under fiat from the King. Ultimately this was to prove to be a notable difference from Germany's form of government, no matter that the Western world lumped all the Axis powers together in a heap.

The visit was a success. The Germans were impressed with the parades, banquets, and other entertainments offered. Hitler spoke of the "Roman State" created by Mussolini and said their friendship would benefit both Italy and Germany. At Naples Mussolini displayed the Italian fleet and particularly his submarines, of which Italy had the largest fleet in Europe. Hitler was really impressed with the Italian navy and went away feeling that it was powerful enough to challenge Britain on the sea. His generals were not impressed with the Italian army; they had gained a bad impression of that army's operations in Ethiopia and in Spain. Undisciplined, badly organized, and questionable in battle was their opinion.

On May 9 the Germans went to Florence, and Mussolini accompanied them. At the end of that day, the Germans boarded their train to return home. At the parting, the two dictators clasped hands, and when Mussolini said "Henceforth no force will be able to separate us," Hitler's eyes filled with tears. During the meetings, Hitler mentioned Czechoslovakia casually, and Mussolini let it be known that Czechoslovakia did not interest him. Ribbentrop brought with him the draft of an alliance that would include a military partnership, and Foreign Minister Ciano gave it to Mussolini, who said he intended to go through with it. But in the end he rejected it because the British were about to bring up the recognition of the Ethiopian acquisition at the League of Nations. Ribbentrop was furious, but Ciano told him that the partnership between Germany and Italy was so secure they did not need a treaty.

The result, as far as Hitler was concerned, was salutary. He felt that he and Mussolini had once more agreed and that Mussolini was again giving him the green light to pursue his ambitions in northern Europe, for which he was grateful.

A few days after Hitler's departure, Mussolini made a speech in Genoa, in which he attacked France and laid down the gauntlet to the West. It might not be true that the democratic powers were preparing an ideological war against the totalitarian powers, but if it was true, then they would find Germany and Italy marching together, Mussolini said.

That speech impressed Hitler mightily and caused concern in Paris and London. The problem, the Western powers now found, was that they did not know where Italy stood. They should have known; they should have been able to reconstruct their own past policies by which they had thrust Italy into partnership with Germany with their refusal to stand up and be counted against Hitler when Mussolini did so. Now it was very late indeed, as was indicated by fascist Italy's embrasure of Hitler's peculiar racism.

Italy and Italians were not by nature inclined to be racist. Hitler had observed in his first meeting with Mussolini that Italians were different from Germans, and he had indicated loftily that was because they had a touch of the tar brush in them. This implication of inferiority had irritated Mussolini and was one of the reasons he did not like Hitler personally.

But racism came to Italy along with empire. In the earlier years Italy's attitude toward various races had been one of the points that differentiated it from the racist Anglo-Saxons. In the first Italian colonies—Libya, Eritrea—the Italians mingled freely with the Arabs and the other native people. The practice of *madamismo* was common; most civil and military officers had black mistresses with whom they lived openly. But this policy changed in 1935 when large numbers of soldiers and workers came to East Africa. The flood of mulatto children that resulted caused the government to act to separate the races. In 1936, the Minister for African Affairs laid down new rules. Whites and blacks must live separately. They could not frequent the same places of amusement. A law of April 1937 provided stiff penalties for any white caught living with a black. Children of mixed marriages could not be legitimized or even recognized by the white parent. That year the laws became more and more strengthened. The Italians invented apartheid: Whites and blacks had to live in separate areas; Italians were forbidden to drive buses that carried blacks or to travel on the same buses.

By 1938 Mussolini had convinced himself, and his fascist entourage, that racism was natural and proper. The one most active Fascist who refused to accept the racial policy was Italo Balbo, who, as a highly placed government official, tried to encourage the assimilation of the Arab and Berber populations of Libya. By the end of the 1930s, racism was a fascist policy, although a very uncomfortable one, since it went against the grain of most Italians.

In the Dodecanese Islands of the Aegean, which had been conquered from the Turks in 1912, Italy ruled over a Greek population and tried to Italianize it, particularly after Count De Vecchi became governor of the Aegean Islands in 1936. Thereafter a strict campaign to make Fascists and Italians of the Dodecanese Greeks was inaugurated. But real racism came to Italy in 1938, as Mussolini tried to follow a Hitlerian policy that he really did not believe in. In fact, in Hitler's first visit to Italy, Mussolini had cautioned him against pursuing racial policies in Germany. Mussolini numbered among his friends and associates many Jews, and, in the early days, he had told biographer Emil Ludwig that they were a great asset to Italy. Religious freedom was guaranteed in the Italian Constitution, and the Vatican policy held Roman Catholicism open to people of all creeds and races. Modern Italy then had a tradition of racial amity. Half a dozen Jews had been among the fifty founders of the fascist movement, and two of the women who played important roles in Mussolini's life—Angelica Balabanoff and Margherita Sarfatti—were Jews. But suddenly in 1938, Mussolini came out with a campaign of anti-Semitism. Why?

The reason can be found in the politicization of the international Jewish community against the takeover of Ethiopia. This created real resentment in Rome and played into the hands of the pro-Germans and fascist antiliberalism. By 1938, although Mussolini had decided that he must stand with Hitler, this is not the reason Mussolini turned to anti-

Semitism. The Jews had to take the blame for that themselves. There is no indication that Hitler or anyone in his following tried to put any pressure on Mussolini in this regard.

∽

Italian anti-Semitism began early in 1938 when the extremist fascist newspaper *Tevere* responded to anti-Fascist campaigns in the Western press, which they identified as run by Jews, and began an anti-Semitic campaign. Shortly afterward the *Informazione Diplomatica* noted editorially that the government was watching recent Jewish immigrants and would ensure that the Jewish influence on national life did not become disproportionate to their numbers.

Mussolini followed this with statements trying to prove that there existed a pure Italian race. "We must get into our minds," he said in October 1938, "that we are not Hamites, we are not Semites, we are not Mongols. And then, if we are none of these races, we are evidently Aryans, of Mediterranean type, pure."

By this time the government was harassing the Jews, although never conducting an extermination campaign such as Hitler. The Minister of Education prohibited the entry of foreign Jews into Italian schools. Foreign Jews were forbidden to live in Italy, the Aegean Islands, or Libya. Jews who had arrived in Italy after 1919 were deprived of Italian citizenship, although the families of Jews who had served in World War I remained untouched by decree. Jews were forbidden to join the Fascist party, they could not marry Italians, and they were forced out of all scientific, literary, and artistic organizations. They could not teach in state schools. Their ownership of land was strictly limited and they could not employ more than one hundred persons. They were forbidden to serve in the armed forces.

This policy was very unpopular with the Italian people, who by nature were easygoing and tolerant. It was unpopular with the Vatican, and it was detested by the King. Some of Mussolini's own ardent followers even took exception to it, including Italo Balbo, who had several close Jewish friends and, in defiance of Mussolini, made a practice of meeting them in the most public of surroundings.

The anti-Jewish campaign was never very successful nor was it pursued with a great deal of vigor, although two sets of anti-Semitic laws were passed in the fall of 1938. Still, it meant suffering to the Jews who had escaped Hitler's Germany and chosen to settle in Italy, and many of them left for England, France, Palestine, or the Americas.

Much more important than the racial question in that fall of 1938 was the situation in central Europe. Hitler made much of the plight of three million ethnic Germans who lived in the Sudetenland of Czechoslovakia. Mussolini knew after the Nuremberg Nazi Party Congress that Hitler was determined to destroy Czechoslovakia. He also knew from the British government dispatches to the British embassy in Rome that the British were not going to do anything to stop it. Thus Mussolini knew, and told his intimates, that Czechoslovakia was only going to be a beginning for Hitler and that he would not stop until he had avenged Germany for the treatment at Versailles.

On September 14, British Prime Minister Chamberlain met with Hitler in Berchtesgaden where the British agreed to give the Sudetenland to Germany. But, now, having achieved his demand, Hitler increased his demands, and war seemed to threaten.

On September 15, an article dictated by Mussolini appeared in *Il Popolo d'Italia*. It advised the British to give in. He called Czechoslovakia the creature of Versailles, "a sausage state." It was not worth going to war about. Hitler wanted a plebiscite. Let the Czechs hold one, Mussolini said. On September 18, Mussolini made a speech at Trieste in which he cast Italy's lot with Germany and demanded a plebiscite for the Sudeten Germans.

In the last week of September 1938, Europe seemed to be about to go to war. Germany was mobilized and so were France and Czechoslovakia. The British fleet was on the move. The Russians were asking Romania to allow transit of their troops. Only Mussolini was calm, and it was not until September 27 that he even ordered an alert. Although he was publicly pledged to Germany, he did nothing to show it, and the German military attaché in Paris complained because Mussolini had done nothing to pin down any French troops on the Italian border.

On the morning of September 28, it looked like war. Then British Prime Minister Chamberlain asked Mussolini to intervene with Hitler. The British ambassador telephoned Count Ciano, the Italian foreign minister, and asked that Mussolini speak to Hitler. Mussolini agreed, and an hour later telephoned the Italian ambassador in Berlin and told him to see Hitler and request a delay of twenty-four hours before marching into Czechoslovakia.

Ambassador Attolico rushed to the German Chancellery where Hitler was in conference with the French ambassador. Attolico insisted on interrupting. Hitler came out, received the message, and said, "Tell the Duce that I accept his proposal." Thus Mussolini had averted war.

Meanwhile Chamberlain made more overtures to Mussolini. He offered to come to Berlin along with French and Czechoslovakian representatives and arrange for the transfer of the Sudetenland to Germany. Mussolini again acted and through Ambassador Attolico suggested a four-power meeting: Britain, France, Germany, and Italy. Attolico again intruded on Hitler and again the proposal was accepted, provided that Mussolini would himself attend the conference. Hitler offered him the choice of meeting in Frankfurt or Munich, at Il Duce's pleasure. Mussolini chose Munich, and that is where the conference was held the next morning, September 29, 1938.

The world cheered this movement, except for the pope, Stalin, and the Czech government, which protested the move to act regarding their country without their representation. Mussolini was the man of the hour, having persuaded Hitler to refrain from his military conquest of Czechoslovakia. French Prime Minister Daladier and British Prime Minister Chamberlain had abandoned their Czechoslovak ally. And in this Mussolini saw total decadence.

What could one expect from a country like England, which built cemeteries and hospitals for pet animals and where legacies were bequeathed to parrots? "You can be sure that decadence has set in." Mussolini's theory was that World War I had killed off so much of the British male population that there were four million more women of marriageable age than men. "Four million sexually unsatisfied women, artificially creating a host of problems in order to excite or appease their senses. Not being able to embrace one man, they embrace humanity." He was joking at the time, but Mussolini's well-developed sense of humor often hid serious thoughts, and his contempt for the British had now become profound.

Early on the morning of September 29, Mussolini was met by Hitler at Rosenheim, halfway between the Italian frontier and Munich. It was more than a gesture of respect; Hitler wanted to confer with Mussolini before they met the Western allies. They traveled in Hitler's private train and he explained his intentions with maps.

The Siegfried Line had been completed, and he did not fear attack from the West, he said. (This was not true; the line was fragmentary and even at the time of the Polish crisis Hitler feared a Western attack.) If the democracies attacked, then he would counter, and the campaign would be over before they had completed their mobilization, he said. This was sheer bluff on Hitler's part, and he was obviously practicing on his Italian ally to get his reaction. He said the only reason he insisted on moving now was to avoid encirclement by the West. He also showed on his maps how he would destroy the Maginot Line, which was also all bluff.

Hitler talked on and on. He said he would destroy Czechoslovakia because it immobilized forty German divisions. The tenor of his tirade was that he and Mussolini were in all this together. Mussolini said neither yes nor no, but listened. Finally Mussolini interrupted to ask Hitler's minimal demands regarding Czechoslovakia. Ribbentrop handed him a paper. The demands had been set down by Goering, Baron Konstantin von Neurath, the former foreign minister, and State Secretary Ernst von Weizsäcker.

∞

The conference was disorganized and noisy. Hitler was impatient, Daladier kept going into an anteroom for drinks of Pernod, Chamberlain yawned. Only Mussolini seemed calm and slightly bored, as if he knew the outcome from the beginning.

Mussolini had opened the conference by stating the demands of Germany. The meetings broke up into bloc meetings, then reassembled, and broke again. The telephone system in the building broke down and messages were carried by hand. Mussolini dominated the conference, and Hitler yielded to him time and again. Mussolini made the telling point that they were only talking about three million Sudeten Germans, not all of Czechoslovakia. Hitler did not want the rest of it and would not take it as a gift. Hitler nodded and said nothing. As André François-Poncet, the French ambassador to Germany, put it, everything that happened at the conference showed that Mussolini was the master of the situation and Hitler followed his leads.

Mussolini was the only one there who spoke all the languages—French, German, and English—and he went from one delegation to the other clarifying points. Finally the agreement was reached, giving Germany eleven thousand square miles of Czech territory, including 70 percent of its heavy industry, 86 percent of its chemical industry, and all of its fortifications against Germany.

Mussolini left Munich after the state dinner that night with the feeling that he had saved Europe from war, a feeling that was expressed the next day around the world. Mussolini was the man of the hour.

∞

A by-product of the Munich meeting was an agreement between Mussolini and Chamberlain, in which Chamberlain finally agreed to recognize the Italian Empire and Mussolini agreed (happily) to withdraw his ten thousand volunteer troops from Spain. But at the same time, Italy's relations with France grew worse, largely because of fascist attacks in the Chamber of Deputies. And after Munich, Germany became much more aggressive in its foreign relations. In the Italian–German arbitration of the Hungarian–Slovakian frontier, Germany took the side of the Slovaks against Italy and Hungary, which was an embarrassment.

That year, too, Germany's Von Ribbentrop proposed a military alliance between Germany, Italy, and Japan. The Japanese were told that it was to be an alliance against America. But the Germans wanted it to strengthen their hand in Europe. Hitler now felt that Germany and Italy had the upper hand in Europe and that this was the time for a formal alliance. Mussolini said no, not yet. It would take some time to prepare the Italian people for such a move. Ribbentrop predicted war within three years, not naming any enemies. Mussolini was ready for war, as a means of extending his empire. When he had returned triumphantly from the Munich Conference, with demonstrations of love and loyalty all the way, he had spoken from his balcony at the Palazzo Venezia and told the crowd a little contemptuously, "You wanted peace. I have brought you peace." But from that moment, Mussolini decided that the way to achieve his expanded empire was through war.

CHAPTER 18

✍

Italy and World War II

In February 1939, Pope Pius XI died and was succeeded by Cardinal Pacelli, who became Pius XII. The mourning for the old pope and the interest in the new one occupied Italian attention during most of February, but Mussolini was now preparing for the war he foresaw in Europe. Attacks on France dominated the news about foreign nations, and they were now accompanied by criticism of the United States, which was just beginning to rearm after the severe cutbacks of the 1920s and 1930s. The armaments race, said the Italian press, was all the fault of the democracies.

When Hitler moved in on Czechoslovakia in March and dismembered that state, Mussolini took no apparent notice. He was determined to increase his own empire and not willing to disturb his relations with Germany. About that time Edda Mussolini, the daughter of the dictator, told a visiting American that the decline in relationships with America, which had been notable since Munich, was attributable to the United States' close relations with England and France. The U.S. embassy indicated that this was probably the view of Mussolini, which indeed it was. He now lumped America together with France and England as potential enemies. On March 21 he told the Fascist Grand Council that Italy must show uncompromising loyalty to the Axis. Italo Balbo, who often spoke his mind, accused him of licking Hitler's boots.

Mussolini grew angry, but he did not reply to the accusation. Because Mussolini had not been informed of the German actions in Czechoslovakia before they were taken, he was annoyed. Hitler learned this and, on March 25, sent a long flattering message, telling of his

175

admiration for Mussolini. This was true, although some writers have tried to denigrate the relationship; Hitler revered Mussolini so much for his development of fascism that had led the way to national socialism, that he kept a bust of Mussolini in his private office.

Late in March the capture of Madrid by Franco's forces brought an end to the Spanish Civil War, which was celebrated wildly in Italy. Mussolini wanted to match Germany's seizure of all Czechoslovakia with a movement of his own, and he chose Albania for his next foray into colonial acquisition. He drafted an Italo–Albanian agreement that permitted Italy to take control of Albania. King Zog of Albania offered objections, but on April 7, Good Friday, Mussolini's troops invaded. King Zog fled the capital and looters took over. There were many tense hours before the Italian troops arrived from the coast. In the next few days, the annexation of Albania to Italy was completed. The move was greeted joyfully by the Germans who said it added to Axis power, and without visible response by France and England. The crown of Albania was added to that of Victor Emmanuel's Italy.

At a meeting in the spring, representatives of the German and Italian general staffs assured each other that their armies were in a state of development. Italy would not be ready for war, General Pariani, Undersecretary of the Army, said, until 1943. Later in the year that same time frame was repeated in discussions between Count Ciano, the Italian foreign minister, and German Foreign Minister Von Ribbentrop. In May 1939, a new military alliance was formed between Germany and Italy. The Germans called it "the Pact of Steel."

By this time Mussolini had given up any attempts to cultivate relationships with France and Britain. The anti-French campaign in the Italian press was extended to become anti-British as well. The theme was the attempt of the democracies to encircle the totalitarian states.

In the face of a growing threat in the spring of 1939, the Polish government turned to England, and early in April, Prime Minister Chamberlain announced that England would stand by Poland if she were invaded and adhere to the Polish–British mutual assistance pact. In Italy this was greeted with further complaints about encirclement of the Axis powers.

In June, Dr. Joseph Goebbels, the German Minister of Propaganda, went to Danzig to make a speech attacking the Polish government for suppressing the rights of the large German population of that city. It was the Sudetenland all over again.

On July 7, Chamberlain appealed to Mussolini to again use his good offices with Hitler to prevent an attack on Poland. Mussolini this time was cold and adamant. If Britain went to war to protect Poland, Chamberlain was informed, then Italy would go to war at Germany's side.

Toward the end of the month of July, Mussolini could no longer ignore the threats Germany was making toward Poland and sought a meeting. But Hitler refused. He had drawn the plan for the seizure of Danzig by force. By August 6, Mussolini's basic concern was how to get out of the offensive alliance he had signed with Germany, because Italy was totally unprepared to wage war, and the Italian people were completely opposed to any military adventures. Mussolini lamented this fact; he often spoke of his Italians as a nation of sheep, and he really wished that he had at his disposal the Legions of ancient Rome. But he recognized the deficiencies and knew he must do something to prevent his embroilment. On August 11, Count Ciano met with German Foreign Minister Von Ribbentrop, who refused to give any information. When Ciano and Ribbentrop were walking in to dinner, Ribbentrop let the truth fly. Ciano had asked him what the Germans wanted, the Polish corridor or Danzig. "Neither," said Ribbentrop, his eyes flashing. "We want war."

And so Ciano knew. He was never to recover from this shock of having been used by the Germans to pave the way for this war that was now coming. When Ciano saw Hitler the next day, the result was the same, although Hitler was more civil to him than Ribbentrop had been. Further, Hitler looked into the future and happily predicted war between the Axis powers and the British and French. He advised Mussolini to liquidate Yugoslavia as quickly as possible.

Ciano left Germany angry and upset. He recognized that the situation of Italy relative to Germany had switched around in recent months. Hitler was now in the saddle and he was paying no attention to what Italy wanted. Ciano wrote in his diary:

"I return to Rome completely disgusted with the Germans, with their leader, with their way of doing things. They have betrayed and lied to us. Now they are dragging us into an adventure which we do not want. The alliance was based on promises which they now deny; they are traitors, and we must not have any scruples in ditching them."

This was Ciano's announcement of his personal switchover to become anti-German. When Ciano reported to Mussolini, the dictator was of two minds. He, too, was angry with Hitler and Ribbentrop, but he felt the need to honor the commitment to Germany to go to war.

On August 18, Italian Ambassador Attolico had a stormy session with Ribbentrop in Salzburg, in which Ribbentrop said war with Poland was inevitable. Attolico said that the war could not then be localized and that Italy would not go to war with Germany. The two men parted enemies, and a few months later Attolico was withdrawn as ambassador at Ribbentrop's demand.

On August 20, Attolico reported to Mussolini, who insisted that Italy must back Germany in the war that was coming. On August 22, Hitler had his ambassador call on Mussolini to ask what he required in terms of arms to carry on the war at Germany's side.

Hitler had been busy working out his agreement with Stalin to partition northern Europe—including Poland, Estonia, Latvia, and Lithuania—which would be divided between Russia and Germany, with the Russians getting half of Poland and Estonia and Latvia. Once this was achieved, Hitler felt free to march against Poland. The Italians told him that if he did, the British and French would come into the war. Hitler scoffed at them. He really did not believe that Britain would ever fight, and he was certain that France was so corrupt that she could not.

This request for Italy's needs to honor the Pact of Steel proved to be Italy's escape hatch. Mussolini prepared a list, and when it was transmitted to Germany, Hitler said he could not supply all the materials. So it was agreed that Italy would not enter the war at this time. Count Ciano had a sense of what the Germans wanted from Italy now—only the pressure she could exert by placing several divisions on the French front. Hitler was now talking like a man insane, Ciano said, a man who had changed to consider only his own immediate problems. Ciano said that no matter what Mussolini's feelings were of being honor-bound to support the pact, Hitler was now beyond rational thought.

On August 30, 1939, just hours before the threatened invasion of Poland, the Italian press for the first time said that Italy would remain neutral in such a war. The Italian people cheered. If there was anything they did not want, it was a war.

On September 1, the situation was made official when Hitler sent a message to Mussolini releasing him from the terms of the Pact of Steel. Immediately Mussolini began to think of himself as mediator, even after France and England entered the war that first week of September. Mussolini's feeling was all with Germany, but he was relieved not to have to go to war. But by not going to war at Germany's side, Mussolini changed forever his relationship with the Germans. Hitler still admired and respected Mussolini, but he told Ribbentrop and others that Mussolini was all there was to Italy, and if something happened to him, Italy was worthless. Hitler's generals agreed; the Italian army was not capable of carrying on a campaign against any modern force.

Whenever taxed with this truth, Mussolini grew angry, but it was the truth nonetheless. The Italians were not by nature warlike, and nothing was done by their officer corps to instill martial spirit into them.

The initial change in the relationship between Germany and Italy was noted by Count Ciano toward the end of September; the Italians had no idea of what was going on in the minds of Germany's leaders and could not find out. "Berlin gives us absolutely no information," Ciano confided to his diary. But on September 30, he had a call from Ribbentrop suggesting that either he or Mussolini come to Germany for a meeting. Ciano did not want Mussolini to go, for Mussolini might be trapped into some change of policy that would be unwelcome, so Ciano went to Berlin that very day. He found Hitler very confident, and very friendly to Mussolini and Italy. What was past was past, Hitler said, and he wanted Mussolini with him in the future.

Italy's neutrality did not go unnoticed in the United States; the Secretary of State sent along to the president Ambassador William Phillips's situation report as of October 5 and a special letter in which he analyzed quite accurately Mussolini's reasons for abstaining from the war. Mussolini, as always, had doubts about his own action, and at the end of October told Ciano he was going to write Hitler and tell him that Italy remained Germany's "economic and moral reserve" and later on planned to play a military role. Mussolini also began shaking up the army to improve the quality of his soldiers. His new commanders reported that if they could have all the material they had asked for and the factories worked double shifts, they could be prepared to go to war by October 1942, but not before. And although Mussolini had always depicted his people to be happy warriors when he spoke to the Germans, privately he called his Italians useless as soldiers. "Have you ever seen a lamb become a wolf?" he asked. "The Italian race is a race of sheep. Eighteen years are not enough to change them. It takes a hundred and eighty and maybe a hundred and eighty centuries."

Yet he was determined, in the winter of 1940, that Italy should go into the war on the side of Germany before it ended, so that he would have the glory of sitting on the victor's side of the peace table and carving up the world as the British and French had done in 1920.

∽

In March 1940, Ribbentrop and an entourage of thirty-five came to Rome, bearing a four-thousand word letter from Hitler, which was largely a justification of his own actions. But he did also play on Mussolini's ambitions, by talking of the coming victory, and indicating that

Mussolini should enter the war. "But if that future is conceived as a guarantee of the existence of the Italian people from the historical, geopolitical, and general moral viewpoints, that is according to the criteria of your people's right to existence, Duce, then you will some day be confronted by the same opponents who are fighting Germany today. I know full well, Duce, that you yourself do not think differently on the subject." And Hitler proposed an early meeting, to cement their friendship and apprise Mussolini of plans and developments in their alliance. It was agreed that a meeting would be held March 18 at the Brenner Pass.

At the meeting, Mussolini asserted his eagerness to enter the war against the Western allies at the earliest possible moment, which would be three or four months away. He suggested that Hitler postpone his offensive until then. Hitler said he could not do that, but that the moment for Italy to intervene would come when the enemy had been smashed in northern France. Then Mussolini could send troops along the Swiss frontier toward the Rhone valley. So it was agreed that once Germany had made a victorious advance, Mussolini would enter the war. On his return from the Brenner, he began talking about war, and empire, and Italy's share of the booty after the Western allies were defeated.

By April 9, when Hitler attacked Denmark and Norway (without notifying Mussolini until it happened), Il Duce was really excited about the prospect of going to war at Hitler's side. He was really giving no attention to the realities of defense posture; his entire thinking was of the glory of empire, not of the planes and tanks and guns that would be necessary to achieve it, or the trained soldiers who would have to man these weapons. Although he had been a soldier and a good one, his appreciation of the military mentality was nothing like Hitler's. Mussolini was a completely political creature, not a military one.

He approved Hitler's actions so far in the war wholeheartedly. "His hands fairly itch," Ciano wrote about Mussolini in his diary.

The news of the German action seemed to please the people of Italy. Mussolini was unimpressed by his own people's reaction. "The Italian people is a whore who prefers the winning mate," he said contemptuously. But as for the date of Italy's entry into the war, it was postponed until the spring of 1941. The fact that virtually no Italians except some of the Fascists wanted to enter the war meant nothing to him. As he told Ciano, what was the use of building a great fleet of ships if you weren't going to use them? And as for the people, "To make a people great it is necessary to send them into battle even if you have to kick them in the pants." He knew very well how the Italians felt about the war, including King Victor Emmanuel, whose feelings were very anti-German and pro-English. But Benito was determined to manipulate Italy in war as he had in peace, even if his people were very poor cannon fodder. "I do not forget," he told Ciano, "that in 1918 there were 540,000 deserters in Italy."

Still, the drive for glory and empire overcame his own sharp analysis of the character of the Italian people. Because he wanted them to become great in a military fashion, he moved in a manner to try to force greatness on them.

By May 13, 1940, Mussolini's itch was almost unbearable. He declared that the Allies had already lost the war and that he must get into it within a month, or he would not be able to share in the spoils. Traveling around the country, making speeches, Count Ciano was becoming impressed with the average Italian's views: against entry into the war. These were views he shared.

But by May 29, Mussolini had established a supreme command of the military forces of Italy, with himself as commander, with his generals headed by Badoglio and Graziani. He was now talking of June 5, 1940, for entry into the war and of making a speech to the Italian people on June 4. He sent a message to Hitler informing him. Since the King had the constitutional responsibility of declaring war, Mussolini sent Ciano to get his approval, and the King did approve, albeit reluctantly. The King observed that the Italian people were being dragged into a war they did not want. But Mussolini was too entranced with the thought of empire to listen to this truth. A day or so later on the golf course, out of hearing of any of the listeners who were always about, a personal friend told Ciano that they ought to form a new political party: "The Party of Interventionists of Bad Faith."

In response to a request from Hitler who was planning a major attack on French airfields, the date of entry into the war was postponed until June 11. Ciano observed the reactions of several people: Governor Italo Balbo of Libya said he would do the best he could, but Ciano knew how much Balbo hated the Germans. The King said he was prepared now for war and that he would greet it like a good soldier. Ciano prepared to join the military. He would command a squadron of bombers at Pisa, which was near Corsica where his father was buried, where he wanted to fight the war. On June 10, 1940, from his balcony at the Palazzo Venezia, Mussolini announced the war to the Italian people and Ciano called in the British and French ambassadors and told them.

It was, said Mussolini: "An hour marked by destiny, the hour of irrevocable decisions. We are entering the lists against the plutocratic and reactionary democracies of the West, who have always hindered the advance and often plotted against the very existence of the Italian people. At a memorable meeting in Berlin I said that according to the laws of fascist morality, when one has a friend, one goes with him to the very end. We have done this and will do this with Germany, with her people, with her victorious armed forces."

Mussolini was already feeling victorious. Ciano was downcast by the attitude—"The news of the war does not surprise anyone and does not arouse very much enthusiasm. I am sad, very sad. The adventure begins. May God help Italy."

∽

Like most of the leading Fascists, Ciano liked playing soldier on a part-time basis. On June 11, he went to Pisa and then engaged in several bombing attacks on French territory. But except for the bombing, nothing happened. Hitler was surprised and not very pleased. When Mussolini had said that he must enter the war by June 11, Hitler had thought Mussolini had an operation all planned—the invasion of Corsica, or Tunis, or Malta. He had assumed this, and because he had made it clear that what happened in the Mediterranean was Mussolini's affair, he had not thought to inquire. And when nothing happened, Hitler began to agree with his generals that Italy was a military ally of very little use.

On June 18, Mussolini and Ciano went to Munich for meetings with Hitler. Mussolini insisted on using Italian forces to attack the French in the Alps, although Badoglio was opposed to it and Generals Roatta and Pintor said they were not ready to fight.

Mussolini also insisted that his favorite Littorio division be employed, and so it was moved from the valley of the Po to the Alpine foothills, getting in the way of the Alpine division, which was already deploying for the attack.

On June 18, the Italians attacked, the attacking force commanded by the Crown Prince. The attack was a monstrous failure, even though the French troops they faced were already conscious of the defeat of their country and application to the Germans for peace. The prince and his forces managed only to occupy the towns of Modane and Briancon and were stopped cold at Mentone. They got no further, and Mussolini was furious and humiliated.

Of course, now at Munich he could not ask for vast chunks of French territory, as he had anticipated doing when he contemplated going to war. Privately Hitler told him that he would have to be content for the moment with a mere token of victory. Hitler wanted to turn the French into allies, and thus he wanted to deal gently with them, after first taking Germany's revenge for Versailles by signing the armistice in the same car in which the armistice of 1918 had been signed. But he promised Mussolini that when the war ended and the spoils of Europe were finally divided up, Italy could take what she wanted from the French possessions in Africa.

Mussolini was sensible enough when the French peacemakers arrived in Rome. Since there had really been no war, he said there should be no hoopla about the peace. The meeting was to take place almost secretly and the press would be told to play it down. By Mussolini's order the Italians were restrained and dignified and so were the French. But the net result of the war against France was humiliation and frustration. Hitler had rejected all Mussolini's overtures for territorial concessions. He received only the few miles of territory that his troops had conquered and the demilitarization of a fifty-kilometer strip along his European and North African frontiers with France.

Mussolini sent Ciano to Berlin in July to see where Italy and Germany would go from here. Ciano found Hitler undecided. Now he really did want peace, as Ribbentrop said. But Britain was not going to surrender.

At Berlin Ciano talked about possible Italian operations and mentioned Greece and North Africa. Hitler said the Mediterranean and the Adriatic were matters of purely Italian concern and that anything Mussolini did there was acceptable. Mussolini offered to send an expeditionary force to join the Germans in the next round of fighting, but Hitler turned him down. He really did not know where the fighting would be next, although he was thinking about an invasion of England. His reason for declining Mussolini's offer was that the problems of supply and management of two different armies were very serious. This, of course, was true, as the Allies found out in their attempts to pair British and American methods, and as Hitler would discover in North Africa and Russia. But the truth annoyed Mussolini, who was champing at the bit to get his Italians into the fray, no matter the cost.

The blank check that Hitler had given Mussolini in the south was soon withdrawn, and Italy was cautioned not to stir up the Balkans until Hitler had decided on his next move. So in the summer of 1940, Hitler dithered and ultimately decided to let Goering try to knock out the British Royal Air Force (RAF) preparatory to an invasion of England. Meanwhile in the south, in the Mediterranean, the war was on dead center. At the end of June, Italo Balbo was killed when an Italian anti-aircraft battery at Tobruk fired on his plane, mistaking it for an English aircraft. That stopped matters cold in Libya.

Mussolini kept calling on his generals for war in East Africa and in North Africa, and the generals kept saying they were not ready. Marshal Graziani steadfastly refused to move. Mussolini frantically talked of invading Greece, of invading Yugoslavia. But through Ribbentrop, Hitler said no, there must be no movement other than the coming battle against Britain. For the first time Mussolini was put in the position of having to knuckle under and accept second fiddle in the Axis scheme. Always before, Hitler had coated the pills with sugar, giving Il Duce the satisfaction of feeling needed, even when the need had passed. Now all had changed, and Italy was relegated to a supporting role. It was the beginning of the end of Mussolini's dream of empire.

CHAPTER 19

✧

Mussolini Invades Greece

In the summer of 1940, Mussolini was eager to get into the war against Britain. The reason was simple enough. He had missed out on the spoils in the defeat of France by not entering the war soon enough, and he did not want the same thing to happen again with the defeat of England, which he fully expected to come with an invasion of the British Isles.

The Italian fleet was so important an element in British war planning that they would soon have two forces arrayed against it, the British Mediterranean fleet and Force H, a special unit of capital ships. The Italians had two modern battleships available and four more nearly completed. They had a powerful force of cruisers and destroyers and the submarine fleet, with 116 submarines, which was the largest in the world. These forces were stronger than the combined British and French Mediterranean fleets. The only class of ship the Italians lacked was aircraft carriers, and the British had two of these in the Mediterranean.

From the outset, the sea war in the Mediterranean was real and bloody. On June 12, a British cruiser and destroyer force shelled the Italian military base at Tobruk. An Italian force of cruisers set out to engage but failed to make contact. But off Crete, an Italian submarine sank the cruiser *Calypso*.

At the end of the war against France, the British tried desperately to gain control of all the French fleet. They managed to take over several French ships that were in British harbors, and some in Alexandria. But at the base at Mers el Kebir, when the French were threatened by the British, they refused to surrender, and the British opened fire, sinking the three battleships. But the new *Strasbourg* and five destroyers escaped to the French naval base at Toulon.

On July 9, 1940, the British and Italians engaged in another sea action, between the Italian battle squadron and Admiral Cunningham's Mediterranean fleet, in which the battleship *Giulio Cesare* was damaged before the action was broken off. Italian planes bombed the other British force, Force H, which was escorting convoys to Africa.

Again, on July 19, two Italian cruisers and the Australian cruiser *Sydney* and five destroyers met in an action in the Mediterranean. The Italian *Bartolomeo Colleoni* was sunk, and the *Sydney* was damaged before the action was broken off.

The real fighting in the war, then, was going on in the Mediterranean and beginning in England with the Battle of Britain, by which Hitler hoped to destroy the RAF Fighter Command and prepare for his invasion of England. Mussolini was aching to get into the war, fully expecting the Germans to succeed.

At this time Mussolini was really the sole government of Italy. He kept five different ministries to himself: Interior, Colonies, War, Navy, and Air Force, and none of the other nine ministries could take any policy action without his express approval. He was also prime minister and commander in chief of the armed forces. The result was almost total impotence of the government. Whenever Mussolini was not available to make decisions, no decisions were made.

The Germans advised Mussolini to keep his military activity confined to Africa, which they saw as a major theater of operations. Hitler suggested that Mussolini launch a campaign to capture the Suez Canal, but Mussolini wanted to be in on the glory of operations against England; thus, he insisted on offering bombers to Goering to fight with his Luftwaffe and submarines to Admiral Dönitz to operate with the U-boat fleet in the Atlantic. Three hundred planes were sent to Belgium in October 1940, to assist in the breaking of the British Royal Air Force. But the Italian planes were not suitable for the strategic bombing of Britain, even less so than the German, which were too light for the job. General Kesselring, commander of the Third Air Fleet, made use of the Italians only to bomb targets in the hinterland and, after a few weeks, sent them back to Italy. The real problem was that the Italian air crews were not trained in the same methods as the German. The Germans were using radio beams to direct their bombing, but the Italian aircraft were not fitted with that sort of equipment. The Germans regarded their beam system as an important military secret that they did not want to share. Consequently, the Italian air force was returned to the Mediterranean, where it belonged. There, although the Allies never made much of it, the Italian air force was formidable. It was effective in the attacks on Malta and other British targets, particularly in 1940 and early 1941, when very few RAF planes could be spared from the Battle of Britain for the Mediterranean theater.

As for the submarines, they were almost equally useless in the northern waters, through no fault of the Italian submarine service. The Italian submarines were larger and more spacious than the German but not suited for operation in the stormy cold waters of the Atlantic. But the most difficult matter was the method of operation. Dönitz's U-boat captains were so disciplined that they never questioned his personal command of the wolfpack efforts. But the Italian submarine skippers were not used to this sort of operation. They went out to fight on their own, and their cruise discipline was not to Dönitz's liking. Therefore, after a few months, he sent the submarines, too, back to the Mediterranean, even though several of the Italian captains had scored quite effectively against British convoys and on the American station.

The real truth of both operations was that the Germans were incapable of fighting a war with allies, unless they controlled their every action. For that reason, Mussolini's intention to fight a parallel war alongside the Germans made a great deal of sense. The trouble, as it turned out, was that Mussolini had so far disrupted his military organization with his one-man rule, that the Italian forces, and particularly the army, were incapable of fighting any modern force. As they were to prove in Africa, under competent direction, such as that of Field Marshal Erwin Rommel, the Italians fought very well when their heart was in the battle. But the inadequacies of the Italian army, with obsolescent artillery and inferior tanks, would hamper the operations in Africa from the beginning and, coupled with the failure of Italian military leadership, would contribute greatly to the Axis failure there.

In 1940 most of the Italian army was sitting in barracks in Italy while Mussolini champed at the bit. There were, however, 350,000 troops in Ethiopia, although 70 percent of them were Africans. Mussolini insisted that summer that they get into action. The action was frustrated in Libya when General Balbo was killed in the plane crash, setting back the military planning there.

On August 3, the Duke of Aosta began an invasion of British Somaliland with 175,000 men against the British 25,000-man force. The
Italians advanced toward Zeila on the north, Hargeisa in the center,
and Odeina on the south. In two days they captured Zeila and Hargeisa.
But on August 15, the British put up a strong defense at Tug Argan
before yielding the town to the superior Italian force. On August 16,
the British began to embark at Berbera for evacuation to Aden, and
Royal Navy Cruisers took off 5,700 British soldiers and civilians, leaving most of the native troops to the mercy of the Italians. The British
had suffered minimal casualties to their own troops. But they *had* lost
the war in this area, and Prime Minister Churchill was furious. When
General Archibald Wavell, the Middle East commander, attempted to
justify the British actions, Churchill transferred his anger, thus began
the bad blood between prime minister and field commander that would
lead ultimately to Wavell's ouster in the Middle East.

In Libya that summer Marshal Graziani refused to start an attack
on the British in Egypt because, he said, he had nowhere near enough
trained men or enough tanks and artillery for the job. Mussolini fretted
in Rome and held endless conferences with Count Ciano, the foreign
minister, planning military actions. He thought about attacking Yugoslavia. He considered attacking Greece. He expressed a real fear that
the war would now end before he had gotten into the fighting and that
he would once again fail to gain more empire. His dream was that the
British Empire would be dismembered and that he would receive the
lion's share of the Mediterranean and African sections. He had an eye
on the Sudan, Uganda, and Kenya, Aden and the Red Sea, and Tunisia
and Egypt in the north, plus some part of northwest Africa to give him
an outlet on the Atlantic.

On August 16, Mussolini sent a message to Hitler that he would
resolve Italian differences with Greece by exploiting incidents that the
Italians would provoke. In answer, he received a stern warning from
Ribbentrop to cease any troublemaking in the Balkans until the problem of Britain had been resolved. So once again Mussolini was stymied.
This was all the more unbearable to him because the British were attacking the Italian industrial plants in Turin and Milan, and the British
fleet was bombarding the ports at Bardia and Fort Capuzzo.

On August 17, the Greeks partially mobilized their forces after one
of Mussolini's submarines sank the Greek cruiser *Hellas* with no prov-
ocation. There were more actions in the Mediterranean, mostly involving British bombardment of Italian bases, and Italian air attacks on
the British fleet. None of them was decisive. In September, Prime Min-

ister Churchill ordered an attack on Dakar in French West Africa, to try to capture that port for the Allies. The French government sent elements of its fleet to the scene and defeated the British ignominiously. This was proof of Hitler's contention that the Vichy government could be a vigorous ally to the Axis. When the Vichy air force attacked Gibraltar on September 24 and 25, it was further proof and stilled Mussolini's complaints.

September came and still Graziani had not moved in North Africa, although the Duke of Aosta's force invaded Kenya and captured the small town of Buna. At sea, the British Mediterranean fleet was increased to three battleships and two carriers. The Italians had five battleships and several big cruisers, and Admiral Cunningham, commander of the British forces, was very much aware of the Italian naval threat.

As Mussolini had warned Hitler he would do, he increased the Italian military force in Albania by forty thousand men in answer to the Greek mobilization. He also began a media campaign against Greece, intended to persuade Italians that an aggressive Greek government was threatening Italy.

On September 13 the Italians under Graziani reluctantly began an attack toward Egypt. Graziani had five divisions in the line with another eight in reserve in Libya. But knowing his troops' capability, he complained that this move was suicidal. The British western desert force of two divisions, under General Richard O'Connor, fell back before the superior Italian assault. On the first day the Italians occupied Sollum. The Italians also continued to advance in Kenya, and the Italian newspapers were filled with trumpet calls of victory. On September 16, the Italians captured Sidi Barrani in Egypt. But their offensive had nearly run its course, the Italian supply lines were extended, and there was only one good road from Libya into Egypt. Had the Italians been prepared for war, with a quarter of a million soldiers in Cyrenaica, they could have achieved all Mussolini's war aims, the capture of Alexandria, and the capture of the Nile delta. But they stopped and went on the defensive, which seemed inexplicable to the British at the time.

At sea, the war was heating up. The planes of the British carrier *Illustrious* attacked Benghazi in Libya and sank four Italian ships in the harbor, including two Italian destroyers. In retaliation, the Italians sent torpedo bombers out and seriously damaged the cruiser *Kent*.

As Count Ciano wrote in his diary, "never has a military operation been conducted so much against the will of the commanders" as the one in North Africa. On August 18, Graziani's Tenth Italian Army had come to the end of its supply line, and he stopped the assault and began building fortifications.

At this point, Mussolini was joyful. He had a war, and his Italians were winning it. Ribbentrop arrived in Rome with plans for an alliance with Japan and Germany. It was really directed against the United States, to keep her from entering the European war or threatening Japan's expansion in China.

Then plans began to go awry for Germany and Italy. In late September Hitler realized that, despite all Marshal Goering's bluster, his Luftwaffe had lost the Battle of Britain, and he suspended the plan to invade the British Isles. Franco was supposed to come into the war on the side of the Axis, which would take care of Gibraltar, but Franco refused to get involved. At a meeting at Brenner Pass, Mussolini spoke about his plans for Egypt: He would attack at Mersa Matrûh in a few weeks, and he would then attack Alexandria and the Nile delta. Hitler offered him armored forces, but Mussolini shrugged them off. For his parallel war, he wanted to keep the Germans out of Africa. Thus all the glory of victory there would be Italy's, and Mussolini would have a major voice in the doling out of the spoils, giving him the Mediterranean empire he wanted.

Mussolini said did not need any help. Therefore, Hitler got the idea that Mussolini would fight the war in Africa. What was he, Hitler, to do to keep the war going? In the breach, he recalled an old idea, that he and Russia could not coexist. The idea had been given credence in 1939 and after by Stalin's immediate and ultravigorous actions in northern Europe, preempting more than his share of Poland, taking over Estonia and Latvia and attacking Finland. Since Hitler could not force the British down, he decided to attack Russia, which should be an easy prey.

Toward the end of September, Hitler made another of his lightning moves without telling Mussolini. He sent troops into Romania to guarantee the safety of the German oil supply from the oil fields at Ploesti. Mussolini was very angry at not being consulted. In retaliation against his difficult partner, he planned an operation against Greece. On October 15, in a meeting at the Palazzo Venezia, he made the final decision to attack. Italian troops were to seize the Ionian Islands and Salonika and then take over all of Greece. The date was to be October 26. Marshal Badoglio pointed out that twenty divisions were needed for this operation and he only had ten divisions. This was because Mussolini had become so overconfident with his victories in Africa that he had begun demobilizing. Without consulting Badoglio or anyone else,

he had ordered half the Italian army—six hundred thousand soldiers—
disbanded. And now Badoglio had to call up one hundred thousand new
troops, most of them untrained. This was part of the crazy quilt pattern
of military operations in which Italy was embarked because of Mussolini's husbanding of power.

On October 15, 1940, Mussolini summoned his ministers and told
them that they had two weeks in which to prepare for war with Greece.
His military estimate was that the Greeks would have an army of only
thirty thousand to oppose them, but in reality the Greeks were mobi-
lizing three hundred thousand men. Mussolini claimed that the operations had been planned down to the last detail. But planned by whom?
He did not have a representative of the air force or the navy at the
meeting, although this was to be an amphibious landing and control of
the air was necessary to bring it off. And so inexperienced was the
general put in charge of the landings, that he said a whole division could
be disembarked at Albania's single port in one day, whereas it actually
took one month. Nobody mentioned the season, or the coming of the
chill autumn rains to the mountains of Greece and Albania. Nobody
mentioned the demobilization that was still going on. Mussolini announced that he was taking full responsibility for this action, which
was supposed to reassure the Italian people.

This time, Mussolini told Ciano, he would have a surprise for Hitler. He would not announce beforehand what he was going to do. Two
could play at that game. Hitler had acted first and talked later one time
too many in Romania, and now Mussolini was aching to give his German friend a taste of his own medicine.

On October 19, Mussolini drafted a latter to Hitler that mentioned
his coming attack on Greece, although he was very vague about the
date and did not send the letter for three days. It was delivered in Berlin
on October 24 while Hitler and Ribbentrop were on their abortive mission to meet with Franco. In the hope of deflecting Mussolini, Hitler
had Ribbentrop telephone him en route and suggest an immediate
meeting. Mussolini, knowing that his timetable called for his troops to
march into Greece on October 27, suggested October 28. And when the
Germans arrived at Florence, he was standing beaming on the platform
to announce "Victorious Italian troops crossed the Greco–Albanian
frontier at dawn today."

Hitler was dismayed, because, as he had told Ribbentrop on the
way to the meeting, this Greek scheme of Mussolini's was crazy. The
Italians would get nowhere in the Greek mountains in the rainy season
and the following winter snow. But when Hitler was faced with the

facts, he congratulated Mussolini and voiced none of his concerns. Mussolini was in very good humor, and the conference went off very well. Hitler was in a generous mood and he assured Mussolini that he would sign no peace treaty with France unless all Mussolini's territorial demands were met, and he regarded those demands as really minimal. But for the moment it was important that France be cultivated, for, among other problems, there was still the bulk of the French fleet to be dealt with. (Before the war, this French fleet was the second strongest in Europe.)

At the end of October, Count Ciano made a trip to Albania to see how the fighting was going. It was very slow; the Italians were already bogged down in the rain. After some investigation, Ciano learned that Mussolini was being subverted by the Italian general staff. Badoglio, the head of the Army, had not believed war was necessary with the Greeks and, thus, he had made no special effort to prepare. The problem, of course, was that Mussolini kept the authority to himself but still relied on his top officers and gave them the responsibility for preparing for his moves.

On this trip to Albania, Ciano played air force pilot and made a bombing raid on Salonika. On the return his formation was attacked by Greek fighters, and two of the fighters were shot down.

But on the ground, the war against Greece was going badly. An Italian attack was ordered on Corsica, and it was a failure. By the eighth day of operations the initiative had passed to the Greeks. At Mussa, a frightened battalion of Albanians panicked and this began a general Italian retreat. Mussolini fired the general in charge and sent General Soddu to assume command of the army there. His first recommendation to Rome was for some Alpine troops. In the Epirus sector, General Visconti remained in command and expressed hopes for a victory at Jianina.

The Greek assault petered out by November 9, but Mussolini was very angry. His yes-men, the generals, had promised him an easy victory. At this point his problems were complicated by a growing apathy among the Italian people about the war, and economic conditions. This was not helped on November 12 by a British carrier plane attack on the naval base at Taranto in which the battleship *Cavour* was sunk and the battleships *Littorio* and *Duilio* were badly damaged.

On November 18, Foreign Minister Ciano went to Salzburg and then to Hitler's eyrie at the Berghof. He found Hitler very gloomy and now inclined to be negative about the Balkans, because of Mussolini's ill-timed attack on the Greeks, which caused the British to reinforce

Greece with aircraft and troops. Hitler said nothing about his own plans, which called for a lightning attack on Russia the following May. They discussed the possibility of making an alliance with Yugoslavia, which aroused Hitler's enthusiasm. Ciano went south for a few days to the signing of the tripartite pact by Hungary, Slovakia, and Romania and then back to see Hitler again. At this time Hitler had it all planned to bring Paul, the Yugoslav regent, to Berlin and work out the details. As Ciano left Hitler, the dictator gave him a letter to take to Mussolini, which was extremely critical of the Greek venture. He said unequivocally that Mussolini had posed new problems for the Axis partnership. Now he wanted to see some victories in Albania and a resumption of the Italian campaign in North Africa; thus, he was going to send some Stuka bombers for the Italians, with, of course, German pilots. What he was worried about was British air bases in Greece. Nothing could be done before March 1941 to solve that situation, except to make an alliance with Yugoslavia and partition Greece, giving Yugoslavia the port of Salonika.

What Mussolini should do now, said Hitler, was resume the campaign in Egypt and reach Mersa Matrûh, from which Alexandria and Suez would be in air range. In the spring then, an offensive could begin against Egypt, and bombers could attack the British Mediterranean fleet. He offered German bombers.

Badoglio, who had lost patience with Mussolini's methods of running an army, resigned his command at the end of November 1940 and was replaced by General Cavallero. The battle in Greece and Albania continued to go badly for the Italians, and Hitler, as a first move, sent fifty transport planes to Italy. A few days later General Milch, the real operating head of the Luftwaffe, came to Rome to arrange for a strong Luftwaffe contingent to be sent to Italy to assist in the war in North Africa.

That first week of December, General Ubaldo Soddu, the commander in Albania, sent an urgent message to Rome. He was defeated, he said, and had to seek peace. Mussolini dispatched an emissary to Berlin asking for immediate help. The ambassador, Dino Alfieri, saw Ribbentrop, who was caustic about the Italian problems, and then Hitler, who chastized the Italians for their whole Greek venture. Then he said he would send as many transport planes to Albania as the fields would hold, to extricate the Italian troops from disaster. He demanded a meeting with Mussolini.

On December 9 General O'Connor launched an assault on the Italians with two divisions of well-trained troops. On the first day they captured ten thousand Italian prisoners, and in three days, they wrecked five of the seven Italian divisions on the front. Fourteen thousand prisoners were taken on the third day. By December 17, the British had taken Sollum and Fort Capuzzo, and the Italians had retired to the fortress of Bardia. Tobruk fell on January 7, and by that time the British had captured 113,000 prisoners, and Graziani was talking of retreating to Tripoli.

In the two weeks that followed, it became apparent in Rome and Berlin that the Italian army in Africa had collapsed. The Greeks stopped their assault in Albania to regroup, and Hitler promised military aid to Mussolini. But the price was high. The Italians would have to send millions of workers to Germany to help produce the military supplies for the Italian army.

Thus Mussolini's dream of the parallel war, with Italy fighting and winning in the Mediterranean as a full partner of Germany, came to a sudden and ignoble end. From now on, as the year 1941 began, Italy would be a very junior partner in the Axis. It was a bitter pill for Mussolini to swallow but there was no recourse but disaster.

PART V

Decline

The fait accompli that Mussolini presented to Hitler at their October 1940 meeting at Florence did not seem to bother Hitler at the moment, but it had the most far-reaching effects on the Axis war effort for the months to come. Hitler suspected that the Italian campaign in Greece was bound for disaster. It was launched at the wrong time of the year, and the German generals did not have much confidence in their Italian counterparts. So Hitler almost immediately began to make optional plans to stave off an Axis defeat in Greece. He brought Hungary and Romania into the Tripartite Pact so that his troops could cross their territory to attack Greece. He strengthened his buildup of troops in Romania. He began to work on Bulgaria to join the pact. He started the diplomatic work to get Yugoslavia to join, for he sensed from the outset that the Italian attack would give the British the chance they had been waiting for, to put air bases in Greece. And British air bases in Greece threatened the Ploesti oil fields, something Hitler could not abide, particularly with his Operation Barbarossa, the invasion of Russia, coming up.

Mussolini had really created a major problem, which would be solved only if he won a lightning victory in Greece. But he did not. And thus he changed the whole war. And as the war changed, Mussolini's relationship to Hitler changed abruptly.∽

CHAPTER 20

Mediterranean Nightmare

In early January 1941 Mussolini waited for good news from Greece. But it did not come. Instead came the word that the Italians had been routed and were surrounded at the ports of Durazzo and Valona. The Italians began to take heavy casualties, and before the end they would have twenty thousand men killed, forty thousand wounded, twenty-six thousand captured, and eighteen thousand victims of frostbite. At home Italians were singing a new ditty, altogether illegal, but no one seemed to care:

> Oh, what a surprise for the Duce, the Duce,
> He can't put it over the Greeks.
> Oh what a surprise for the Duce, they do say,
> He's had no spaghetti for weeks.

On January 1 Mussolini received a long letter from Hitler wishing him a happy new year and telling him to buck up, because the fortunes of war ebbed and flowed. It did not sound like a relegation of Mussolini to a second-rate position. One of the oddities of the relationship between Hitler and Mussolini was Hitler's loyalty to the man from whom he had learned the secrets of totalitarianism. In the fall of 1940 when Ciano and Hitler had met at Vienna, Hitler gave Ciano a sealed letter to Mussolini and although the content was critical, Hitler observed, "From this city of Vienna on the day of the *Anschluss*, I sent Mussolini a telegram to assure him that I would never forget his help. I confirm it today, and I am at his side with all my strength." And as Hitler said this, he had tears in his eyes. What this new letter said, after criticizing Mussolini for getting the Axis into a mess, was that Hitler was going to get him out of it by sending military supplies and men to fight in Africa. So no matter what had happened, the Axis brotherhood was still intact.

But in spite of the close personal relationship between Hitler and Mussolini, 1941 brought a complete change in the relationship of Italy to Germany. It was obvious that it had been triggered by Mussolini's ill-considered invasion of Greece.

∽

The year opened with a flood of economic experts from Germany descending on Rome and fanning out throughout the Italian peninsula. They began to interfere in every aspect of Italian life. They were joined by German military experts, who arrived to prepare the way for dispatch of air and armored units to fight in Africa. The Germans obviously believed that they would ultimately have to take command in Italy to save the day. So despite the letter that indicated Hitler's continued personal regard for Il Duce, Mussolini had become his captive, and it was a relationship that would not change. But as captive, Mussolini served as well as he was able. For example, Hitler wanted an attempt made to persuade Franco to bring Spain into the war. Mussolini went to Bordighera to meet Franco, presented all the arguments, and got nowhere. Franco would occupy Gibraltar if the Axis powers would capture Suez first. And that was the end of Axis efforts to enlist Franco Spain.

In Albania and Africa the war continued to go badly. On January 11, Hitler made the first move to take a hand by establishing the Afrika Korps. Two armored divisions under General Erwin Rommel, who had distinguished himself in the French campaign, would go to Africa to support the Italians there. Before they could arrive, Benghazi fell to the British and the whole of Cyrenaica fell into British hands. Further south, the Italian Empire was crumbling. Italian Somaliland was lost, and Eritrea, and soon Ethiopia would fall, and Emperor Haile Selassie would return to his capital.

The decision of Hitler to actively enter the war in the Mediterranean was greeted by the Italian government with relief, although by and large the Italians did not like the Germans or their interference. The American embassy reported to Washington that the widespread nervousness and confusion of thought resulting from the military defeats in Albania and Africa abated somewhat with the knowledge that the Germans were supplying air power in the Mediterranean and would soon bring troops.

In the first week of 1941 Bardia fell to the British. In the fourth week Tobruk fell. That week Ciani handed a letter to Mussolini that explained a great deal about his armies in Africa and Greece. It was from a Professor Faccini of Leghorn, whose eighteen-year-old son was mobilized in January and sent to Albania as a soldier the same day. He had absolutely no training and had never seen a firearm and did not know how to use one.

But the next month, the Axis fortunes in Africa improved, through a combination of circumstances mostly resulting from the Italian invasion of Greece. General Rommel arrived in Rome and, after a few days, went to Africa where he awaited the 15th Panzer Division and the 29th Light Division.

As soon as his troops began to arrive, Rommel was ready for action, and his forces first met the British on February 20, near El Agheila. Although Rommel was ordered to do nothing but fight a defensive battle, he ignored these orders and prepared to attack, because he sensed that the British momentum had been lost.

∽

And so it had, because early in February 1941, Britain had decided that Greece must be assisted in its fight against the Axis. Hitler had very quietly begun to set the stage for his attack on Russia late in 1940. To protect his stake in the Balkans, and live up to the agreement with Italy, he made arrangements to pass through Bulgaria. The Bulgars signed the Tripartite Pact, which linked their fortunes to the Axis. Now the Axis had the alliance of Bulgaria, Hungary, and Romania, which served to protect Hitler's southern flank as he attacked Russia. All that was needed was the immobilization of Yugoslavia and Greece. Regent Paul signed the Tripartite Pact too, pledging Yugoslavia to the Axis on March 26. But Hitler had been forced into movement too soon here, for much of the population was pro-British, and Regent Paul was much disliked. As soon as the signing became known the Yugoslavs rebelled, overthrew the government of Regent Paul, and declared young Peter to be king and ruler. Hitler was enraged by this unexpected act that threw his plans off, and he vowed that he would destroy Yugoslavia.

Besides this, the British, at the insistence of Prime Minister Churchill, had been building up the Greek forces to help them in their battle against Italy. They were warned by their military leaders and diplomats that if they continued, they would risk an attack by the Germans, who had many divisions in Romania, Hungary, and Bulgaria in preparation for the attack on Russia. The Greeks knew that the Germans might attack them if they accepted a great deal of British aid, but the pressure from Mussolini in the last months of 1940 had persuaded Prime Minister Metaxas to accept British air bases and British troops. The only way the British could provide this help was by taking the men from the British contingent in Africa, and in February Churchill insisted on sending so many troops out from North Africa that Generals Wavell and O'Connor had to suspend their assault on the Italians just as they were on the brink of victory, of capturing most of Mussolini's army and eliminating the Italian presence from Africa.

The British agreed to send one hundred thousand troops to Greece, and these also must come from Africa. As soon as Hitler realized what the British were up to, he decided that he would have to make a major thrust. To do that, he postponed the date for his invasion of the Soviet Union until June 21. Hitler then threw his resources into destroying Yugoslavia for its perfidy to him and driving the British out of Greece. He had not wanted to invade Greece, but the British threat was too great to his coming Russian campaign. Mussolini had argued that he could handle Greece with his new offensive planned for March, so Hitler had at first waited. Mussolini himself went to Albania to supervise the battle and twelve new divisions were thrown in. But the result was far from satisfactory and by March 16, the offensive was called off. Hitler then decided to act, to destroy Yugoslavia, and push the British out of Greece; on April 6, the German attack began.

Meanwhile, by moving the best British forces out of Africa, Churchill had so weakened the force there that Rommel, with his combination of Italian and German troops, could go on the offensive. When he arrived in North Africa in February, he saw a beaten army. But he sensed that the British force had been seriously weakened and he moved later in March. His success was spectacular. The British abandoned Mersa Brega, and the Germans and Italians began the reconquest of Cyrenaica. Rommel swiftly learned the strengths and weaknesses of his Italian troops. In combination with German leadership, they could be superb, but because of the failure of the Italian high command to instill in them a fighting spirit and adequate understanding of modern weapons, they were terrorized by tanks and were likely to panic and flee in the face of a sudden tank attack.

∽

On April 6, 1941, the Germans struck Yugoslavia and Greece, and in a lightning campaign, they thoroughly defeated the combined Greek and British forces. On April 26, the British troops were evacuated to Crete. But in May the Germans attacked Crete, and in another lightning campaign they captured that island. The surviving British forces moved back to North Africa, early in June. That summer Rommel continued to advance, until he reached El Alamein, the key to the Nile delta. If he could make one more push, he would capture Cairo. But there he was stopped, mostly by lack of fuel and ammunition.

By that time Hitler's invasion of Russia had begun, and Mussolini had been inveigled by his own pride into sending an Italian army to fight with the Germans, alongside the Romanians, Hungarians, and Slovaks. Once again it was a matter of his concern lest he be left out of the victory celebrations and the booty. On August 25, Hitler invited Mussolini to Rastenburg, his eastern front headquarters, an occasion on which Mussolini sought to strengthen his force in Russia. Hitler refused more troops because of the difficulties of logistics, since their weaponry was different. They talked about the war in Africa, and Hitler had to say he could do nothing there until Russia had been taken care of.

In the West, America and Britain had just issued their Atlantic Charter, which pledged the democracies to fight for the freedom of captive peoples and the right of self-determination of all peoples everywhere (which, unfortunately, after the war turned out to be a bit of war rhetoric but at the time was very effective).

Mussolini, who had an excellent sense of public relations, proposed a European New Order, in which the Axis would wipe out bolshevism and establish peaceful collaboration with European nations. Otto Dietrich, Hitler's press chief, welcomed the idea, but Ribbentrop did not like it, probably because he had not thought of it himself. He undertook to scuttle the plan, which was supposed to be announced as soon as Mussolini reached Italy. When he was at Klagenfurt, just a few miles away from Italy, he learned that Ribbentrop had stopped the communiqué. He was furious. He refused to discuss the matter with the Germans in his entourage, and he said the train would stop and the journey would not be resumed until the communiqué was issued as drafted. Hitler was told, and he overruled Ribbentrop. There were messages in that altercation for Mussolini. When he stood up to Hitler, he usually got his way. And it was obvious here, as it had been to Count Ciano for a long time, that many of Italy's difficulties with the Germans did not derive from Hitler but from the authoritarian egotist Ribbentrop. Unfortunately, the messages were not perceived.

The confusion and the unhappiness of Italians about the war continued and grew. Students rioted in several cities when they were called up by the military a few weeks before the end of term. Their reason was the refusal of the authorities to grant them their credit for courses taken even though they would be unable to take the final examinations. But much more important was the discovery of a band of armed anti-Fascists just outside Rome. Carabinieri went to the area to investigate and were fired upon by machine guns. Several carabinieri were killed. When the others returned, soldiers were sent and two groups were captured, one of seventy people and one of thirty. The anti-Fascist movement had begun to feed on the unhappiness of most of the people with the war. In October 1941 the American embassy quoted Vatican sources to say that 70 percent of the Italians were now opposed to fascism. The loyal were the Blackshirts, the officials, and others whose position depended on their loyalty.

"The regime is blamed," the report said, "basically for having taken the country into war and specifically for political ineptitude in launching the Greek and Libyan campaigns. One penetrating comment puts it thus: 'The people feel that against their own better judgment they were led by Il Duce and the party leaders to believe that fascism had forged them into a race of warriors; now they knew they never were nor will be.'

"There is widespread feeling that Italy would be better off if England won the war."

Later in October Ambassador Phillips referred to unrest bordering on revolutionary ferment in Italy. He reported on the rise of unrelated anti-Fascist organizations among university students, in the armed services, and among workers. The people were sick of the war. But then on December 3 came an event that indicated the war was going to be very long. The Japanese ambassador called at the Palazzo Venezia and told Mussolini that Japanese negotiations with the Americans were about to be broken off and that war was imminent. The Japanese government wished to invoke the Tripartite Pact and have Italy declare war on the United States as soon as the break occurred, as well as sign an agreement not to conclude peace separately with the United States or with Britain. Then war came on December 7, 1941. Mussolini greeted it with a seemingly light heart and began speaking of a long war—he who only months before had declared that Italy could not stand a long war.

The answer of the Italian people to Mussolini was a further breakdown of civilian morale. In December, the chief of the carabinieri conducted a study and reported to Mussolini that the country had lost faith in the Fascist party, which was no longer seen as an important element in national life. Even Mussolini's son-in-law, Count Ciano, began to speak disparagingly of Il Duce. Here, however, the attitude was largely because of Mussolini's open infatuation with Clara Petacci, which now seemed to influence a great deal of his life. He seemed to live in a dream world most of the time.

In Trieste, with great publicity, the government conducted a mass trial for seventy persons, mostly of Yugoslav descent, on charges of irredentism and terrorism. It was held in the open—which trials by the Special Tribunals almost never were—obviously a method chosen to warn the general public; the concentration was on intellectuals and students. The testimony was carried by all the Italian newspapers. As if more evidence were needed Virginio Gayda, the leading fascist newspaper columnist, seized upon an American newspaper report of the trial to deny the obvious that it was all intended to intimidate the Italian people.

Concern was being shown by the government about the increased anti-German feeling since thousands of German troops had been pouring into the country. It was known that the Germans had taken control of the Italian air force, and the former chief of staff had been fired for objecting to it. The people of Sicily, where most of the German air units were sent, found the Germans intolerable, and most of them refused to have anything to do with them. The American embassy reported that most of the people were longing for a British landing on Sicily.

To counter this, Mussolini made a tour of the provinces to rally the people. His appearances aroused the usual enthusiasm among the crowds, for he really was a spellbinder as an orator, but when he returned to Rome after the tour he said he had accomplished nothing. He recognized that he had created a monster in his personal government and that there was nothing he could do about its disintegration now.

"I have no longer any doubt in regard to the lack of discipline sabotage and passive resistance all along the line. The regime is exhausting itself, wearing itself out, and literally consuming scores of comrades in the party organizations and the ministries, and we are almost back where we were originally," he told the party directorate.

The Germans in Italy reported home about the bad state of Italian morale, and at the end of January 1942, Hermann Goering arrived for a visit to try to talk up the war and convince Mussolini and the others that victory was in sight. But Goering was now fat and greedy, wearing a monstrous sable coat, which reminded Ciano of the sort that motorists wore in 1906, and prattling about his jewels and his art collection. So the Goering visit accomplished nothing.

∽

German control of the Italian war effort brought an agreement that Malta would have to be captured. Hitler was finally convinced of this when Mussolini told him that about 60 percent of the supplies and reinforcements sent for Rommel in North Africa had gone to the bottom of the sea, the convoys attacked by elements of the British fleet or the air force based at Malta. Rommel had been pressing for such action for months. Hitler allocated the German 1st Parachute Division for the task and it was training at Viterbo. The operation's code name was Hercules, and it was scheduled for July during the full moon.

In the meantime General Rommel had survived the anger of the high command over his success in North Africa. General Jodl had told him to conduct a defensive war, which took little toll of supply, but Rommel had gone on the attack with spectacular success that still embarrassed the high command because of the cost. Jodl sent General Paulus to Africa on a survey. Paulus came back to recommend that Rommel be relieved, but it was so obvious that Paulus wanted Rommel's job that nothing was done. Finally, Rommel had ceased his attack at the end of the year as demanded. But he was now ready to go again, even though short of supplies because of the failure of the German and Italian air forces to protect the convoys.

On May 26, 1942, Rommel attacked again. Again with a shortage of supplies, he managed to keep going by capturing British supplies until he was able to report on June 17 that he had won the battle and was besieging Tobruk. Four days later he reported the capture of Tobruk, thirty-three thousand British and British Empire prisoners, ten thousand cubic meters of gasoline, and supplies for thirty thousand men for three months.

At this point Hitler made a major error. He shelved the Hercules project to capture Malta and advised Mussolini to press Rommel to keep up the offensive in Egypt until the British Eighth Army was destroyed, which he indicated would happen very soon. Thus, he backed off from the one effort that probably would have given North Africa to the Axis in that summer of 1942. Everything was staked by the Axis, against Rommel's wishes and against the advice of the Italian high command, on a swift victory in Egypt. Malta remained the principal threat to Axis convoys and kept Rommel from ever achieving a solid basis of supply, and so he was deprived by Hitler, with Mussolini's acceptance, of the victory.

On June 29, General Auchinleck, fighting a rearguard action, managed to stop Rommel at El Alamein. Rommel was running out of the supplies he had captured, and because of the failure to take Malta, the aircraft from that base were steadily sinking the Italian ships carrying oil, ammunition, and tanks to Rommel's forces. He had shot his bolt. The opportunity vanished in the resupply and strengthening of the British front in Egypt.

For three weeks, Mussolini remained in Libya, waiting for the word of victory, but finally he accepted the inevitable: Rommel was stymied, and he went to Greece, where he complained to Hitler about the harsh German occupation that was brewing rebellion on every side. Hitler was now so preoccupied with his difficulties in Russia that he paid no attention to Mussolini's complaints. German officers were behaving most uncivilly to their Italian counterparts. The occupation was supposed to be an Italian affair but the Germans paid no attention to the Italian civil administrators.

So in the fourth week of July, Mussolini returned to Rome a sick man. His case was diagnosed variously, and he was finally treated for ulcers and dysentery. He lost more than forty pounds. Apparently the underlying cause of all of it was anxiety and frustration, for over the past year, Mussolini's life had changed completely. He was no longer the master of Italy but a vassal to Hitler.

On August 30, 1942, against all advice and the state of his supply, Rommel again tried to renew the assault but was thrown back by the now strengthened British forces. Never again would he go on the offensive in Africa.

Conditions in Italy began to deteriorate. Food was in short supply and black markets sprang up everywhere. American reporting on Italy, of course, stopped with the declaration of war, but American diplomats in Switzerland, although their reports were more judgmental than informative, thought they were keeping track of Italy.

"The lower, classes, too ignorant to understand the situation, suffer, grumble, but follow along, both because of innate cowardice and also because they believe the regime is sincere in its claim that it has the welfare of the people at heart and is honestly trying to raise wages and endeavoring to reduce the cost of living."

For all practical purposes, the foreign reports of what was happening in Italy were too late and too opinionated to be of much use.

By autumn, Italy and Mussolini had nearly given up hope of victory in Africa. The highly touted attack by General Montgomery at El Alamein was to be expected, because the British had been building their forces steadily while Rommel could not even get gasoline across the Mediterranean to run his tanks. It was evident to him and to the Italian generals that it was time to withdraw from Africa while the troops could still be gotten away. But Hitler stopped the move. He had an obsession. "Where the boot of a German soldier has trod, there will be no retreat," he said, and he began sacrificing thousands of troops in Russia and Africa on the altar of this fixation. The whole war was approaching the turning point at Stalingrad. Hitler had failed to capture that city, despite overwhelming power exerted against it. And November 1942 brought two major developments that promised disaster for the Axis. The Americans and British landed in French North Africa, and the Russians began a major offensive against Stalingrad.

By the end of 1942, the Italian people were thoroughly sick of the war and all they wanted was for it to end. Heavy air raids in October wrecked much of the Fiat plant at Turin and a nearby aircraft factory, and a direct hit wrecked the railway station. A freight car loaded with explosives exploded and added considerably to the damage.

Genoa had been harder hit than Turin, with a particularly stunning disaster in the tunnel air-raid shelter of the Galleria delle Grazie, where hundreds of people had collected during the air raids. Canisters full of tar had been placed along the quayside to serve as a smoke screen. They were fired up and the fumes blew into the shelter, suffocating nearly a thousand people.

A report from Italy to the *Manchester Guardian* said the Fascists had tried to make the air raids a point of anti-British propaganda, which was running hot then. In the schools the British were depicted as a nation of heavy drinkers and haughty in demeanor. Schoolchildren were given little badges—*Dio maledica l'Inglaterra,* God Curse England—but most families did not want the children to wear them, because they suspected the badges came from Germany.

Bread was rationed in Italy, with the ration for a day being less than the usual consumption for one meal. The crops of the peasants were sometimes seized. Officials examined parcels to see if people were smuggling food, and of course they were, because the black markets proliferated all over the country. A kilogram of beans cost thirty lire, the equivalent of a day's earnings for a skilled worker. Shoes were made of processed cardboard and lasted about three months. A sweater cost five hundred lire, the price of a new suit before the war. Gas for cooking in the cities was only available five hours a day.

Italians no longer listened to Italian radio for the war news, because it was totally unreliable. They did not think much of the BBC either, so they mostly listened to rumors and waited for the bitter end.

CHAPTER 21

The End in Africa

Anti-German feeling was running so high in the fall of 1942 in Italy that when an Italian who had married a Swiss woman and gone to live in Switzerland came back with his wife for a visit, they encountered a problem. Sitting in a restaurant in Milan they began talking in Swiss German. An Italian came up to their table and warned: "This is Italy. No German is to be spoken in this restaurant." Only when they identified themselves as Swiss was a crisis averted.

And when a pair of visitors to Italy returned to Switzerland that autumn, they reported:

"Italy is still only a German province. Mussolini is nothing else than a subaltern of Hitler. Only the presence of the Nazis and the German troops protect Mussolini from the disillusionment of the people. Were the Germans to withdraw today, Mussolini would be overthrown tomorrow."

This report was made before the American landings in Algiers and Morocco that completely shocked the Axis partners.

The crisis began at 5:30 on the morning of November 7, 1942. As Mussolini later wrote:

In Italy the moral repercussions of the American landing in Algiers were immediate and profound. Every enemy of fascism promptly reared his head; the first of the traitors, minor figures, even though some were National councillors, emerged from the shadows. The country began to feel the strain. As long as only the English were in the Mediterranean, Italy, with Germany's help, could hold firm and resist them, though at the cost of ever greater sacrifice, but the appearance of America disturbed the weaker spirits and increased by many millions the already numerous band of listeners to enemy radio.

A few hours after the landings, Ribbentrop telephoned Mussolini again to demand in Hitler's name that he or Ciano come to Munich for an emergency meeting to plan strategy. Mussolini was sick (the bad times had brought back his ulcers), so he sent Ciano to do the job. By the time Ciano arrived, Hitler had already decided what he was going to do, and without the influence of Mussolini, which might have made a difference, there was no arguing.

Italy would occupy Corsica and a small portion of France to the Rhone River valley, and Germany would occupy the rest of France. Hitler said the step was necessary to keep the French from joining the Allies. He also planned to seize the French fleet at Toulon, but when he tried, the French scuttled their entire fleet—ten capital ships, twenty-nine destroyers, sixteen submarines, and eighteen other vessels.

Hardly had these changes been accomplished than Hitler felt the need of another conference, but again Mussolini was sick and sent Ciano. He told Ciano to make an attempt to get Hitler to leave Russia. But on December 18 when Ciano arrived, Hitler spurned this advice. He was completely wrapped up in the struggle for Stalingrad, which the Germans were losing. They also soon would lose their entire Sixth Army and never again be able to make a major offensive in the East. But Hitler did not speak of this; he spoke of victory in the East.

By the time Ciano returned from Germany, defeat was in the air of Rome. The Allies were attacking Italian cities and towns from the air, and the war weariness of the people was obvious to all. Opposition was more or less public, and anti-Fascist leaflets, which had been stringently searched out in the past, were found everywhere.

A German observer noted, "Italy as an ally stands and falls militarily with the fate of North Africa and the political future of the Axis is and remains bound up with the life of Il Duce. If Germany wishes to think of the alliance beyond the lifetime of the Duce, then a weighty and most delicate problem arises." And that problem was simply, to whom should the Germans turn?

The Italians were looking at the future, too, but from a different angle. In the military and even in the Fascist party, movements were afoot to unseat Mussolini and he knew it very well.

All the troubles made his ulcers worse. The war news did not help. But in spite of his illness, Mussolini seemed to have a special antennae that recognized threats to his survival, and just now two cabals were active in plotting to unseat him. One was led by Giuseppe Bottai, one of the original Fascist leaders and a member of the cabinet, and the other was led by Roberto Farinacci, the tough right wing party leader. On January 8, 1943, Ciano lunched with them. They discussed the attempts of General Cavallero to unseat Mussolini. All this was brought to Mussolini's attention, but at the moment he did nothing but telephone Ciano, to let him know that Il Duce knew what was going on.

With his government near collapse, Mussolini was sustained by one factor: He still had the confidence of the King, who said that if Mussolini were to disappear complete chaos would follow. As noted, Hitler felt the same; he had said earlier that all that held Italy to the alliance was Il Duce.

Mussolini held a cabinet meeting on January 23, 1943. The discussion was grim. Tripoli had just been evacuated. Stalingrad was falling to the Russians and the German Sixth Army was trapped. Some ninety thousand survivors of the siege would surrender in a few days. Advisors were talking about alarming reports from Hungary and Romania and telling Mussolini it was time to extricate Italy from the iron embrace of the Germans. But Mussolini was loyal to his alliance. He knew, better than the others, that there was no place for him to go. He would have to stand or fall with Hitler.

An allied démarche at this point most likely would have been successful and would have pulled Italy out of the war, under conditions that the Germans would not have been able to take over the country. But the Allies lacked the imagination to follow their own diplomatic reports. Further, they were entrapped by their own rash action in declaring that they would settle for nothing less than "unconditional surrender" from any of the Axis powers. So although the officials of the U.S. State Department saw that Italy was ripe for action, there was nothing they could do but suggest that the official Allied propaganda line stress a promise that Italy would survive as a nation after the war.

So Mussolini settled on a course of action: He would blame the military leaders for the defeat in Africa and he would get rid of the men around him that he no longer trusted.

On January 31, 1943, Mussolini informed the King that he had replaced General Cavallero as chief of staff with General Vittorio Ambrosio. Five days later he called Foreign Minister Ciano into his office and fired him but gave him the sop of the embassy to the Vatican. That day he made many other changes, and the new government emerged with Mussolini holding the foreign affairs portfolio himself. Bottai was dismissed from the Ministry of Education and Grandi from the Ministry of Justice. Half a dozen other ministers were fired. The ones Mussolini really wanted to get at were Ciano, Bottai, Grandi, and Buffarini-Guidi, the Minister of the Interior, who controlled the police.

Mussolini's action strengthened his ties with the Germans, who had taken particular offense at Grandi. But now, a new problem came into the picture. The Italians were trying to put down unrest in Yugoslavia, and they regarded Tito as their basic enemy; they wanted to cooperate with Colonel Mihailovich and his Chetniks. The Germans, however, insisted on the impartial liquidation of all the partisans. Hitler regarded this matter as so important, expecting an allied landing soon in the Balkans, that he sent Ribbentrop armed with a sixty-page letter that was to form the basis of discussion, to come to a meeting of the minds with Mussolini about policy in Yugoslavia. So it was apparent that although the Germans no longer regarded their Italian ally as a trustworthy military supporter, Hitler continued to respect Mussolini's judgment, even when he disagreed and would not follow it, as was the case with Mussolini's advocacy of making a peace with Russia.

The meetings were not very successful, the Italians resisting the German proposal to wipe out all the partisans. As Mussolini observed, fighting partisans was a futile and nonproductive activity. Ribbentrop came away from the meeting with the feeling that the Germans were losing control of events in Italy, and when he indicated this to Hitler, the führer again asked for a meeting with Mussolini.

Mussolini then proposed a stroke that should deal a serious blow to the Allies. It would be to seize Gibraltar and hold Tunisia. But to do this, Hitler would have to have many troops, and the only place they could come from was the Russian front. Therefore, said Mussolini, it was all the more necessary that Hitler conclude a peace with Stalin and free the Axis to fight the West.

On April 6, Mussolini went to Salzburg to meet Hitler again. In the conference at Klessheim, again Il Duce stressed the need to get out of the trap in Russia and bring forces west to attack Gibraltar. It was becoming apparent that the war aims of the two partners were diverging rapidly. The Italians wanted concentration of forces in the Mediterranean. The Germans were determined to smash Russia, although the tide was all running the other way. They did not like Mussolini's plan to bring Hungary and Romania into prominence in the New Order. The Germans suspected that the Italians, and the Hungarians and the Romanians, might try to seek a separate peace. They realized that the Italian public support for the war was diminishing daily.

The Klessheim meeting was a tonic for Mussolini as all his meetings with Hitler seemed to be. He arrived at Klessheim sick and dispirited. And when he left, according to Dr. Goebbels, who was pleasantly surprised at the change, "he was in high fettle and ready for anything." Goebbels credited Hitler for showing Mussolini that their fates were inextricably linked, but there is more evidence that Il Duce had realized this a long time before.

⌒

Mussolini returned in mid-April 1943 to an Italy that was becoming ever more critical of his leadership; General Ambrosio was indicating his dislike of Mussolini's policies. What he and others wanted was for Mussolini to disengage from Hitler.

In mid-April the Axis forces in Tunisia reached Enfidaville, where they would make their last stand. On April 18, an enormous convoy of one hundred transport aircraft flew from Sicily to carry supplies to the beleaguered Axis troops, but half of them were shot down by the allied air forces. The next day the Luftwaffe and the Italian air force tried again, with the same result.

The troops were behaving very well. Montgomery launched an attack on the Enfidaville position, but it was repulsed with heavy losses. But by April 22, the British and Americans were attacking various hill positions, and slowly they were making progress. On April 22, the Italian and German air forces tried again to supply the troops and again lost thirty transports. The battle was furious and with reinforcements the Axis might have held out for some time longer. But Hitler's mind was on the eastern front, and he had no reserves and no aircraft to spare any more for the Mediterranean. So on May 12, German General von Arnim surrendered the German forces. Mussolini promoted General Messe to field marshal, a trick he had learned from Hitler, to prevent him from surrendering the Italian forces, but this ploy was no more effective than it had been for Hitler with General Paulus at Stalingrad. There came a time when to hold out was simply to give up the troops for massacre, and Field Marshal Messe was not ready to do that, so the Italian army also surrendered on May 13. The Axis then lost 250,000 troops to surrender, troops who could have been brought back to the mainland three or four months earlier.

In Yugoslavia the Germans began a campaign against the partisans, sending in 120,000 troops to try to clear the mountains of Mihailovich and Tito partisans. The Italians wanted no part of the operation and were not asked to participate.

The discontent had grown worse at the end of April when Mussolini called for more air support from the Luftwaffe to save Tunisia, and Hitler turned a deaf ear. The reason for the deaf ear was that Hitler was fully occupied on the eastern front. But as Rommel had observed months earlier, Tunisia was a lost cause, and the Axis would have been better to get out when they could have saved their armies.

∽

Mussolini did his best to prop up the home front. He fired Carmine Senise, the chief of police, replacing him with an old Fascist and friend of Balbo's, Renzo Chierici. On May 3, 1943, Mussolini made a major speech from his balcony at the Palazzo Venezia, as usual to a spellbound audience.

In response to the cheering, he jutted his jaw and shouted: "I hear vibrating in your voices the proclamation of your old and incorruptible faith. The bloody sacrifices of these hard times will become victory. It is true and it is true that God is just and Italy immortal." The speech was long on rhetoric and short on substance, but what was there to say? It was his last appearance on the Palazzo Venezia balcony.

But a police report contradicted what Mussolini was saying about loyalty. The Communists were making enormous inroads in the industrial section of Italy. People had lost faith: the Fascists had sacrificed the confidence "even of their own followers because of the excessive robberies of the bosses and the patent injustices that have been committed." Even the party faithful had now lost faith in Mussolini's ability to pull a rabbit out of the hat.

For Hitler, the end of the war in Africa signaled a change in approach. He had been told by his generals that the Italian army was finished, exhausted by the fighting in Greece, Russia, and Africa. The troops in Italy proper were in no condition to withstand the allied landings that were now expected. Hitler must make plans to take over the defense of Italy himself and thus keep the Allies from coming up from the south to challenge his Fortress Europe. Hitler trusted Mussolini, but he was the only one in Italy that Hitler did trust. As the Axis was falling apart in Tunisia, Hitler offered Mussolini five divisions for the defense of Italy and was rejected. Divisions meant nothing, said Mussolini. What he needed was air power.

On May 12, Admiral Dönitz, now commander of the German navy, came to Rome in Hitler's behalf. Dönitz was impressed with Mussolini's attitude, which Dönitz found to be optimistic, composed, frank, and amicable. Dönitz properly assessed the situation: Mussolini had refused the five divisions, Dönitz reported, because he wanted to remain master in his own house.

Hitler said nothing to Mussolini, but he began to make contingency plans to occupy Italy, and he demanded that Italy take part in the Yugoslavia operations. Mussolini replied evasively but agreed to live up to the agreements they had made about joint operations to protect the communications lines in the Balkans.

All this new tension had a very bad effect on Mussolini; his ulcers flared up and he was very sick for several weeks in May and June. Meanwhile the King was beginning some negotiations of his own, aimed at detaching Italy from the Axis. He quietly called in some of the old prefascist political leaders. They advocated the replacement of Mussolini by a military government to keep order. But the King did not like the idea and decided not to intervene unless he had some constitutional reason to do so. That would mean a vote in the Chamber of Deputies or the Grand Council of Fascists.

In May it became apparent, although the Allies tried several plans of disinformation, that the invasion of Sicily was going to come soon. The fortified island of Pantelleria nearby had been under air attack for some time and was running out of water and food. The commander of the island asked permission from Mussolini to surrender and the permission was granted on June 1. Two days later the island of Lampedusa fell.

On July 9, 1943, the Allies landed on Sicily. The Italian regular troops fought bravely, but their image was tarnished by the coastal battalions that manned the shore defenses. Most of these units surrendered without picking up their weapons.

The Italian and German commanders planned and executed a very effective withdrawal from Sicily, bringing away all their fighting troops, but Hitler was furious that the island was lost. Any sacrifice of any territory infuriated him, and when Sicily fell, he sent a message to Mussolini that was the most insulting he had ever ventured. If the Italians did not intend to fight, he said, he would send no further troops to Italy. Mussolini did not say so, but he did not want any more Germans in Italy nor did any other Italians. What everyone but Mussolini wanted was disengagement from Hitler and an accommodation with the Allies. The problem with that, as the Allies would soon learn, was that Winston Churchill and President Roosevelt had locked out any chance of a negotiated peace with their demand for unconditional surrender.

On July 16, a group of old Fascist leaders presented themselves to Mussolini and asked that he convene the Fascist Grand Council in this time of crisis, so that all the old leaders could participate in affairs. Mussolini had been managing one-man rule for too long. Facing such determination, Mussolini yielded and agreed to convene the council in the second half of July.

∽

At Rastenburg on the eastern front, Hitler was forced to take some time from his manipulation of his forces against the Russians to consider the Italian problem. The question was, how much influence did Mussolini still have, and could he make the Italians fight for their country? If so, the problem was relatively simple. Hitler would send troops, supplies, and aircraft to defend Italy, for it was in the German interest to delay the allied advance from the south as long as possible. Did Hitler still have hopes of winning the war? Not really, but this was a matter that was not discussed. What was discussed was the need and the possible means for delaying the Allies east and west. The army high command wanted to take over Italy, but Hitler was wiser than they, and he realized the Germans would have to withdraw to a short line in the north, and then the whole Balkan issue would be opened again.

So through the German ambassador to Rome, Hitler sought another meeting with Mussolini. It was arranged for July 19 in a villa at Feltre near Venice. The men around Mussolini now agreed that Italy was at the end of her string and must disengage from the war. If Mussolini would do that with Hitler and successfully, all right. If not, the others decided, he must go and be replaced. The conspiracy of Italian leaders had been building for weeks. This day, General Ambrosio and the others had decided that if Mussolini did not produce an end to the war, then General Hazon would lead a coup d'état that would greet Mussolini when he returned to Rome, and most of the important generals and public security officials were involved.

Mussolini left Rome by air without seeking any advice from his people, and they had not a clue as to what he was going to do.

On the morning of July 19, General Ambrosio and Counselor Bastianini were met by Ambassador Alfieri, who had flown in from Berlin. They all agreed that Mussolini must make a firm stand to get away from the Germans. However, the Germans also came to the meeting with a plan: All power in Italy must be placed in the hands of Mussolini. What that meant was that the King must be removed from interference, and then German reinforcements would be sent to Italy, and the German high command would control the Axis forces.

Hitler announced that he must return to Germany that afternoon and they had best get down to cases. But for two hours, nothing was said about the important matter of Italy's participation in the war. Mussolini knew better than his associates Hitler's mind, and that to raise the matter of disengagement would infuriate Hitler and bring about an immediate occupation of Italy. There was no point in trying to argue this issue. The Germans would never let them go.

The formal session began in the drawing room of the villa at 11 A.M. Hitler was supported by General Keitel, General Warlimont, General von Rintelen, and General Mackensen. Ribbentrop was not present. Hitler began with one of his two-hour perorations, which was interrupted by word brought to Mussolini of a major allied air raid on Rome—the first. Hitler seemed annoyed that he was interrupted, not realizing that the raid represented allied power and offered the Italians more hope of an escape from his control.

Hitler began his usual statement that he would not yield an inch of territory. He attacked the Italian conduct of the war, and he talked about secret weapons that would turn the war around.

Hitler's combination of promise of victory (which no one believed if they could understand it; there was no translation and most of the Italians did not understand German) and diatribe against the Italians was brought to an end by the call to lunch at 1 P.M.

Mussolini and Hitler lunched alone. Just before they met, General Ambrosio issued a sort of ultimatum to Mussolini to get Italy out of the war in fifteen days. Mussolini replied, "Can you suppose that I have not long been tormented by this problem. My apparent indifference masks an intense agony of spirit. For the sake of argument, suppose we were to make a separate peace. It looks so simple. Are we prepared to obliterate at a single stroke twenty years of fascism? It's so easy to talk about a separate peace. But what would be Hitler's attitude? Can you believe that he would allow us to retain our liberty of action?" And that, of course, was the key to everything.

At lunch Hitler did all the talking as usual. He spoke about the new secret weapons (V-2) which would "raze London to the ground" and about the new submarines (schnorkel) that would turn the U-boat war around. But they never got down to the issue—how to get Italy out of the war. And soon it was time to go and the party broke up. On the train to Treviso, Hitler and Mussolini talked, but only about the aid that Germany would give to Italy.

In another compartment, Keitel and Ambrosio talked, and Keitel said flatly that the Italians could expect no help unless they met the German conditions.

1. The Italian and Germans were each to supply two divisions for a defensive line.
2. The Italians must assure supplies and a defense in Calabria and Apulia.
3. This was total war and all power must be in the hands of the military. In reference to Italy that meant the Italian Seventh Army. The Germans would set up a liaison staff with the Seventh Army.

Then Ambrosio said that all must rest with the Duce, but what was important was adequate air protection. Keitel said brusquely that they would talk about that only after all the German conditions had been met.

At 5 P.M. Hitler and Mussolini said good-bye to each other at the Treviso airfield. After the Germans had left, the Italian party rushed up to Mussolini to find out what had been said. Mussolini assured them that the meeting had been productive.

"This time he promised faithfully to send all the assistance we ask for."

∽

So nothing at all had been decided. Mussolini returned to the city upset by the news of the bombing of Rome. His advisors were also upset for a different reason. General Ambrosio said Mussolini had gone mad. He had not mentioned to Hitler the Italian need to get out of the war.

Mad? That was not the case. Mussolini knew that the Axis was losing the war, but he had staked the future of Italy with Germany, and he knew very well that in an Italy that surrendered to the Allies there would be no place for him. So he had followed the natural course of self-interest.

The generals had an alternative plan. If Mussolini did not comply with the demand that he get Italy out of the war at the Feltre meetings, then they would overthrow his government. General Hazon had been left with instructions of what to do, and it was supposed to be accomplished by the time the party returned to Rome.

The message was sent to Rome to put the alternative plan into effect, but when they got back to Rome they learned that General Hazon had been killed in the air raid, and that nothing had been done.

Nothing.

PART VI

Fall

The collapse of the Axis armies in North Africa had been an enormous shock to the Italian people, but the invasion of Sicily was the final straw; whatever enthusiasm had remained for the war effort vanished overnight. The detested Germans were everywhere, and the major concern of the people was to get them out of Italy and get Italy out of the alliance with Hitler. Mussolini still boasted that he had the people with him, but he had long ago sacrificed their loyalty on the altar of his ambitions. He had now come to the realization that his Italians could not be made into gladiators, but it was much too late. He lived almost completely in a dream world, surrounded by guards and sycophants, who dared not tell him the truth: that he was the most hated man in Italy. Even his Blackshirts resented his one-man rule, and when they contemplated the results—the occupation of part of Italy by the enemy—they, too, turned against him. His most recent shuffling of the government had destroyed what was left of continuity, and now he was almost completely alone.∽

CHAPTER 22

∽

The Night Fascism Died

The Germans wasted no time. A few hours after the arrival of the train that brought the delegates back from Treviso, General von Rintelen appeared at the Palazzo Venezia and demanded the response to General Keitel's three provisos for further German military assistance.

1. The Italians must increase their forces to form a strong defensive line. They would supply two more divisions and the Germans would supply two.
2. Supplies and creation of a powerful defense must be assured in Calabria and Apulia.
3. Southern Italy must be placed under martial law. This was total war and all civil activity must be placed under the command of the Italian Seventh Army. The Germans would set up a liaison staff with the Seventh Army.

Mussolini argued that Hitler had given his word that the Germans would then send the assistance he wanted, mostly in aircraft. General Ambrosio argued that they had no assurance the Germans would do anything, and that this program would put them under the control of the Germans. Mussolini said they had no recourse but to accept. Both men seemed to know that the Italian relationship to Germany had really ended, and that a whole new situation faced them. The German plan actually was no longer to have an alliance, but to use Italy in preparation of a suitable defense line, to keep the enemy as far away as possible from the Third Reich. Toward that end, Hitler preferred to keep the Fascists in power and Mussolini at the head of the state, rather than to step in and declare an occupation of Italy.

On July 21, 1943, Roberto Farinacci, leader of the right wing of the Fascists, called on German Ambassador General Mackensen to report that the Fascist Grand Council had been summoned to meet that week. He gave the picture of a Rome in which Mussolini had been persuaded to introduce the spartan measures that would be necessary to invigorate the Italian war effort. Mackensen reported to Berlin that affairs were moving in the right direction in Rome. The Germans were half-prepared for a crisis in Rome, but this meeting and Mackensen's report of it were comforting enough that they called off their alerts for plans to take over control of Italy.

Several friends and Mussolini's wife Rachele warned him that he was in real danger, but he preferred to believe that he could exercise the old magic on the Fascist Grand Council and the King. But the King was convinced that Italy had to be taken out of the war and had to break off her relationship with Germany, and he had told General Ambrosio that it was time for Mussolini to go.

Dino Grandi prepared a motion that he would submit to the Fascist Grand Council, restoring much that had been destroyed by Mussolini—the cabinet, the Parliament, the corporations, and the assumption by the King of command of the armed forces. He gave a copy of the motion to Carlo Scorza, now one of the men close to Mussolini, and he showed the document to Mussolini, who rejected it forthwith.

One by one the old Fascists were consulted, and they found that they all agreed: Mussolini must give up part of his power, he must take the Council seriously, he must admit others to the government of the country.

Grandi sought and received an audience with Mussolini, who listened to his proposal. The war was lost, said Grandi, and the job now was to transfer the responsibility for it from the people to the regime. The interview was to last fifteen minutes but lasted an hour and a half, during which time Field Marshal Kesselring, who had the next appointment, sat and cooled his heels in a waiting room.

Mussolini seemed to agree with what Grandi had said, that fascism had failed. But then he said, "However, the war is not lost. You would be right and the solution of putting everything into the hands of the King would be acceptable, if the war were lost but in fact it is about to be won, because within a few days the Germans will launch a weapon that will transform the situation."

∽

So Grandi and the old Fascists were working quite openly for the replacement of Il Duce by themselves as a council to run the country. Meanwhile the generals were independently plotting, with the King's approval, to depose and arrest Mussolini.

General Angelo Cerica, the new commander of the carabinieri who had replaced General Hazon, was brought into the plot. By July 24 the plotters were ready to call on Marshal Badoglio and offer him the post of Head of the Government.

The Grand Council was convened at 5 P.M. on July 24, 1943. Before the meeting Rachele made one last effort to save her husband, telling Mussolini he should arrest all those who had been talking about the meeting and what they were going to do. This group of conspirators was very nervous. Grandi had been to confession and left a last letter for his wife in case he was killed. He took two hand-grenades to the meeting with him. When he got to the Palazzo Venezia, he found it was full of militiamen everywhere, and he had the sinking feeling that Mussolini was going to act against the conspirators. Bottai whispered to him, "This is the end."

Just after five o'clock, the chief usher appeared in the chamber carrying Mussolini's briefcase. He was followed by Il Duce, who was attired in the uniform of supreme commander of the Fascist Militia. Scorza called out the usual greeting, "Salute Il Duce!", and all present shouted the reply, "We salute him."

Mussolini looked neither to right nor left, nor did he recognize any of his servitors. He sat down in the embroidered armchair on the raised dais at the head of the table, arranged his papers, and after the roll call of members was ended, he began to speak.

He spoke without passion—almost as if he were a third person— reporting on events. He said the war had become critical, and what had seemed impossible had happened—Italy had been invaded. The enemies of fascism had closed ranks, and they had even suborned some Fascisti, he continued. "At this moment I am certainly the most loathed man in Italy."

He reserved his criticism for the military leaders. He had never wanted supreme command of the military forces, he said. That had resulted from a suggestion by Marshal Badoglio. He had never directed military operations. Only once had he interfered with operations and that had produced a victory. When he fell ill in October 1942, he had thought of giving up the command but had not done so because it seemed like deserting the ship in a storm.

As for aid from Germany, which was under discussion at the moment, he said they must admit that Germany had been very generous with her aid since 1940 and he quoted figures: fifteen hundred antiaircraft guns, and he listed all the raw materials. He did not mention the aircraft and tanks the Italians had requested and not gotten.

Then he turned to the attitude of the people toward the war. Their heart was not in it he knew, but their heart had never been in a war, and he cited the 1914–18 war to prove it.

"This is the moment to tighten the reins, and to assume the necessary responsibility. I shall have no difficulty in replacing men, in turning the screw, in bringing forces to bear not yet engaged, in the name of our country whose personal integrity is today being violated."

In conclusion he turned to Grandi's memorandum. The Council had a choice, he said. They could give it to the King. He could then decide to support Mussolini, or to throw out the regime.

This statement had lasted for about two hours. When he was finished there was silence. Nobody was convinced. The comment was that the speech had been disastrous, but that was not the real issue. The real issue was that these men had already decided that Mussolini must go. What they also had decided, although not all of them knew that, was that fascism had come to an end in Italy.

Marshal De Bono then spoke, defending the military leaders. De Vecchi spoke next, taking issue with him. Then Grandi arose; he said it was not the army but the dictatorship that was responsible for Italy's plight. Italy had been betrayed on the day that it had been cast into the arms of Hitler. Il Duce had plunged them into a destructive war without regard for the feelings of the nation. And then Grandi read his statement calling for the restoration of the organs of the state and transfer of command of the military to the King.

He then added an attack on Mussolini's personal rule, which, he said, had wrecked fascism and brought about the loss of the war. But the Grand Council was as responsible as Mussolini. What was needed now, he said, was to rebuild the nation.

Bottai followed in support of Grandi, and Ciano talked about the Pact of Steel in which Hitler had promised that there would be no war until 1942. "We are not the betrayers but the betrayed," he said.

Farinacci, representing the far right, then followed with his motion to emphasize solidarity with Germany and called on the King to assume command. He demanded the resignation of General Ambrosio, a single Axis high command, and a unified direction for the war. He finished with an attack on Grandi for bringing about this crisis of fascism in the middle of the war.

After another speech in favor of Grandi's motion, Mussolini announced that the party secretary had proposed an adjournment until the next day.

Grandi objected. "The destiny of our country is in our hands," he said. "Let us go on until we vote."

Mussolini hesitated, and then agreed. "As you will," he said.

The speeches went on until nearly midnight when Mussolini called a recess for fifteen minutes and retired to his study. He was followed by Scorza, Galbiati, and Alfieri, who urged him again to persuade Hitler to set Italy free. Buffarini-Guidi urged Mussolini to arrest the whole council. Mussolini made no such move, although he had been advised to do so several times that day.

At the end of the respite, the debate resumed, and got more ragged the longer it lasted. Various plans were offered. Grandi handed Mussolini his resolution with the names of the nineteen signers.

Finally Mussolini called on Scorza to put the matter to a vote. He reminded them that he could have had them all arrested. He knew some of them wanted to get rid of him, he said, but the King was his friend. "Yes, the King is still in favor of me. I have never had friends, but the King is my friend, and I wonder what those of you who oppose me tonight will think tomorrow."

So Grandi's motion was put to a vote. Nineteen voted for it, and seven voted against.

Mussolini sat glowering. Then he spoke.

"You have provoked the crisis of the regime," he said. "The session is closed."

Scorza was about to call for the "Salute to the Duce!" when Mussolini checked him: "No, you are excused," he said and went into his study.

Why had he behaved as he did? Seemingly he was indifferent to the proceedings that endangered him. A few months later he spoke to one of his aides who also had ulcers. He said he was sick that night, having had an attack earlier in the day.

> After my statement, the discussion started. I seemed to be assisting at my own trial. I felt as if I were in the dock and at the same time a spectator. I suffered physical pain from the ulcer, but my brain was very lucid. I distinctly heard Grandi's ruthless indictment, but all my

energy was suddenly drained away. You know that this is one of the results of our ailment. It totally saps all energy while conserving a lucidity which I could describe as completely transparent.

But there was another reason. In all his years of power and his pretensions, he had never failed to be honest with himself. He knew that he had failed at Feltre and that his accusers were right in what they said. And he was tired, and sick, and not inclined to quarrel. He gathered up his papers then. It was three o'clock in the morning, and he went back to the Villa Torlonia with Scorza. No matter what had happened that night, he was at least confident of the King's support.

Rachele met him as he came in and could tell by his face that the night had brought disaster. She questioned whether he had had them all arrested. He said no, but that he would do so. And then after checking to see if there had been any allied air raids, he went to bed, exhausted. "There is nothing more that I can do. They are set on my ruin. I am afraid my orders do not count any more."

∽

He did not realize even then that the Grandi group had been presenting an opposition case to him and were all prepared to be overruled, and perhaps imprisoned for their temerity. Grandi had told the councillors in advance what he was going to do and had even shown Mussolini a copy of his motion. But he had so little confidence in success that he had not told the King, or even caused him to be informed, until the afternoon of the meeting when he sent a copy of the motion to the King just before going to the Council session.

After the Council meeting ended, at four o'clock that morning, Grandi had gone to the Duke of Acquarone, minister of the Royal Household, and informed him of what had occurred. He requested that the facts be brought to the King's knowledge and that the King be told of the opportunity to eliminate the dictatorship and restore the Constitution. But time was important. Otherwise Mussolini might appeal to the Germans for assistance. "Not a minute must be lost," he said.

The Duke of Acquarone agreed to make an immediate report to the King, but he could not promise any action. He asked who Grandi believed should be the premier. He should be a soldier, said Grandi, who had prestige with the people and with the army.

Would Grandi participate in the government? Acquarone asked.

No, he said, he had now performed his ultimate public service and he would not, but he would serve as an intermediary with the Allies to bring the war to an end. Since Grandi had been foreign minister and ambassador to Britain, Acquarone knew that he had more access to the Allies than any other Italian had, so that was not a matter to be taken lightly. Grandi then said that advantage must be taken of the shock value of the move, before the Germans could act, and he urged the King to issue immediately the decrees ending the dictatorship. At the request of the duke, Grandi drafted two decrees, one ending the dictatorship and the other restoring the Chamber of Deputies to power. He recommended Badoglio for the job of prime minister, and then he left the palace. He knew nothing of the real conspiracy that was occurring within the military.

The next day, Sunday, July 25, 1943, dawned sunny and hot. The newspapers said nothing of the events of the night before but were full of the surrender of the Axis forces at Palermo in Sicily.

∽

The conspirators met to consider what Mussolini would now do. Acquarone had informed the King of the meeting with Grandi and had secured the King's signature to the decree abolishing the dictatorship. He joined General Ambrosio at his headquarters, and shortly afterward they took to Marshal Badoglio the signed royal decree appointing him prime minister. The three men then put into operation the plan to arrest Mussolini.

Mussolini was up early that morning and drove to the Palazzo Venezia. Scorza did not appear but telephoned to say that some of the councillors were having second thoughts about their votes. "Too late," said Mussolini. "Too late."

After some consideration of the previous night's meeting, Mussolini then arranged for an audience with the King at five o'clock that afternoon. The King asked that he not come in uniform, which aroused Rachele's suspicions about the King's intention. But Mussolini was not concerned. He spent the day talking with supporters about what should be done and refused to consider arresting the nineteen councillors who had voted against him. At noon, he saw the new Japanese ambassador and gave him as accurate a picture as he could of the war. He said he was still trying to persuade Hitler to bring the war to an end, and he asked Japan's assistance in this project. Then he went home to lunch, stopping off in San Lorenzo to feel the pulse of the people. He got out of his car, distributed some money, chatted a few minutes, and was satisfied that he still had the people with him. General Galbiati asked him how he stood with the King. Mussolini replied:

"I have never done anything without his complete agreement. For more than twenty years I have been to see him once or twice a week. I have consulted him on every matter of state and even private questions. He has always been solidly with me."

It was three o'clock by the time he got back to the Villa Torlonia, late for lunch again.

Meanwhile the conspirators were preparing for his arrest. It was agreed that the arrest should be made by the carabinieri, the most respected military organization in Italy. General Carboni would take over the Rome garrison. All the carabinieri in Rome were ordered to stay in their barracks on the pretext that their new commander intended to make an inspection. Thus, there was a reserve force in case of trouble. Two junior officers were briefed on the arrest.

The plan called for the use of an ambulance and a detachment of fifty carabinieri in a truck. The ambulance and the guards would be parked in the driveway of the Villa Savoia, the King's palace. The Queen objected to the arrest being made on the grounds of the royal residence as an act unworthy of a sovereign. But the King gave his consent.

And so the afternoon drifted by, with people in the parks and squares, at the motion picture houses, and sitting in the cafes drinking and reading the newspapers. The rest of Mussolini's afternoon was spent at home assembling the papers he might need in his conversation with the King. He thought the King might choose to take over the military command himself, but he would feel relieved at relinquishing it. Other than that, he had no concerns about the coming meeting.

At five o'clock his car was at the main gate of the royal villa, which had been opened in anticipation of his arrival. He was accompanied by his private secretary while the three cars carrying his escort and the detectives remained outside. He noted more carabinieri around than usual but that did not strike him as strange.

The King, wearing a field marshal's uniform, was waiting for him in the doorway. Together they went into the drawing room, up the stairs.

Mussolini began to give an account of the military situation and the session of the Grand Council. The King interrupted him. It was useless to go on, he said. Italy was defeated. Army morale had collapsed. The Alpine regiments were singing a song to the effect that they would no longer fight for Mussolini. At the moment, the King said, Mussolini was the most hated man in Italy, without a friend except himself.

"I will ensure your personal safety," said the King.

He had to demand the Duce's resignation, the King said, and he had already appointed Badoglio to head the government.

Mussolini tried to argue.

"I'm sorry," said the King. "But the solution could not have been otherwise."

The audience was over. The King accompanied Mussolini to the door. As he left the residence, Mussolini seemed resigned to accept the situation.

Outside, his chauffeur, who had been lured into the porter's lodge on the pretext of a telephone call, was seized and held until the next scene was over. The ambulance was backed up so that Mussolini could enter at the rear, and two carabinieri officers moved forth as Mussolini emerged from the villa. "His Majesty has charged me with the protection of your person," said one of them.

"That's not necessary," said Mussolini, heading for his car.

"No, you must come in my car," said the officer.

Mussolini said nothing further but went to the rear door of the ambulance, where he stopped. He faced six police officers, and he saw there was no point in objecting. He mounted the step and sat down, accompanied by the carabinieri officer. The second carabinieri officer went to the front of the ambulance and sat beside the driver, and the six police officers then entered the ambulance. The doors were shut and the driver drove off at high speed through the deserted streets of Rome.

After a short drive, the ambulance arrived at the Podgora Carabinieri barracks in Trastevere. Mussolini was brought out and taken to the officers' quarters, where he was placed under armed guard. A little later that day he was moved to the barracks of a cadet school. That evening he was visited by a doctor but said he did not need any medical attention. He talked to the doctor about the situation. The new government, he said, was a good one and should handle affairs well. There might be demonstrations in the valley of the Po but these could be easily suppressed.

The doctor left, and Mussolini remained shut up in the office of the commandant of the school, under guard. No one said he had been arrested. But that evening when an officer came to ask him what he would like to eat for supper, he saw the sentries outside the door. He refused food and sat in the colonel's room until 11 P.M. when he climbed into the colonel's bed and turned out the light.

In the streets of Rome all had gone unremarked. The route from the Palazzo Venezia to the palace had been lined by the usual police cordon that was set for Mussolini everywhere, which remained, waiting in the heat. Then a car passed down the line and all the police were told to go back to their station, because Il Duce would not be returning to the Palazzo Venezia that evening. Rome was quiet. The people assembled in the open air restaurants at the Piazza Venezia and ate pasta, drank wine, and gossiped about prices, the black market, and the war news. The band of the antiaircraft militia was giving a concert and the police band was playing that evening in the Pincio. Children were cooling off in the fountains, and street musicians were playing their tunes. There was no threat of an air raid. Rome was almost as quiet and beautiful as it had been on Sunday evenings before the war.

No one except the King and the conspirators knew that everything had changed.

CHAPTER 23

∽

The Rescue

In the streets of Rome, twenty-one years of fascism suddenly disappeared overnight. The news of the change in government was broadcast by Badoglio at 11:00 that night, but it was already coursing through the streets. He announced that he had been chosen by the King to carry on the government, and that the war at German's side would continue unabated. This was a lie—he was already trying to get in touch with the Allies to arrange a surrender. But it was a necessary lie, for the Germans were still nervous, despite Mussolini's promises. German Ambassador Mackensen learned of the arrest of Mussolini while cooling off in his swimming pool. In a cafe a writer listened to the broadcast, then suddenly picked up a chair and smashed it over the head of a Militia officer, something he had been wanting to do for years. A typical conversation that night would go like this:

"Have you heard the news?"

"You mean about Mussolini?"

"Yes. Wonderful! You know I was never a Fascist, really."

"Neither was I."

That night thousands of fascist badges were thrown away. Carlo Scorza, the secretary of the Fascist party, and the one man with the power to call out the Fascists to rescue Mussolini, did nothing. He visited General Cerica, was told that Mussolini had been arrested, and was told to issue a statement that there was to be no bloodshed. He complied meekly and immediately went into hiding.

Rachele received an anonymous telephone call telling the news, and nothing else. General Galbiati, who could have called out the Fascist Militia, was overwhelmed by a show of force and gave up his com-

231

mand to a regular soldier, General Armellini. By midnight, a crowd had marched to the Quirinale Palace to proclaim loyalty to the King. Some Fascist officials were quietly arrested and others disappeared. Manlio Morgagni, director of Stefani news agency, committed suicide. Alexander Pavolini, editor of *Il Messaggero*, disappeared. Roberto Farinacci fled to the German embassy and was transported to Germany. Host Venturi, former Minister of Communications, walked the streets that night to see what was happening and observed that all was calm and there were no disturbances. The feeling in Rome seemed to be intense relief.

At one o'clock in the morning, Mussolini was awakened from his sleep in the colonel's bed in the carabinieri academy by a messenger from General Badoglio:

> Cavaliere Signor Benito Mussolini:
> The undersigned head of the government wishes to inform Your Excellency that what has been done in your regard had been done solely in your personal interest, detailed information having reached us from several quarters of a serious plot against your person. He much regrets this and wishes to inform you that he is prepared to give orders for your safe accompaniment with all proper respect to whatever place you may choose.
>
> Badoglio

Mussolini responded that he wanted to go to Forlì, to the Rocca delle Caminate. He would make no difficulties, he said. He wanted only to live in peace for the rest of his life. To others he began speaking of himself as though he were talking about a dead man.

But difficulties immediately presented themselves. The prefect of Forlì said that if Mussolini was brought there, he would be lynched. And Badoglio began to believe that Mussolini might represent a valuable card in his negotiations with the Allies for the surrender that he had promised the King he would bring about. So on the evening of July 27, Mussolini was driven in a convoy to Gaeta, where he was handed over to Admiral Franco Maugeri and put aboard the corvette *Persefone*. He was taken to the island Ventotene, but when the admiral learned that the island was garrisoned by Germans, Mussolini was not landed but instead taken to Ponza, a penal colony, where he was kept for ten days. The government did not harass him. He received a telegram on his sixtieth birthday, July 29, from Goering. He spent the time contemplating, thinking about his religious beginnings and translating Carducci's *Odi Barbare*. He asked the parish priest to say a mass for his son Bruno, who had died in an air accident over Pisa.

A few days later he received from Hitler a set of the complete works of Nietzsche bound in blue morocco leather. These had been delivered by Field Marshal Kesselring to the King and sent along.

On August 6, the Badoglio government learned of a German attempt to rescue Mussolini and moved him to the island of La Maddelena, which upset the King, because he had a corvette lying at Civitavecchia and a refuge villa on that island. But the information that the Germans were searching for Mussolini was correct. When Hitler heard the news of the arrest, he had erupted in fury. First he wanted to take over Italy immediately but was dissuaded by advisors who suggested that Badoglio was behaving properly and that there was no need. Still, Hitler ordered General Kurt Student, the paratroop commander, to go to Rome and take command of the paratroops there and be prepared to seize Rome. He had one other mission: to find Mussolini and rescue him. For that purpose Hitler sent to Rome Colonel Otto Skorzeny, who had distinguished himself in Holland and Belgium with remarkable paratroop victories and several times since in adventurous roles. Skorzeny came to Rome and immediately began to search for Mussolini.

Skorzeny arrived in Rome on July 27 and met that night with Obersturmbannführer Herbert Kappler and Standartenführer Eugen Dollmann, Himmler's SS representatives in Italy, and enlisted their aid.

First swearing them to secrecy, Skorzeny had explained how the day before, Hitler had called him into his presence and explained the problem:

"Mussolini, my friend and loyal comrade in arms, was betrayed yesterday by his King and arrested by his own countrymen. I cannot and will not leave Italy's greatest son in the lurch. I will keep faith with my old ally and dear friend—he must be rescued promptly or he will be handed over to the Allies."

Dollmann asked if Ambassador Mackensen and Field Marshal Kesselring had been informed of the mission. They had not, said Skorzeny, and it was vital that they not be told. Hitler felt that both men were too friendly to the Italians and would botch the job. No, only General Student and these three men and Skorzeny's deputy knew what was being planned.

∽

So the game began. Skorzeny sent back to Germany for special men and special equipment, which were assembled in a few hours by Hitler's personal order. Twenty hand-picked instructors from the secret training school that Skorzeny ran for the State Security Service, tropical uniforms, civilian suits, weapons, laughing gas, tear gas, thirty kilograms of plastic explosive, and even two complete outfits for Jesuit priests had been assembled and were already in Rome.

For twenty-nine days, the Germans searched for Mussolini. Meanwhile Hitler had also decided that Mussolini's family must be gotten out of Italy. Rachele was under house arrest at Rocca delle Caminate, and it was relatively easy for an SS unit to spirit her out of the country and to Munich. That was not enough. Hitler was also determined to save the other members of the family. Vittorio was brought to Germany. And Edda and the grandchildren were also to be brought. This development provided a new problem. The Badoglio government had placed Galeazzo Ciano under house arrest on the Via Angelo Secchi. But Edda and the children had the freedom of the city, and on the morning of August 27 they pretended to be going for a boating trip on the Tiber. Instead they were picked up by a car, which also picked up Ciano twenty yards from his door and sped to Ciampino airfield, where a JU 52 transport was ready.

At Munich they were installed in the Villa Starnberg under the charge of Obersturmbannführer Wilhelm Höttl. It was not long before Höttl learned of the existence of a diary Ciano had been keeping since 1939. Edda had been so unwise as to indicate that they had complete reference to all Ciano's conversations of four years with the Nazis. Since he had been foreign minister, the diaries must tell of his relations with Joachim von Ribbentrop, who was the mortal enemy of Ernst Kaltenbrunner, state security chief, and Höttl's boss, Heinrich Himmler.

Seeing in the diaries a way to discredit Ribbentrop, Höttl had approached Ciano for a deal: The diaries would be deposited in a Swiss bank, and when Ciano and his family were safe in the Argentine they would be turned over to the Germans. But then Ribbentrop found out about the diaries and moved to stop the arrangement. In a meeting with Hitler, it was made clear that the Cianos would not be allowed outside Germany. They went back to Munich and waited.

Meanwhile, Skorzeny was forever just missing Mussolini. He learned that Mussolini had been held at the carabinieri school and then taken by corvette to sea and was held at Ponza; Skorzeny missed him by a few days. But on August 10 they had a report that the garrison at La Maddalena had suddenly been strengthened and that local telephone workers had an order from the admiral commanding the base to install a direct line between his office and the Villa Weber outside the central switchboard. Rumor had it that Il Duce was a prisoner there, and had been since the afternoon of August 7. He was also reportedly guarded by 150 carabinieri.

Skorzeny's plan called for six E-boats anchored at Anzio to make an official visit to La Maddalena. A flotilla of minesweepers would bring a group of SS men from the Corsican brigade and both groups of small craft would leave the harbor on a naval exercise. Then, at a signal, the E-boats would give covering fire and the men from the minesweepers would land and storm the Villa Weber and rescue Mussolini.

Skorzeny scouted the area himself. He had to be sure that Mussolini was actually there. Everything was soon ready to put the plan into effect. He tracked him down through the interception of a letter by the German postmaster of Rome, from Mussolini's daughter Edda to an address in La Maddelenà. Skorzeny then flew to the area and over the house where Mussolini was staying. He came into the town later and looked over the villa. One of his young volunteers actually saw Mussolini sunning himself on the veranda.

But the Italians got wind of the plan, probably from Skorzeny's flight low over the Villa Weber. They decided to move Mussolini by seaplane on August 28 to Lake Bracciano, north of Rome. He was then taken to an inn next to a funicular railway that ran to the top of the Gran Sasso, where a ski resort was located. Again Skorzeny was on the track, and German planes began flying over the area, which alerted the Italians one more time. They moved Mussolini then to the top of the mountain, where the Campo Imperatore Hotel was located. All the paying guests were ejected, and Mussolini had the place to himself, with the staff and his guards. He was given a luxury apartment on the second floor. He spent his time in the dining room playing cards with his guards. Everyone was relaxed and seemed to relish the idea of the coming ski season. Mussolini talked of skiing and several of the guards brought up their ski equipment.

∽

September 1943 arrived, and with it change. On September 3, the National Liberation Committee was formed of Communists and Socialists, primarily dedicated to directing partisan activity against the Germans.

On September 8, Hitler was suddenly pressed to action by the news that the Italian government had surrendered to the Allies. Hitler moved to seize Italy, and in three days, Rome was in German hands.

That same day, Skorzeny had his answers. He had sent an army physician to the Gran Sasso on the pretext that the German army might want to take over the hotel as a training spot for mountain troops. The doctor had seen the guards in the village of Assergi at the foot of the mountain but had been told by the carabinieri at the funicular railroad base that he could not go up the mountain and that if he did not leave immediately he would be arrested, German or not. Skorzeny had concluded that Mussolini was indeed held here. He took a reconnaissance flight over the Gran Sasso and noted a field not far from the hotel that seemed proper for glider landing, so he decided on a glider rescue. A motorized party would seize the lower funicular station and the gliders would bring in 120 troops and Skorzeny to lead the rescue from the top.

On September 12, Skorzeny and his gliders took off the German-held airfield at Pratica di Mare and soon were over the Gran Sasso. The first glider went into the prescribed field and crashed, because it was too steep. The three other gliders in that echelon then circled and went down to the base of the mountain to land, but Skorzeny and eight other gliders landed near the hotel and rushed to rescue Mussolini. The first man out of the glider was Italian General Soleti; behind him was a German officer with a pistol pressed to his ribs. "Don't shoot," shouted Soleti.

Mussolini heard the commotion and opened his second floor window, leaned out, and also shouted to the carabinieri not to shoot. They had no intention of shooting. They had been ordered that if the Germans came they were to surrender and not get hurt. Some of the carabinieri fled down the mountain, but the rest surrendered without a shot being fired.

Skorzeny entered the hotel, took the stairs three at a time, and flung open the door of Room 201. He found himself in a small hallway with hatstand and wardrobe, a yellow-tiled bathroom on one side, a double bed, leather easy chair, a photo of the dead Bruno Mussolini framed in black, and in the center of the room three men—Inspector General Giuseppe Gueli of the carabinieri, another officer, and Mussolini. Skorzeny surged forward:

"Duce, the führer sent me. You are free!"

Mussolini embraced him. "I knew my friend Adolf Hitler would not leave me in the lurch," he said. Skorzeny was shocked by Mussolini's appearance. What a change from the old pictures! He had actually seen Mussolini once, on his balcony in the Palazzo Venezia. The man he saw now was unshaven, his bald head had grown a fuzz, and he was sallow and wrinkled: He looked more like a homeless man of the street than a dictator. Skorzeny told Mussolini that his family had been taken to Vienna, and he could go there to join them. He said he wanted to go to Forlì. Skorzeny said his orders were to take Mussolini back to the air base and that a Storch aircraft would be used for the purpose. Mussolini finally agreed and prepared for his departure.

It was late afternoon before the Storch was loaded, overloaded in fact, with Mussolini and the big Skorzeny. Skorzeny had insisted on climbing in the plane even though it was a two-seater. The overloaded plane charged down the sloping field. Fifteen feet from the edge, the pilot put his flaps down to bring the plane up and pulled on the stick. The right wheel struck a rock, the left wing canted down. The Storch then bounded off the edge of the ravine and plummeted toward the valley; the pilot pushed the stick forward, increased the speed, and then pulled the plane out of the dive; they flew down on the deck, too heavy to make altitude. At about 5:30 in the afternoon they landed at Pratica di Mare airfield. There Mussolini was transferred to a Heinkel aircraft, and Skorzeny joined him for the flight to Vienna.

They arrived in Vienna shortly before midnight and Mussolini spent the night in the Hotel Continental. That night Hitler telephoned Mussolini jubilantly. He had kept his promise to do anything in the world for Mussolini and he had brought him safely to a haven out of the hands of his enemies.

The next day, Mussolini was flown to Munich, where his family had been taken. He did not know it but within the Nazi establishment a hot discussion was being held about his fate. Dr. Goebbels wanted Mussolini eliminated. He argued that such a course would enable the Germans to do what they wished with Italy, annex territory and take it over as a colony. A regime headed by Mussolini would fall heir to all the rights in the three-power pact, which Goebbels found to be ridiculous and unnecessary.

Hitler, however, was of a totally different mind. On ideological grounds he could not and would not abandon Mussolini, the father of fascism. If he did so, he told the others, it would be an open invitation for the enemies of naziism to redouble their efforts to bring the regime down. No, Mussolini must be rehabilitated and returned to power.

CHAPTER 24

⚬

The Republic

On September 14, 1943, Mussolini flew to Rastenburg, the führer's eastern headquarters. Hitler was waiting for him outside his bunker with Mussolini's son Vittorio. Hitler and Mussolini embraced after a separation of less than two months that seemed like two years because so much had happened. Hitler was shocked at Mussolini's appearance. He had lost thirty pounds and his collar hung loosely around his wrinkled neck. Those piercing black eyes seemed larger in a shrunken head, and he looked like an unshaven derelict of the streets. Mussolini knew very little about events, or the progress of the allied invasion of Italy, which was taking place in the far south. In a few weeks his outlook on life had changed completely. He had accepted the collapse of the Italian war effort, and he was now certain of an ultimate German defeat in the war. All he wanted for himself was to return to the countryside of his north Italian home and live out the rest of his life in serenity. Gone were the trappings of power, the private railroad trains, gaudy uniforms and trumpets, and adoring crowds. Peace was all that mattered to him now.

But it was not to be. That day Mussolini and Hitler met for two hours. Hitler had expected Mussolini to be filled with wrath and eager to wreak vengeance on the men who had betrayed him. Hitler and Ribbentrop were particularly angry with Ciano, whom they accused of betraying the German–Italian alliance for years. Hitler expected Mussolini to feel the same. But not so. He found Mussolini disgustingly philosophical about his downfall and not inclined to blame the Fascists who had surrounded him and demanded the fatal meeting of the Grand Council. Hitler had great difficulty in showing him that these men

239

were traitors to the Fascist party, especially Grandi, who had set the wheels in motion. Hitler's reaction was that "he [Mussolini] is not a revolutionary. Italy never was a power, is no power today and will not be a power in the future."

Hitler still hoped, however, that Mussolini was only suffering a temporary lapse. That evening, Mussolini was brought a small group of faithful Fascists who had been gathered by the Germans at Rastenburg to help him form the core of a new fascist regime. They were led by Alessandro Pavolini, lately Minister of Popular Culture. The Italians called on Benito to lead them to revenge and a new glory, but Mussolini was uncertain. To join the battle again? The vision of a peaceful old age beckoned him to Forlì. He refused to commit himself, and when they pressed, he temporized. "I cannot make any decisions. I lack too many elements to form a judgment. Let us see tomorrow."

The next day, Mussolini met again with Hitler, who was disappointed and spoke sharply. "What is this sort of fascism which melts like the snow before the sun?" he demanded. "For years I have explained to my generals that fascism was the soundest alliance for the German people. I have never concealed my distrust of the Italian monarchy; at your insistence, however, I did nothing to obstruct the work which you carried out to the advantage of your King."

"We cannot lose a single day," Hitler said. "It is essential that by tomorrow evening you make an announcement that the monarchy is abolished and an Italian fascist state with power centered on you has taken its place. This way you will guarantee the full validity of the German–Italy alliance."

Mussolini tried to delay. He would need time to think it over.

"I have already reflected," said Hitler. "You'll proclaim yourself Duce once again. Then you will be just as I am, both head of state and of the government. And its constitution must be provided for within a week."

Hitler then insisted that the traitors of the Fascist Grand Council be tried.

Mussolini was still undecided, and he spoke frankly.

Hitler then gave Mussolini two options. He could return to the fray, and work for an Axis victory, and Hitler would promise that Italy would not suffer for Badoglio's coup d'état. Once the war was won, Italy would be restored to rights, fascism would be reborn as the national polity, and the traitors would be brought to justice. But if Mussolini refused to play his new role, Italy would be treated as an enemy. In the meetings at Feltre, Hitler had described his new weapons, the V-2 rockets, which were going to win the war against Britain. "It is up to you," he now said to Mussolini, "to decide whether these weapons are to be used on London or tried out first on Milan, Genoa, or Turin. Northern Italy will envy the fate of Poland if you do not agree."

Italy would be occupied and the government would be taken over by Germans. As it was, on September 10, Hitler had taken steps to protect the the German frontier. The two frontier provinces of Italy, Venezia Giulia and the South Tirol, had been placed under Nazi gauleiters, Friedrich Rainer at Trieste and Franz Hofer at Innsbruck.

Mussolini saw that he really had no choice. To refuse Hitler was to turn Italy over to immediate disaster. He saw himself now as a buffer between Italy and the barbarous Germans, whom he had always distrusted but into whose alliance he had been thrust by the arrogance of the Western democracies. He was becoming more alive and alert now, and he spoke of the need to build a new Italian army. On this point Hitler was not convinced. He had enough of Italian soldiering. So the question of a new Italian military force was left in abeyance.

On that evening of September 15, an official communiqué was issued in Rome, announcing that Mussolini had reassumed power over fascism in Italy. He ordered the appointment of Pavolini as provisional secretary of the Fascist Republican party, reinstated the functionaries of his government dismissed by Badoglio, instructed the party to support the German army and the war, and to investigate the conduct of the membership in the coup d'état and the surrender to the Allies, and reorganized the Fascist Militia, which had been dismissed by Badoglio. Renato Ricci was to command the Militia, and the officers of the armed forces were told that they no longer would pay allegiance to the King.

So the restoration was complete and everything was the same as before on the surface, but in reality everything was different. Hitler no longer looked on Mussolini as his political equal, and he suspected the truth, that Mussolini had really wanted to break off with the Germans and take Italy out of the war. Hitler separated the future from the past, and his personal admiration for Mussolini persisted because of his respect for what Mussolini had accomplished in establishing the first fascist state. But the führer no longer trusted the Italian people and regarded Italy as territory for conquest and exploitation; he began to talk about the outright annexation of Venezia Giulia into the Third Reich, thus extending the German border to the Adriatic. But the real difference was that Mussolini no longer had power over the Italian people, and unless it could be restored, he was not a man to be regarded seriously in the political field. To the Germans he had now become a tool of limited usefulness.

The next day, Mussolini prepared to leave for Bavaria, which would be the initial center of the new Fascist Republican government. He was examined by Hitler's personal physician, who found him reasonably healthy, suffering only from a circulatory disorder and a bowel problem, which Goebbels observed was common to all revolutionary politicians.

On September 17, Mussolini was flown to Munich, and the Hirschberg castle near Weilheim was taken over for his family use. At the airport he was met by Filippo Anfuso, his old private secretary, who had elected, alone among those close around Mussolini in the past, to join in the rejuvenated fascist movement. He saw the change in Mussolini immediately. Instead of jutting out his jaw and fixing Anfuso with that arrogant glare of the past, Mussolini shook him warmly by the hand and asked him to sit down. Long gone was the sixty-foot gap between the Il Duce's door and the desk at which there were no chairs for visitors.

The castle might as well have stood out alone in the Bavarian countryside. There was no contact with the outside world save through the Germans, by a German telephone line, an SS liaison officer, a German military guard, and the German foreign office. The Germans were aware of all the comings and goings, and everything that happened inside the castle.

One of Mussolini's first visitors was Count Ciano, whom he had branded a traitor because of his opposition to the Germans and to carrying on the war. He was allowed to come through the interposition of his wife and Il Duce's daughter, Edda Mussolini. Ciano protested his loyalty and Mussolini allowed himself to be convinced, much to the disgust of Hitler and the other German leaders. But these Germans were still in awe of the aura of Mussolini, no matter what they said, and they accepted his change of heart, at least for the moment.

To old Fascists from the early days, Mussolini unburdened himself and revealed his present concept of the past. He had always been a Socialist at heart, he said, a Socialist of the pure school, which served only the interests of the nation. He should have liquidated the monarchy in the beginning, but he was afraid to do so, knowing how much the Italian people revered the institution. He could have done it after the success of the Ethiopian adventure but then he had felt that to do so would be only furthering his personal ambitions. Now, he had no desire but to serve Italy and the Italians, and he spoke longingly for the socialist days of the past.

Mussolini's first public airing of the return to socialist principles was in a broadcast beamed to Italy by Radio Munich on September 18. He spoke of the overthrow of his government and then began discussing his new philosophy. Italian traditions, he said, were more republican than monarchical. It was the Republicans who had brought about the unification of Italy. Now he proposed to set up a republican state, fascistic in nature "thus going back to our origins." His new government would go to war again at the side of Germany, Japan, Hungary, Romania, and Bulgaria. The armed forces would be again organized around the Fascist Militia, and the traitors at home would be punished. In the future, labor would be the basis of the national economy and the state.

When Dr. Goebbels heard about this broadcast and examined the German text, he was very pleasantly surprised. "The Italian Fascists," he said "will draw new hope and fighting spirit from this speech."

Recognition of the new government came within days from Germany, Japan, Manchukuo, Bulgaria, Romania, Slovakia, and Croatia. If anyone thought this was knee-jerk, then the abstention of Hungary would give them another thought. Hungary held off because of the need to clarify some territorial claims between Italy and Budapest. The real problem was that the Italian legation in Budapest had remained loyal to the Badoglio government, and a new set of diplomats had to be organized. Soon recognition came from Thailand, Burma, and the Nanking regime in China.

A few days after the broadcast, Mussolini appointed Anfuso to be ambassador to Berlin for the new government. His new appointees fanned out to get on with the jobs, and Mussolini retired to the castle to await developments. Pavolini and German Ambassador Rudolf Rahn went to Rome to see what could be done to reorganize the Fascist Militia. They met with several of the old Fascists and were advised against trying to restore fascism. The Italian people were not interested. Ricci, trying to reorganize the Militia, was able to recruit only a handful of members.

On September 22, Rahn telegraphed Berlin that it was very difficult to put together the fascist elements in Rome. Many of those Mussolini wanted for government posts were hesitating about accepting. Rahn, therefore, advocated the announcement of the new government. So on September 23, the new government officially was inaugurated.

The Ministry of Interior, a key post, was given to Guido Buffarini-Guidi, a lawyer from Pisa, and he was the best of a mediocre lot. They had been unable to find anyone to take the Ministry of Foreign Affairs, so Mussolini assumed the portfolio himself. Fernando Mezzasomma became the Minister of Popular Culture (Propaganda). The rest were leftover bureaucrats of the second and third tiers from the past. General Graziani was the best known of all of them; he was persuaded to take the War Ministry. And two undersecretaries, both popular war heroes, handled the air and navy arms.

The list promulgated. Mussolini then left for Forlì wearing a Militia uniform without any decoration or emblems and a borrowed black shirt. He was met by Ambassador Rudolf Rahn and SS General Karl Wolff, who were to be his personal guardians from this point onward. Truly, he was now the captive of Hitler. As if there was any doubt, like Pu Yi, the emperor of Manchukuo, he was surrounded by a Praetorian guard of his "ally," a detachment of the *Leibstandarte* Adolf Hitler.

And what was to be Mussolini's role in this new puppet state? He summarized it for Ambassador Rahn: His responsibility was to maintain law and order in the rear of the German armies. Mussolini realized that Germany must have sole leadership in the conduct of the war. But he must have control of the administration and finances of the new government. Otherwise, he said, there was no point in having a government at all.

∾

Mussolini wanted to return to Rome. In the weeks since his downfall Rome had become a cockpit of rumor and confusion. When he was rescued on the mountain he had asked how matters were going in Rome. Badly, said his German informant. What was happening? Mussolini had asked. Looting, said the German. And what of the Fascists? asked Mussolini. There were no Fascists in evidence in Rome, said the German.

The Badoglio government had continued in power, negotiating with the Germans and the Allies both, until the surrender to the Allies was announced on September 8. The Germans had then swung into action, and in a few hours had disarmed the Italian army forces, then given them a choice of fighting under the Germans, or disbanding and going home.

After the announcement of the surrender, the King and Queen and Badoglio had taken refuge in the Ministry of War, which was supposed to have the deepest air raid shelter in Rome. Outside Rome there was some fighting by Italian units against the Germans. In the next two days, the Italian army and the partisans who were armed by the army dealt so heavy a blow to the German 2nd Parachute Division that the division could not be sent, as it was supposed to be, to the Salerno front to oppose the allied landings. Who said that Italians would not fight? What they needed was leadership and a reason, and in the battle against the invading Germans they had both.

Before the night was out, the only escape route from Rome that remained was west to the Abruzzi Hills, along the Tiburtina River. In the darkness of night the King and Queen left the capital in a family limousine, flying the azure royal standard. Badoglio and other members of the government fled in other cars in the motorcade. They drove to Chieti near Pescara on the Adriatic coast, the King lamenting on the way that he had discarded Mussolini, who had served him faithfully for twenty-one years, only to meet total disaster. At Chieti they boarded the destroyer *Baionetta* that would take them to safety in Brindisi, far from Rome. Thus the King and Prime Minister Badoglio had escaped, leaving Italy to the mercy of the Germans.

By September 11 the whole country was occupied. In a period of forty-eight hours, ninety Italian divisions had been wrecked and their stores and weapons taken over by the Germans. Four million Italian soldiers were deserted by their government. Of these, seven hundred thousand were sent to Germany as prisoners of war. And at no point in the whole proceeding had they been given orders to fight against the Germans. So the whole royalist plan had been to "play off the Allies against the Germans and wriggle out between."

Indeed, Italy, in her hour of need, had been betrayed by the King and the prime minister. And it was all planned. Later it was learned that the King had shipped two trains of more than twenty cars each to Switzerland, bearing royal treasures. Badoglio's wife and family were sent to Switzerland, too. The King and the prime minister then chucked the blame for the betrayal off onto General Carboni. So hoodwinked were the Allies that Churchill and Roosevelt both sent messages of congratulation to the King and Badoglio when they should have clapped them in jail for the sellout that had deprived the Allies of any benefit from the Italian surrender.

As for Rome, the Germans were thinking about declaring it an open city, so Mussolini's suggestion that he return there was rejected by Hitler. Besides he wanted Mussolini closer to the German frontier.

The proof of acuity of Mussolini's intuition that the Germans would never let Italy out of the alliance came late in September when Mussolini wrote Hitler asking for an end to German interference in the internal affairs of his new Italian republic:

If we want to reconstruct the civil life of the country, the new government I have formed must have the necessary autonomy to govern.

The Republican government, which I have the honor to lead, has only one desire and one aim, to see that Italy resumes her place in the war as soon as possible. But to reach this supreme result it is essential for the German military authorities to confine their action to the military sphere only and for all the rest to allow the Italian civil authorities to function.

If this is not accomplished, both Italian and world opinion will judge this government incapable of functioning and the government itself will fall into disorder and even more into ridicule.

Hitler did not even reply to the letter. Everything that Mussolini had said in it was true, and, in fact, the condition he presupposed had already come about. All the countries that had recognized the new Republic were now strangely silent. Not one of them sent a diplomatic representative or offered to establish diplomatic ties with the new Italian Republic. The most bitter pill was handed Mussolini by Spain's Generalissimo Franco, who refused to extend more than de facto recognition. Mussolini, said El Caudillo, was a shadow, and he could not last long. Behind him there were few decent Italians. He was now only an appendage of Germany. When Mussolini's representative reminded Franco that Il Duce had recognized his Spanish government immediately after it was formed in 1936, when the issue was very much in doubt against the republic, Franco had nothing to say. So from the outset it was, as Mussolini said, a government deemed ridiculous by the world.

Mussolini's reaction to all this was silence. But in his heart he knew what was happening and he retreated into a solemn pride. He refused to revive his *Il Popolo d'Italia*, which had been closed down by Badoglio. He said it was possible for him to sacrifice himself in this tragic situation of Italy, but he would not sacrifice his newspaper to German censorship, because "for thirty years it has been a flag and a flag must fly freely."

As for himself, he was resigned to play the role Hitler had chosen for him. On October 9, he left La Rocca by car for Lake Garda, accompanied by a few aides. The residence chosen by Field Marshal Rommel for Il Duce was the Villa Feltrinelli, a medium-sized house faced with pink marble, located in a small park on the bank of Lake Garda about a mile north of Gargnano.

His government was scattered all over. The Ministries of Foreign Affairs and Popular Culture were at Salò. The cabinet office was at

Bogliaco. The Interior Ministry was at Maderno. The Armed Forces Center was at Desenzano, the Ministry of Education at Padua, and the Ministry of Public Works was far away in Venice. But right on top of Mussolini were his German guardians. Ambassador Rahn was at Fasano, about six miles from the Villa Feltrinelli. General Wolff was stationed at Gardone, seven miles down the lake. Next door to the Villa Feltrinelli was Colonel Jandl, the German liaison officer, and the German soldiers were all about, manning an antiaircraft gun on the roof of the villa, and guarding—whether guarding Mussolini from the world or from escape seemed sometimes debatable. All communications were in the hands of the Germans.

Colonel Jandl saw Mussolini every day, and in his first report to Berlin said he had Mussolini "under control." He had a staff officer living in the villa, through whom he could keep track of all the visitors, telephone calls, and activity in Mussolini's house. Soon the noise and the sequestration became intolerable to Mussolini, and he insisted on establishing his office in a neighboring villa away from the noise. There he spent his days as he bent himself to several tasks: the relations with Germany, the organization of the party, creation of a new socialist system, and rebuilding the army.

Now Italy was controlled by the Allies in the south and by the Germans in the north, with Rome the center of a hinterland between, still held by the Germans. In the south the Badoglio government obediently declared war on the Germans, and began supplying labor troops and pack trains to the Allies. Its government had virtually no effect on the Italian people. It was nearly the same in the north. Officials of the Todt Organization and the German Ministry of Labor swarmed over the countryside, pressing Italians into service for labor in Germany. The army demanded whatever it wanted. In northern Italy the Germans actually ruled Alto Adige (Upper Tirol) and Trieste (Venezia Giulia), and German troops occupied several cities. As the partisans became more active in the Piedmont area, the Germans spoke about setting up a third military zone. Mussolini objected that this would undermine his government, but the Germans paid no attention. On October 10, 1943, military government was established in all northern Italy.

∽

Life in German-controlled Italy now became a matter of survival for the people, with no effective government to help them. Lobo Davila, the Portuguese minister to the Italian court, traveled home to Lisbon that fall. Rome, he said, was a cock pit, with Fascist and anti-Fascist groups moving about the city. The Chigi Palace, the foreign office, was totally deserted; the archives and the furniture had been removed, and the shutters were closed.

Rome had been through two periods since Mussolini's fall. The first was those few weeks when the Badoglio government had attempted to step in and take over. The second phase had come when the Germans took over and forced the functionaries in government who were not Fascist to get out of their offices. The offices were transferred to the north, then under German control, with many of the bureaucrats forced to leave their families in Rome.

As for the diplomatic corps, when the Salò Republic had been announced, some of the missions were closed down. The Turkish ambassador and the staff left Rome, leaving a caretaker, not a chargé d'affaires. The Spanish minister returned to Madrid, leaving a secretary in Bologna in charge of such relations as Madrid had with Mussolini. The Hungarian minister left a chargé d'affaires in Rome, the Romanian minister retired to the Vatican. The Finns, Afghans, and Swedes remained in Rome, where they had nothing to do because the Republic was in the north, and what remained of the monarchy was in the Naples area.

The Portuguese minister's journey from Rome to Switzerland was made by car in November, 1943. He found that they could travel only in the daylight hours, because of the danger from bands of partisans who roamed the countryside by night. Even daylight travel was dangerous because of raids and air raids by allied aviators machine-gunning the roads. His car also had to make many detours to avoid the German military fortifications north of Florence. As for food supplies, Lobo Davila found that the further they got from Rome the more the food situation improved. He was stalled for four days at Milan, waiting permission to pass into Switzerland, and there observed the total control by the Germans of north Italian life.

Lobo Davila was most impressed in this Italy by the sense of weariness of the Italians. There were exceptions; some favored the Salò Republic and fascism, and more seemed to want to join the anti-German struggle. But most of the people were apathetic. Their old idol was fallen, and that idol had proved to have feet of clay when he dragged Italy into the war nobody wanted. As for the Allies, the Italians had no faith in them either, disillusioned by the allied failure to move when Mussolini was deposed.

∽

Mussolini pondered the best method of moving into this vacuum and re-creating a government of Italy. The Germans, more interested in maintaining order and their fortifications for defense against the allied movement north, were totally unsympathetic. As far as they were concerned, Mussolini's republic was of use only if it restrained the Italian population of the north from rebellion.

Mussolini's complaints drew an explanation from Italian Republic Ambassador Anfuso in Berlin. The Germans, he said, were unsympathetic because the Republic had not taken an energetic position against defeatism and compromise inside the country. Things would be much better when the Italian army was organized and began to fight alongside the Germans. But Mussolini had first to bring forth a semblance of coherence to his government. After some thought he decided on a socialist manifesto. He prepared this, along with Italian aides, and it was ruthlessly edited by Ambassador Rahn, who said he had been obliged to cut out many references of a socialist tone, and to strike entirely a section composed by Il Duce about territorial integrity.

In the end, the manifesto contained eighteen points. A Constituent Assembly would be convened. Its first task would be to declare the dissolution of the monarchy and proclaim a social republic. The head of government would be nominated, to be elected every five years. This, of course, would be Mussolini.

Sovereign power would be in the hands of the citizens. No citizen could be held under arrest for more than seven days except by court decree. A new system of elections would be devised, to avoid the failures of parliamentary democracy and the excesses of authoritarian government. The political education of the people would be in the hands of the party, but one did not have to belong to the party to secure employment or privileges. The religion would be Roman Catholic, but all other religions would be respected. For the duration of the war, Jews would be regarded as enemy nationals. The Republic would seek the realization of a European Community and a federation of all nations subscribing to certain principles: (1) the elimination of British intrigues on the continent; (2) abolition of capitalism; (3) exploitation of the resources of Africa for the benefit of Europeans and the native peoples, the native peoples to have complete respect; (4) private property would be guaranteed; (5) public services and war industries would be nationalized; (6) land ownership depended on agricultural performance; (7) the state would create an adequate housing program; (8) the trade unions would be amalgamated into a general Confederation of Labor; and (9) the social legislation passed by the Fascists over the past twenty years would remain in force.

In a newspaper article Mussolini described the manifesto as meeting the needs of the working classes. "Fascism, relieved of much tinsel, has returned to its revolutionary origins."

The manifesto was greeted by some old Fascists with new enthusiasm. In Turin a labor leader said this was very much like Russian communism and predicted that the plutocrats would be liquidated and socialism introduced. Other Socialists approved, and Mussolini told a journalist that this manifesto represented his reconciliation with his socialist past.

The Congress was called on November 14, 1943, in Verona. There were obviously a large number of Socialists and Communists in the crowd, because the proceedings were disorderly and interrupted by much heckling, some of them shouting at the Duce to get rid of Clara Petacci, some shouting for socialist policies. The one positive and overwhelming development of the Congress was the general call for vengeance against the "traitors" who had created the crisis of the Fascist Grand Council. Animosity was focused on Count Ciano, Mussolini's son-in-law, who had antagonized virtually everyone in the party by his arrogance over the past dozen years. In the end, the manifesto was passed by acclamation.

But in the proceedings a vast gulf appeared between Mussolini and his followers. He had the power of introspection to recognize that fascism had ultimately failed, been corrupted, and lost all its vigor, and that was why, when he was arrested, no one had stepped forward to rescue him save the Germans. He recognized, too, that Hitler respected only physical strength, and that his Republic would have no standing with the Germans unless it had an army. But he faced the insuperable dilemma: The Germans did not trust the Italians enough to help create an army, and the Italians had absolutely no wish to continue to fight alongside the Germans. They wanted peace above all things, and so one of the cornerstones of Mussolini's manifesto was built on sand. But there was nothing Mussolini could do about this, since continuation of German support meant to give lip service at least to the Republic's continuation of the war.

The party emerged from the Congress badly split. On the one hand were the men who stood for internal reconciliation, a policy with which Mussolini privately agreed. But on the other side were Roberto Farinacci, who had never ceased to be "the mad dog" of his youth, and Pavolini, who also wanted to return to the old totalitarian system and make it even more repressive. The old Fascists of Milan, Pavi, Turin, and other northern cities—the real backbone of the movement—agreed with the Farinacci group.

In Milan the newspaper *Fascio*, successor to *Il Popolo d'Italia*, published an article that parroted the philosophy:

"He who talks of forgetting, or refers to appeasement and the universal embrace, commits the crime of treason towards his country and a second betrayal of fascism. This is not the hour of the pen, but the sword."

Mussolini did not attend the Congress but sat glumly in the villa on Lake Garda and observed the fragmentation of his movement. He compared himself to Napoleon held captive on the island of Elba where he had held court but wielded no power. Strong action on Mussolini's part, a threat to withdraw from public life, might have welded the party together, but he was no longer capable of such strong action. He was too fearful of his German masters, and the consequences to Italy. He knew that if he quit, the Germans would dissolve the whole mechanism and take over Italy. At this point, fully realizing the impotence of his position, Mussolini came into what was really his brightest hour. For his country, he was willing to sacrifice everything.

CHAPTER 25

∽

Revenge

That autumn of 1943 the German occupation of northern Italy was complete and very efficient. American observers in Portugal and Switzerland reported, "German threats and repressive measures have discouraged sabotage and disorder, but the population's hostility toward Germans is pronounced."

Only in one area was there fighting between Germans and Italians, in the province of Cuneo, where a regiment from France was battling for survival. All the important Italian cities were occupied by German troops. They had little contact with the civilians. Order was maintained by the Italian police who were responsible now to the Mussolini government. As for the people, they strictly avoided contact with the Germans, and most of the city people had moved to the suburbs to escape the Germans and aerial bombardment from the Allies. The Germans were careful. They moved their troops about in large units, heavily armed and mechanized, and avoided the error of letting individual soldiers and small groups move about to be attacked by the partisans, who now literally infiltrated everywhere.

The Germans requisitioned everything—tires, chemicals, mechanical tools, and all the other necessities of the military. Industrial production was kept going by German threats to destroy the factories if it lagged, and by the import of German technicians who cracked the whip over the Italian workers. The degree of hatred of the Germans was rising steadily, but there was nothing to be done. Any act of sabotage was rooted out and dealt with summarily. The rage in the country was leading toward an uprising, but the time had not come; the Germans were still too strong in northern Italy.

The reconstituted Fascist party of north Italy began to take revenge on its enemies in actions reminiscent of the old days of the movement. The federal secretary of the party in Ferrara was shot for treason. A squadron of the bullyboys in the Blackshirts from Padua assassinated eighteen known anti-Fascists. In this atmosphere the trial of the "traitors of the council" was inevitable, even had it not been ordered by Hitler. The Council of Ministers decreed:

"The coup d'état of July 25 has faced Italy with the greatest betrayal in recorded history. A sinister plot involving certain generals, party leaders, and ministers struck the regime in the back, creating disorder and confusion in the country in the agonizing moment when the enemy was setting foot in the soil of the fatherland."

The judgment of history would rest on the King, but the lesser traitors had to be brought to fascist justice.

Ambassador Rahn assessed the men chosen to serve on the Special Tribunal to try these men. He told his German bosses it was composed of "proven and fanatical Fascists of the old guard and most possess the highest war decorations and will offer the guarantee that particularly in Ciano's case the death sentence will be pronounced."

The problem was to find enough of the "traitors" to stage the trial. Dino Grandi, the central figure in the conspiracy, had escaped with his family to London on false passports provided by the King. Alberto de Stefani was hiding in the Chinese Nationalist embassy in the Vatican where Umberto Albini had also taken refuge. Giuseppe Bottai had vanished to join the French Foreign Legion, that refuge of men who want to disappear. But, altogether, six of those who had voted against Mussolini on that fateful night in July were rounded up, including Count Ciano, who had sought safety with his family in Munich and had been held in house arrest there by Hitler since.

As the trial approached, Hitler declared himself satisfied that his sort of justice would be done in Italy and promised not to interfere with the judgment. He was interested in only one thing, to be sure that Count Ciano was given the death penalty and executed, not because he was disloyal to Mussolini, but because the Germans had discovered how much Ciano hated them. Ribbentrop insisted that he had caused incalculable harm to the German cause. Mussolini also declared that personal considerations were all put aside. His daughter Edda had pleaded Ciano's innocence of treason, and he was inclined to believe her, but he saw that the currents were running too deep for him, so he backed off and promised not to interfere.

Ciano never doubted the verdict from the beginning. In prison, on December 23, he addressed a last letter to the King, claiming his loyalty and placing the blame for the war, and all of Italy's misfortunes: "One man, one man alone, through his insensate personal ambition, his thirst for military glories, condemned in his own mouth has deliberately led the country to the abyss." This was his father-in-law, Mussolini. Ciano concluded by telling the King that he had been keeping a diary for four years, detailing all the machinations and pressures and had arranged for it to be published soon after his death. He asked royal protection for his family.

Edda tried desperately to save her husband, and he had another friend, Frau Beetz, who had been assigned to him by the police chief of Rome, ostensibly as interpreter. She became very intimate with him and tried to save him by dealing with Himmler, who hated Ribbentrop and believed there might be material in the diaries to use against his enemy. A plan was drawn for SS men to spirit Ciano away, and the claim would be then made that the Fascists had done so. But the plan fell apart because Himmler had second thoughts and demanded proof that the diaries existed. Proof was proffered, but Hitler intervened and ordered the rescue mission canceled. So it all failed for Ciano.

On January 8, 1944, the trial opened in Verona's Castelvecchio. The nine members of the tribunal, all in black shirts, sat on a raised dais facing the public with the prisoners on the right and the press on the left. The public seats were filled with Fascists. The prisoners were examined. They were allowed defending lawyers but could not call witnesses. The court had a hard time finding a lawyer willing to represent Ciano and finally had to appoint one. One by one the old councillors were questioned and all testified to their loyalty to Mussolini. Marshal De Bono appeared in his military uniform with medals and spoke of his devotion to Mussolini. Carlo Pareschi, the former Minister of Agriculture, said he had voted for the measure only because it was a transfer of military power to the King. He never thought it would mean Mussolini's ouster. The most pitiable case was that of Giovanni Marinelli, who was so deaf that he had not heard a word of what went on at the Council meeting and had voted for the measure because he thought that Mussolini wanted it passed. The last prisoner to be questioned was Ciano, who denied treason in any sense.

What emerged at the trial was a picture of unhappy men, not knowing what to do in a difficult situation, and trying to put pressure on the government to end the war. No indication of conspiracy was presented. Even the president of the court was shamed by the turn of the evidence, which did not indicate that there had been any conspiracy afoot and that all had been done openly.

But the next day a document involving Marshal Cavallero did refer to a conspiracy among the generals to get rid of Mussolini. It named Badoglio and General Ambrosio. There was nothing in this document, nor was any evidence given, to link this military conspiracy with the Fascist Grand Council but the prosecution was triumphant. There had been a conspiracy—that was the important thing. And, of course, by voting to throw the military into the King's hands, the Council then threw the government into the hands of the conspirators. This, in the eyes of the prosecution, made these men as guilty as if they had known what they were doing.

On January 9 the defense lawyers were allowed to speak for the clients, but they were very careful, none of them wanting to imperil his future, and so no fireworks ensued. The court retired at 10 A.M. to consider the verdict. There was some argument over some of the defendants, but in the end the court determined to give all of them the death penalty, except Tullio Cianetti, one councillor who had written Mussolini to apologize for his vote; he retracted it and asked to be sent to the front in atonement, just after the event. He was sentenced to thirty years' imprisonment, and all the other defendants were sentenced to death. Marinelli, the deaf man, was so deaf that he could not hear the verdict and when told that he would die he fainted.

Edda Mussolini Ciano made a last-ditch effort to save her husband, sending letters threatening Mussolini and Hitler with release of embarrassing documents about their various conspiracies of the past. That same day of the verdict she escaped to Switzerland. The convicted men all appealed their sentences. Ciano refused at first to sign the appeal but was persuaded that the absence of his signature would imperil their chances of success, so he relented and signed. Actually, the others may have made a fatal error here. Had Ciano not signed they might have been successful in their appeal. For Ciano was the one the hardline Fascists and the Germans insisted be killed. After the appeal was presented, the prosecution needed someone to reject it and sought vainly among the Italian military for a general who would do so. The prosecutor finally found a local Militia general who signed the rejection of the appeal and ordered the execution.

In the Scalzi prison, the defendants waited through the night of January 10. At nine o'clock on the morning of January 11, the public prosecutor appeared with other officials and announced that the appeal had been rejected, and that the sentences would be carried out. The prisoners were handed over to the Italian police, and the SS guard that had supervised them until now withdrew.

Then followed the last scene in this shabby drama, as confused and ignoble as the whole Italian situation had become. The Germans had assigned an SS officer to attend and witness the execution, and he reported:

"Judges, police officials and Fascists thronged the prison grounds. The condemned men were thrust into the cells and manacled. An untidy procession headed by Don Chiot (the chaplain) filed into the courtyard. Ciano was cursing loudly and Marinelli [the deaf man] was in a state of collapse. At De Bono's insistence, Ciano quieted and turning to the chaplain said, "We have all made mistakes and we are all swept away by the same gale. Tell my family I die without rancor against anyone." [That was a message to Edda that Ciano had forgiven his father-in-law for not saving him.]

I accompanied the Chef de Province and his retinue in the prisoners' vehicle to the scene of execution. It was a shooting range in the Forte San Procolo, a suburb of Verona.

The firing squad consisted of a detachment of militia, some twenty-five men strong. The criminals were made to sit back to front on a chair, with the back of the chair facing forwards so that their own backs were exposed to the firing squad. Their hands were tied to the back of the chair. In the case of Marshal de Bono, who was farthest away from where I was standing, I gather from his head-shakings and reluctance that he was refusing to be bound and only agreed after some persuasion. The only prisoner who caused trouble was again Marinelli, who had to be bound by force by several people, and who shrieked and moaned the whole time. The others maintained a calm demeanor.

The firing squad took up their places in two rows fifteen paces behind the prisoners, their small Italian rifles loaded and at the ready. [What the SS officer did not report was that the Germans so distrusted the Italians that they brought a German squad into the execution ground who stood at the ready, prepared to carry out the executions if the Italians refused.] Just before the order to fire was given, one of the condemned men shouted, "Long Live Italy! Long Live the Duce!"

After the first salvo four of the prisoners fell to the ground, taking their chairs with them, while one remained sitting on his chair, quite unaffected judging from his posture. From the distance at which I was standing I could not make out whether he had been kept erect by sheer equilibrium or whether he had been hit at all.

The men lying on the ground had been so inaccurately hit that they were writhing and screaming. After a short, embarrassed pause, a few more shots were fired from the ranks of the firing squad at the man still on the chair and those on the ground. Finally the cease-fire was given and the men were finished off with pistols of the commander of the squad and a few other militiamen. When Ciano's death and that of all the other prisoners had been confirmed, I left the place of execution.

∽

The reactions of the Germans were all that Mussolini could have wanted. Hitler had expected some attempt to lighten the sentences. He had been so suspicious that a German officer was detailed to examine Ciano's body to be sure that no substitution had been made. But having achieved this vengeance over the man the Germans had hated above all else, when they discovered his antipathy to them, Hitler was pleasantly surprised. He observed to the Italian Ambassador Anfuso that the Republic of Salò had cut its ties with the past and intended to be near Germany in every way.

But in Italy the opinion was sharply divided. The old Fascist hardliners approved heartily. The moderates did not like it. The Republicans of the north hated what Mussolini had done, and in Rome the executions aroused a new sympathy for Ciano.

Personally, the killing of Ciano was a tragedy for Mussolini because he did not really believe his son-in-law was guilty of treason, which he was not. He had never been part of the conspiracy of the generals. But Ciano's opposition had been open, too open, and he had paid the price for airing his hatred for the Germans. In essence, Ribbentrop had had his revenge.

Although Mussolini had been convinced of Ciano's loyalty, he had seen that Hitler was determined to have his son-in-law's life. Hitler had said as much in those brief days in Rastenburg. "If you will not deal with him, we shall hang him here in Germany," Hitler had grated. And so Mussolini had refused to participate in the trial of the Fascist Council members, hoping that somehow something would happen to solve the problem without violence.

"I do not believe and, as you know, have never believed that the condemnation of these men can help the country or the reestablishment of our international situation. The future will prove me right," he said to Ambassador Anfuso.

After the execution Mussolini could not forget what had been done. He interviewed everyone who had participated in any aspect of the trial and punishment. He even defended Ciano to his associates against charges of having enriched himself corruptly or betraying himself.

Politically, the tragedy was great, but personally it was greater. His daughter Edda never forgave him. He sent several letters to her in Switzerland, asking her to write to him. She replied frostily, "I shall be the wife of a traitor and a thief. And I shall be extraordinarily proud of it. I carry the ensanguined name of my husband with pride, it is in honor. And that goes for you and your slaves and masters."

The incident heightened Mussolini's feeling of impotence and drove him into introspection. His interest in religion continued to revive. He had many talks with priests who became friends. "We are Catholics by conviction," he told a delegation of priests who came to see him. "I am a Catholic by conviction, because I believe that Catholicism is the religion which possesses a doctrine capable of resolving all the problems of life, individual and social, national, and international, and in the conflict between spiritualism and materialism it sustains and desires the primacy and victory of the spirit." Yet he resisted going the whole way and returning to the sacraments of the church. When one of the priests asked him to come back to worship, he said. "Let us wait a little, father. There is time, there is time."

But to Otto Skorzeny, who came to see him in the spring of 1944, there was no time. Mussolini appeared to be living in a dream world. He did not seem to take any interest in the political problems of the Republic. His associates said he spent much of his time in meditation. When Skorzeny went back to Germany, he told Hitler that Il Duce had ceased to be the active head of state and had turned into a political philosopher.

That year a rumor started in Rome that Mussolini was dead and everything being done was the product of others perpetuating his name. When Mussolini heard the rumor he did not laugh or snarl as would have been his reaction a few years earlier.

"They may be right," he said. "They may be right."

CHAPTER 26

∞

The Republic
Collapses

Hitler had given Mussolini the impression that what really stood
between them was Mussolini's reluctance to punish the men who
had set up his ouster by the King, but when the Verona trial had been
held and the innocent executed for crimes they never committed, Mussolini discovered that what Hitler had said had no substance. He assumed that his failure to have an army in the field was the source of
Hitler's continued arm's-length treatment, but about that there was
nothing to be done. In spite of active recruiting, the Republic had been
able to enlist only 130,000 soldiers, and, after they were trained, the
Germans sent them back because they had no use for them; besides,
the Italian equipment was ridiculously antique. The fact was that Hitler did not want Mussolini to have an army. He wanted matters to stand
precisely as they were, with the Fascists still having a presence in the
world, but no substance to their government to create problems for the
Germans.

∞

This failure would have played into the hands of the British and American Allies, except for their own failures. The Badoglio government in
Naples had no more respect from the Italian people, by and large, than
Mussolini's Salò Republic. The Allies had sacrificed Italian goodwill
by a series of failures to take strong action in the war. By the spring of
1944, an observer for the British-sponsored Polish government in exile

summed up the Italian situation as a toss-up. The Italians in the south had lost their slender faith in the democracies and were turning to Russia.

"Not only the working classes are looking more and more towards the Russians," said the Polish observer. "Even the middle classes and the intellectuals are increasingly showing their willingness to accept a more communist regime in Italy." (His use of the word *more* suggested a fundamental misunderstanding of the Communists, which at that time afflicted many central Europeans.) And as for northern Italy, "a good part of those who have been forced to join the ranks of the neo-Fascist Republican party under Mussolini foresee the inevitable defeat of the Nazis and are inclined to endorse the establishment of a communist regime."

Here again was a fundamental error made by a Western-oriented observer: No one was forced to join the new Fascist Republican party. And as to the turn toward Russia, it included Mussolini himself, as he reached back toward his beginnings.

The reason for the change in the south was the total failure of the democratic groups there. They had shown no political understanding of the war and had created great confusion in administration. The Allies had not helped by their fuzzy policies toward the Italians. To the people, American and British policies seemed meaningless. "To put it crudely the predominating feeling among the majority of Italians is one of true hate for the Germans, discouragement and a feeling of having been deceived by the British and Americans, and a growing appreciation for the attitude of Soviet Russia, whose propaganda promised a new Europe, built in a socialist image, eliminating the excesses of capitalism."

South Italy had become almost totally dependent on the Allies for its survival and health, said the Polish observer.

He had no better appraisal to make of the conditions in the north where he alluded to "total disorganization in all branches of national life from the military to the economic." He pointed out that the partisans in north Italy could carry on almost unrestricted guerrilla activity because the Germans would not let the Italian police act. Consequently, it was possible for partisans and their leaders to live in the towns and cities without being arrested by the police who knew who and what they were.

Mussolini was put down as "incapable of rallying the Italians around him." The result was, "the already precarious position and conditions in north Italy are aggravated by the existence of fully organized bands of brigands who rove about the country practically unhampered, murdering, robbing, and burning down houses."

But Mussolini was not as insensitive and insensate as his detractors averred. He foresaw the forthcoming defeat of Germany. He sensed that the Italian people were turning toward Stalin. Speaking to his secretary, he noted that because of Italy's voluntary exit from the war, no matter what happened in the peace, Italy was going to be "cracked like a nut" by the Western Allies. The Italians would have to choose a protector, and as far as he was concerned, as an Italian citizen he would not hesitate to choose Stalin. "It is clear that 95 percent of the Italians, if they were called upon freely to determine their future destiny, would opt for Stalin."

∽

Seeing how the wind was blowing with the Germans and that the refusal of neutral nations to either recognize or send representatives to the Salò Republic showed he could get nowhere in the field of international relations, Mussolini began to turn his attention to the civil economy of the Italy he controlled, or rather, that the Germans controlled for him.

His first task was the socialization of the economy, and he turned that over to a new Ministry of Corporate Economy, to which he appointed Angelo Tarchi. What he was trying to do was create more equal distribution of wealth and the participation of labor on equal grounds with capital and management in the life of the nation. He envisaged a new Europe dominated by Soviet Russia and true to the principles of socialism. The new order promised by Stalin would mean that all the liberated countries could play a part. Biographer Ivone Kirkpatrick parroted the Polish observer in saying that "it was a conception wholly divorced from reality." Kirkpatrick was, after all, a British foreign officer and public servant, and it was natural that he should adopt such a view. But the reason it turned out to be true was the nature of the war's end and the peace of America coming into conflict with the peace of Russia and creating the cold war.

In the early months of 1944 there seemed to be a hope that the new Europe could be built without further conflict, and in that setting, Mussolini's views were cogent. Europeans had not forgotten Britain's abandonment of France in the debacle of the spring of 1940 and her self-serving war effort, which had entangled the United States as well. Mussolini fully realized that he was the most hated man in Italy, but he hoped to reverse that opinion in the coming months.

Mussolini's legislative decree for the socialization of enterprise, which applied to companies employing more than one hundred people, called for equal representation on the boards of directors of investors and management and employees. The director would have a vote. The workers' representatives would be elected from a panel. The director and the management committee would answer to the state.

In the south, and by the Western Allies, this plan was greeted with jeers. But the real problem of the plan was that the Germans refused to let the system function. When strikes upset production, they interfered and tried to mobilize the workers on a military system, which, of course, drove more thousands into the arms of the Communists.

From the outset Ambassador Rahn tried to control Mussolini's government. He was restrained by Hitler, who told him that the social and economic measures taken in Italy were to be left to Mussolini.

But the real failure came from the working class. Twenty years of fascism, as Mussolini knew very well, had not dimmed the hatred of the Socialists and Communists for the man who had edited the Socialist party newspaper *Avanti!* and had deserted the fold. Mussolini's effort was greeted as a bit of fascist propaganda. The Communist agitators in the factories helped to extinguish any interest the workers might have had in the scheme. They called strikes that March in Milan and Turin, directed as much against the Salò government as the Germans. The German reaction was swift and brutal, because the Italians were threatening a factory production that was essentially turned to German interests. Hitler ordered action. A fifth of the strikers would be deported to Germany. In the face of this threat the strikes collapsed. This immediate interference with a civil matter proved to the workers that the Salò Republic was a house of cards. One of Mussolini's loyal labor leaders wrote a letter telling him the ugly truth:

"The masses refuse to accept anything from us. The workers assert there will be no nationalization. They think the German influence has been decidedly negative. They said we were not in good faith and hold that the announcement of nationalization was an expedient to draw into our orbit the few 'mugs' who still give us any credit. In brief, the workers consider nationalization to be a mirror to catch larks, and they keep well away from us."

This disruption of his efforts to govern upset Mussolini so much that he decided he must have a conference with Hitler. His request was put through Ambassador Rahn, who added his own recommendation that Hitler should agree, and also that Mussolini should be given something, lest he cease his efforts altogether. In addition to the meeting, it was arranged that Mussolini inspect the cadres of four Italian divisions then in training in Germany. So on April 22, 1944, at Schloss Klessheim Hitler assembled with Ribbentrop, General Keitel, Ambassador Rahn, and General Wolff, the commander of German forces in northern Italy. Mussolini brought General Graziani, Count Serafino Mazzolini, his undersecretary of Foreign Affairs, Ambassador Anfuso, and the military attaché of the Berlin embassy. Mussolini opened the meeting with a statement that he gave in German.

He complained about the German behavior in the Tirol and Venezia Giulia and northern Italy, which the Germans had taken over for military government, and about the continued holding of some Italian soldiers as prisoners. He said openly that his government had little support from the Italian people because it was seen as a creature of the Germans. If the Germans wanted an effective government in Italy they would have to relax their controls. They had asked for a million Italian workers, a quarter of a million soldiers for antiaircraft batteries in Germany, and sixty thousand for antiaircraft batteries in Italy. He could hardly supply these if his government had no credence.

General Graziani then spoke about his difficulties in running a defense ministry without an army, and with all facilities including communications in the hands of the Germans. A dozen battalions were engaged in the war against the partisans, who were better armed and equipped by the Allies than were his soldiers. His new recruits did not even have uniforms.

Hitler then spoke and gave his usual rambling discourse about his own problems.

The next morning Hitler aired his resentments against Italy and against Mussolini for having changed from the self-assured dictator of the past to a political philosopher and from a revolutionary to a moderate.

He said flatly that the Italian soldiers were not reliable. He was adamant about maintaining German authority over the "operational zones" of Italy, where German forces passed through. Perhaps, if fascism again grew strong in the Republic . . .

On the second afternoon Hitler and Mussolini both tried to soften the harshness of their early statements to each other. They pledged their mutual connection and each vowed to stick with the other. They were like children holding hands as they entered a dark room, not knowing what the passage will bring. That evening Hitler and Mussolini dined together, and Hitler talked about the secret weapons that were going to turn the war around. Mussolini listened but later confided to Ambassador Anfuso that Hitler had seemed terribly optimistic to him.

After the meeting with Hitler, Mussolini went to Grafenroehr camp to inspect the cadre of the San Marco Division which was training there. He gave a fighting speech that reminded everyone of the Mussolini of old. He told them that soon they would open fire on "the cruel and cynical Briton, the American, the Frenchman, the Indian, the South African, the Canadian, the New Zealander, the Moor, the Senegalese, the Negro and the Bolshevik bastard races and mercenaries."

This was a taste of the old Mussolini and the troops loved it. He was cheered and cheered, and smiling, he left them to return to Lake Garda, much refreshed by the visit. Of his visit, the Kolnische *Zeitung* said on April 18:

"New strength has been given to the Italians by mustering all the actional forces so as to create a spiritual front which will successfully stem the invasion of the enemy."

But the truth was that the Republic was stuck on dead center and going nowhere. That spring the Italian partisans increased their activity, their ranks swelled by deserters from the Militia and factory workers who had fled to the countryside to escape being shipped to Germany. The Piedmont valley was the scene of a vigorous fight. The partisans attacked the barracks of the Republic's troops. German troops and militia were brought to fight the partisans. The partisans captured the barracks, but the Germans and Republic forces burned sixty-eight houses in the valley, on the assumption that most of them were the houses of partisans. The partisans were becoming better-armed all the time, and in this area even had tanks, which they had taken over from the Leonessa Armored Division, disbanded by the Germans. But most of the arms were allied, air-dropped to the bands, which were in communication with various allied intelligence and special operations units.

More threatening to the Salò Republic was the progress of the Allies. They captured Rome on June 4, 1944, and by July 19 they had reached Leghorn on the Mediterranean coast and Ancona on the Adriatic. The invasion of Normandy had closed the north, and to the east, Hitler's forces were on the retreat before the Russians.

That summer of 1944 the partisan strength was estimated by General Graziano at eighty-two thousand, and they held nearly all of Piedmont. In June, the Germans and the Republic forces had fought twenty-two hundred engagements with the partisans. The war against the partisans became the central activity of the Republic forces. But it was never very effective, because the partisans were better armed and better organized than the Republic.

The Republic was really like a government in exile. It had the trappings of government, but no substance because the Germans would not allow any. They did not want an Italian army. They were becoming more concerned with their own survival every day. General Graziani, after endless talks with the Germans, managed to secure two of the Italian divisions training in Germany for use against the partisans. It was agreed that first Mussolini should pay them a visit. He left Gargnano on July 15 in a special train provided by the Germans on a trip organized by the Germans. For three days he traveled from camp to camp inspecting the troops and making speeches. He was greeted everywhere with cheers by these young Italians. He then took a train to Rastenburg to meet Hitler.

Hitler, his arm in a sling, and looking like death warmed over, stood on the platform as the train arrived. He was accompanied by Ribbentrop, Himmler, Bormann, Keitel, and Dönitz.

Hitler walked to Mussolini's coach and told him that a bomb had nearly blown him up a few hours earlier. He was in no state for a meeting, but he took Mussolini to the scene of the explosion and described the whole affair in great detail. The shattered conference room was still smouldering.

"Having escaped death so miraculously," he said, "I am more than ever sure that the great destiny I serve will transcend its present perils and that all will be brought to a triumphant conclusion."

Later in the day the two leaders met. Hitler spoke of his need for Italian volunteers of antiaircraft batteries to protect the factories. If he got them all, the four Italian divisions could go home and with four German divisions would constitute an army under Graziani. Kesselring would fight a delaying action in Italy as long as possible and the Germans would take steps to recover air superiority. The meeting ended with Mussolini having for once secured all he came to get. That evening they parted, for what would be the last time. Hitler looked long at Mussolini and spoke:

"I know that I can count on you, and I beg of you to believe me when I say that I look upon you as my best and possibly only friend I have in the world."

The first two Italian divisions returned at the end of July and were formed with three German divisions into Army Group Liguria under Graziani's command. Their task was to deal with an allied landing on the northwest coast or an attack coming through the Alpine passes from France. But since these events did not occur, the army group was deployed to fight the partisans, in which they were not very successful, but the war was the more vicious for that. All over the country the partisans attacked Germans and Fascists, and the Germans and the Fascists replied with savage reprisals. In Milan on August 9, 1944, a German truck was attacked. As a reprisal the Germans ordered the execution of fifteen political prisoners. They were shot by an Italian detachment and their bodies were piled in the Piazzale Loreto, where the attack on the truck had occurred.

∽

Mussolini tried his best with the Germans to have at least the semblance of an independent Republic, but he did not succeed. The Germans were too insensitive to the Italians; they kept pressing for manpower to be taken to Germany, they kept interfering with the processes of government in northern Italy. They made such a travesty of Mussolini's efforts that in the summer of 1944 he told his cabinet he was thinking of resigning.

At the same time the battlefront situation was deteriorating steadily for the Germans. On August 15, the Allies landed on the southern coast of France and pushed north. On August 25, Paris was liberated, and by October nearly all of France and Belgium were in allied hands. But more important, on August 25, the Allies in Italy were only 150 miles away, along a line from Pisa to Pesaron.

The Allies halted for the winter just south of Bologna, having captured Mussolini's home at Forlì, which was sacked by the local people.

In an optimistic mood, Mussolini had suggested to Hitler in November that the only front on which the Axis could take the initiative was the Italian front and this could be done with a handful of troops. But Hitler, in November 1944, was in no position to be bothered by the Italian front. Nor was his confidence in Italy restored, although he and his affection and allegiance to Mussolini seemed to be the only permanent attachments he possessed.

∽

Thus, winter 1944 came to Lake Garda.

The allied armies were threatening Bologna and Ravenna, and the entire valley of the Po. The Germans were too busy with their own defense worries to give any consideration to building up the status of the Salò Republic. Mussolini found his activities more and more limited, and he retreated further into himself each month. He was quite isolated from events, and except for his immediate government associates, and the Germans, he was very much alone. It was hard to remember those days in Rome when Romans had cheered his every word. The people of Italy now behaved as though they had never cheered Mussolini and fascism had never existed.

CHAPTER 27

∽

Finis

The winter of 1944–45 was indeed Mussolini's winter of discontent. To begin with, Rachele was acting up. At the time of Mussolini's downfall and captivity she had learned of the affair with Clara Petacci and her fury had been terrifying. Now, Clara had been released from detention by the Badoglio government and brought by the SS to Lake Garda where she had been installed in a villa not far from Mussolini. From time to time he visited her, and she was in communication with him every day by telephone. From Minister of the Interior Buffarini-Guidi, Rachele learned of Clara's presence. She and Buffarini-Guidi visited Clara's villa one day. In the confrontation Rachele demanded that Clara leave the area; Clara refused, and in the quarrel she fainted. Rachele was so angry that she returned to the Villa Feltrinelli and dramatically took poison, but not enough to do much harm. Mussolini, faced with her fury, elected to spend the next few nights in his office.

In turn his anger was directed at Buffarini-Guidi who had interfered, and he decided to get rid of him. He appointed a new undersecretary of Interior, but he could not find anyone of any stature to accept the minister's job, so low had the reputation of the Republic fallen.

The cause of the people's contempt for the Republic was its obvious control by the Germans, who did not even try to be devious in pulling the strings. Mussolini decided to shake off the German shadow, at least in his relations with the people. His first step would be to speak to them, for he knew very well his power as an orator. Very quietly, so as not to arouse German interest, he planned a speech in Milan's Piazza San Sepolcro. On the morning of December 16, 1944, preceded only by a radio announcement the day before that an exceptional event would

271

take place, he appeared before a carefully assembled audience at the Lyric Theater. It was his first public speech since his dismissal by the King. He spoke defiantly of the coming Axis victory over the Western powers. How was it to be achieved? By Hitler's secret weapons. "We will defend the valley of the Po with our nails and with our teeth," he said, and he predicted that in a few weeks he would be back in the Palazzo Venezia and the Allies would have vanished like flies in winter from Italian soil. Then he would revolutionize Italy with social reforms.

As he left the theater he was nearly mobbed by the hysterical crowd. Even known anti-Fascists came up to shake his hand, tears in their eyes. The next day he made a triumphal tour of the city, speaking from the top of a tank at one point, reviewing the troops of the Republic of Salò, traveling in procession through the streets at walking pace in an open car.

But the public ovation changed nothing. Back at Gargnano Mussolini found that he had fewer and fewer options. The German noose was drawn tighter as the war worsened for them. Mussolini and the Germans were now secretly, and without informing one another, making plans for the end of the war in allied victory. General Wolff, commander of the SS forces in Italy, was negotiating with Allen Dulles, the American master spy in Switzerland. Mussolini tried to arrange a surrender with the Allies through the Archbishop of Milan, but the Allies had their usual answer: unconditional surrender.

As spring 1945 came, and the Allies opened their offensive in northern Italy, the Western Allies crossed the Elbe River in Germany, and the Russians were only thirty-five miles east of Berlin. Mussolini continued to try to negotiate a surrender, but he also prepared for a last-ditch stand in an Alpine stronghold for the Salò Republic. Personally he was prepared for death and he welcomed its approach. He gave an interview to Madeleine Mollier, the wife of the German press attaché, which she promised not to publish before his death. "Death has become a friend who no longer frightens me," he said. "Death is a gift from God to those who have suffered too much." He talked to her, as he often did to others these days, about his life, his triumphs, and his mistakes.

"I have never made a mistake when I followed my instinct, only when I obeyed reason. I am responsible as much for the things I did well, which the world will not be able to deny me, as for my weaknesses and my fall . . . I am finished. My star has set. I work and exert myself, though I know it is all a farce. Perhaps I was destined only to point the way to my people. I should have rested content on a firm, secure basis. But have you ever known a prudent, calculating dictator?"

He predicted a united Europe at the end of the war, and a United States that would take a leadership role in world affairs. He predicted that Italy would find herself in the same position she was in at the end of World War I, caught between East and West. Would she become the advance post of the "Anglo-Saxon plutocracies" or the Mediterranean sentinel of the Soviet world? He had lost none of his distaste for Western democracy and held that the future of Italy belonged to socialism.

But as he philosophized and waited for death, he went through the motions of planning for the future. He still held some hope of coming to an accommodation with the Socialists. That could not be accomplished at Gargnano, but only in Milan. On April 14, 1945, he held what was to be his last meeting with the Germans. The German representatives were General Wolff, Ambassador Rahn, and General von Vietinghoff, the commander of German forces in Italy following Field Marshal Kesselring's selection to be commander in chief of German forces in the west. For the Italians, Mussolini was supported by General Graziani and Anfuso, who had recently left Germany to become Mussolini's undersecretary in his role as foreign minister. He unveiled his plans for a last effort in an Alpine redoubt. The Germans, who were making their own preparations to surrender without reference to the Salò Republic, were noncommittal, but General Wolff asked Mussolini not to deal with the Allies through the archbishop. Mussolini said he was planning to move the government to Milan, and Wolff said he should not do that. Mussolini meekly agreed not to move. What else was he to do? The Germans held all the cards in this shrinking deck. They told Anfuso that Ribbentrop was asking for him in Berlin, and Anfuso agreed to leave the following day. He did so and reached Bad Gastein, where he was put under house arrest by the Germans with the rest of the diplomatic corps. He made an attempt to come back but was held up at Riva on the north end of Lake Garda; thus, he missed the last act of the Salò Republic.

∽

Mussolini ignored his promise to Wolff not to move to Milan and on April 16 he announced the move. He had no hopes left but he was going through the motions. He sent for his sister Edvige and advised her to move to Milan with her family. When the war ended, if she needed protection, she was to address herself to Winston Churchill, who had in the past spoken of Mussolini with civility and admiration. He said good-bye to her and told her that he had been ready for some time to die. He sorted through his private papers and had the current ones shipped by truck to Milan; the others were taken by boat out into Lake Garda and sunk.

On April 18 he told his German guards that he was going to Milan for two or three days. In the garden of the Villa Feltrinelli he told Rachele he was going to Milan for a few days. And then he left the villa forever.

At nine o'clock that night he reached the Milan prefecture, a large palazzo on the Via Monforte. Here he clustered around him the remnants of the faithful, a dozen of the new Fascisti but only one of the old, Roberto Farinacci, and his son Vittorio. Outside his office the German SS sentries still stood guard. They had been told that Mussolini was not to leave Italy. If he tried to escape to Switzerland he was to be restrained by force.

But Mussolini had no intention of leaving. He knew his days were numbered and he wanted to die on Italian soil. Clara Petacci had made plans for escape to Switzerland and had found a hut in a tiny community high in the mountains, reachable only by mountain trail, where she proposed that she and Il Duce go and spend the rest of their lives. It was "the asshole of the universe," said her friend Franz Spögler, the German officer who owned the place and gave it to her. At least twenty-five times in the past few months Clara had discussed the hideaway with Mussolini and he had pretended to go along with the plan. Now the men around him spoke about plans to escape to Spain, to Switzerland, and the Val Tellina redoubt.

On April 20, when the Allies cut off Bologna, Mussolini gave orders that the scattered government offices be disbanded. Only those required in the Valtellina would be concentrated now in Milan. Ambassador Rahn came and tried to persuade him to return to Gargnano, but having liberated himself from German control, Mussolini refused flatly to reenter the trap.

On April 21, the Allies entered Bologna and the anti-Fascists rose up and attacked all the Fascist officials they could find. Blood literally ran in the streets. That day General Graziani reported that the German front in Italy had collapsed. In Germany the Russians were at the gates of Berlin, and Hitler was deep in his bunker beneath the ruins of the Reich Chancellery.

It was Mussolini's hope that he could save the Salò Republic by transferring power to the Socialists, and he drafted a letter to that effect. But when the leader of the Liberation Committee heard of Mussolini's proposal, he told his associates that it was to be given no attention whatsoever.

Parma fell to the Allies. Genoa was captured by the partisans. Everywhere the partisans moved, one of their principal aims was to slaughter the Fascists. On April 23 Mussolini again talked about the Alpine redoubt, but he did nothing to arrange to go there. Later that day he visited Clara Petacci, who had come to Milan to be near him. He spoke to Rachele by telephone and told her to leave for Monza, the old royal villa, where she would be picked up by an escort and taken to the redoubt at Lake Como. She left that very night and arrived the next morning.

On April 24, the American Tenth Mountain Division crossed the River Po. Soon now, they would reach Milan. The Liberation Committee was planning an uprising, and when the Allies got wind of it, they pleaded with the partisans to hold off. They wanted Mussolini alive, and twenty-five teams of the American Office of Strategic Services (OSS) clandestine warfare agency were now on the lookout for him; but the partisans wanted him dead and he and his Fascists killed by Italian hands. Luigi Longo, the Communist leader, had persuaded the committee to disregard General Mark Clark's pleas for moderation. That day Kriminalinspektor Otto Kisnatt, chief of the Mussolini German guard, asked Mussolini when he was going back to Lake Garda, and Mussolini told him "never." Then, said Kisnatt, he must go to where the German embassy was located, in Merano on the Austrian border. Mussolini produced a map and traced a route that he said he would follow to Merano. The inspector did not notice that it wound around very near to Valtellina where the redoubt would be established.

On April 25 when the government offices of the Salò Republic opened in Milan, most of the functionaries did not appear, and many of the police had suddenly disappeared from the streets. This day was the fateful one on which Mussolini suddenly decided it was time to go to the Valtellina redoubt. Later that day Mussolini was persuaded to go to the archbishop's palace to meet with members of the Liberation Committee to discuss possibilities of a peaceful surrender. He wanted desperately to reach an accommodation with the Socialists and turn his Republic over to them. "I should like to entrust the Republic to Republicans and Socialists and not to monarchists and reactionaries," he said.

Mussolini arrived at the palace before the Liberation Committee delegates and was received by the cardinal archbishop, who complimented him on his willingness to surrender and possibly spend the rest of his life in prison to save the rest of Italy from ruin. He told the cardinal that he was leaving the next day for the Valtellina, and the cardinal asked if he planned to continue the war in the mountains. "Only for a while," said Mussolini, "and then I shall give myself up."

In another room General Graziani learned then that the Germans had negotiated a surrender of their army in Italy, which was a terrible shock to him.

Finally the representatives of the Liberation Committee arrived, and they all adjourned to the meeting room where the Fascists sat on one side of the conference table and the partisans on the other. Mussolini asked what proposals the committee had to offer. He was told that the committee expected unconditional surrender within two hours. The matter was urgent because the general partisan uprising was about to begin. If the Fascist government surrendered, they would be treated as prisoners of war when they laid down their arms, although some might be singled out later for trials. Graziani then dropped his bombshell, saying that the Germans had surrendered. Mussolini was shocked beyond speech. He broke off the meeting and declared he was going to broadcast the facts to the people. He said he would give the Liberation Committee an answer within the hour, and he left the palace. On the way back to the prefecture, he said that the whole meeting had been a plot to capture him and his government. He was not willing to be arrested again.

Back at the prefecture, he decided against dealing further with the partisans, and rather than have a battle in the streets, he opted to head immediately for the Valtellina. A motorcade was organized, led by an armored car. A truck was loaded with cash, and those who would go to the redoubt left the prefecture—about half the officials of the Republic, the other half opting to stay and deal with the partisans. At eight o'clock that night, April 25, the convoy left Milan. The cardinal's palace telephoned and the caller was told there would be no surrender. That night several Fascist armed bands followed Mussolini on the road to Como; Clara Petacci made her way there, too. At eight o'clock in the morning the prefecture at Milan was quietly occupied by the partisans. Milan was completely in their hands.

On the evening of April 26, the convoy arrived at the prefecture in Como. That evening the local chief of police came in to announce that partisans were infiltrating the city and that it was no longer safe for the Fascists. Mussolini then decided to leave Como, because he wanted to avoid bloodshed in the city. He would go to the mountains, he said. Before he left Como he wrote a last letter to Rachele, under the date,

"26 April Year XXIII of the Fascist Era." He told her he was coming to the end, that he loved her and had always loved only her, and asked her forgiveness for the wrongs he had done her. He told her to go to Switzerland, and if they would not let her in, to throw herself on the mercy of the Allies. The letter was delivered and that night Rachele telephoned him and pleaded with him to escape to safety. He refused. Even his driver had now left he said, and he was all alone. "I see that all is over."

At three o'clock on the morning of April 26 he left Como, and the convoy stopped at Menaggio, where he stayed for the rest of the night hours. Another group led by General Graziani followed him, and Clara Petacci came, too. They were now only ten miles from the Swiss border. They put up at the little Hotel Miravalle. They listened to the radio, and learned that all Milan was in the hands of the partisans, and that the Liberation Committee had decreed sentences of death for all the officials of the Republic and all the Fascist military and paramilitary groups. Some of Mussolini's followers arrived with word that they had been in an encounter with partisans and two of their number had been killed. Mussolini was waiting here for the arrival of his military convoy, several hundred armed men and some artillery and armored cars, which had set out from Milan. But along the way, the military force disintegrated completely and when Alessandro Pavolini arrived at 4 A.M. on April 27 in his armed car, he had only a handful of men left.

That morning a German antiaircraft unit of about two hundred men arrived in Menaggio on its way to safety in the Tirol. Mussolini's German guards decided to join this column and move north. With the disappearance of the military force of Italians, Mussolini gave up the thought of a last stand at the Valtellina. He was now floundering, with no plan at all in mind, impelled by the others in the party and the Germans to evade capture.

The column moved out of Menaggio, now accompanied by Clara Petacci, but was stopped at Musso by a band of partisans. Fire was exchanged, but then a parley began. The Germans said they were only interested in getting through to Germany. The partisans said they would have to go to partisan headquarters a few miles away to continue the negotiations. The officer in charge of the German column did and came back after six hours to report that they could go through. But they would have to stop at Dongo for inspection of their vehicles, because the partisans wanted to be sure none of the Fascist officials of the Republic escaped.

The Germans persuaded Mussolini to put on a German army over-
coat and helmet and ride in one of the German trucks. Clara Petacci
tried to join him but was restrained by the Germans and sent back to
her own car in the rear of the column. At about three o'clock in the
afternoon the column moved, leaving all the other Italians in the hands
of the partisans. Mussolini was now completely alone with the Germans. The convoy halted at Dongo and the partisans searched. They
recognized Mussolini and yanked him out of the truck and took him
to the headquarters of the 52nd Garibaldi Brigade in the municipal
building. There he was soon joined by the other Italians of the party
who had been arrested after the Germans left. Mussolini asked one
favor of the partisans—that they say good-bye to Clara for him. This
was the first news the partisans had that Clara was in the crowd. The
head of the band, who called himself Pedro, saw Clara, and she persuaded him to let her join Mussolini.

That night, the partisans, worried lest they be deprived of their prisoner
by the Americans or by a Fascist group, moved Mussolini to the other
side of Lake Como. He was awakened and his identity hidden by band-
aging his whole head. The party drove first to Dongo, where Mussolini
was allowed to greet Clara, and she insisted on joining him. Then the
party drove to Como, passing through many groups of partisans, each
of which stopped them but paid no attention to the wounded partisan
with his head bandaged who was on the way to the hospital. When they
reached the town of Moltrasio, four miles from Como, they heard firing
and learned that the Americans had arrived that night in Como and
were meeting some resistance from the Fascists. So the two cars then
turned back to the village of Bonzanigo and stopped on the road. Mussolini and Clara and their guards had to climb a steep path to the house
of a farmer one of the partisans knew. At that house Clara and Mussolini were given a double-bedded room and slept while in Milan their
fate was being debated by the Liberation Committee. Actually there
was virtually no deliberation. The top Communist leadership had already decided that Mussolini was to die, along with all the other major
figures of the Salò Republic. A partisan who went under the name of
Colonel Valerio was given the task of taking Mussolini out of the hands
of the local partisans and delivering him—dead—to Milan. Valerio
drove to Como where he demanded Mussolini. The local partisans did
not want to give up their captive, but they yielded to Colonel Valerio
when he said his orders came from the top.

Finally Colonel Valerio was on his way to Dongo and found Pedro, the head of the group that held Mussolini and Clara. When he found Pedro and demanded the prisoners, Pedro said they had been captured by the 52nd Garibaldi Brigade and the brigade would deliver them to Milan. That was nonsense, said Colonel Valerio, "I have come to shoot them." He asked for the list of all the prisoners who had been captured in the convoy, and when he got it, he marked off fifteen names. These people were also to be shot. Valerio then headed for the farmhouse where Mussolini and Clara were being held.

The pair waited all day on April 28. Then at about 4 o'clock in the afternoon Valerio arrived, burst into Mussolini's room, and announced that he had come to rescue him. Mussolini and Clara were hustled into a car and driven down a narrow mountain road in the direction of the lake. The car suddenly stopped outside the Villa Belmonte, a big house standing behind a stone wall. Mussolini and Clara were ordered out of the car, stood against the wall, and riddled with machine-gun bullets. Two men were left to guard the bodies and then Colonel Valerio went back to Dongo, found his fifteen men, lined them up on the square, and shot them.

On the morning of April 29, a moving van brought the bodies to a filling station in the Piazzale Loreto, the scene of the execution of the fifteen Italian hostages by the Germans the year before. The bodies of Mussolini and Clara Petacci were hung upside down from a girder, with the bodies of the fifteen officials beneath them. Men and women came to revile the bodies and even to urinate on them. That night the bodies were removed by the allied authorities and Mussolini was buried in the Musocco cemetery in Milan.

Twelve years later, in 1957, it was decided that Mussolini was no longer a threat, and the body was disinterred and reburied according to his wishes in his home cemetery in Predappio next to the grave of his beloved son Bruno. By that time, fascism was ancient history, and it would have been hard to find anyone who admitted to cheering Il Duce wildly in those demonstrations so long ago. As Mussolini once had said when his supporters demanded bloodshed in the revolutionary days, "No I don't want to end up like Cola di Rienzi." The reference was to the fourteenth-century Roman revolutionary whose reign of a few months had ended when a mob dragged him bleeding through the streets, killed him, and hung his body upside down outside the church of San Lorenzo.

So Mussolini had, indeed, ended up in the way he had feared. By 1957 it was all history. Italy was immersed again in the tangled mire of its own particular brand of parliamentary politics, the Communists were constantly threatening but never really getting anywhere, and nobody remembered the really remarkable fact about the rule of Mussolini—that he had come to power constitutionally, without bloodshed, that his rule, even in the days of his absolute dictatorship had been notable for its lack of murderous intent, and that he had gone out of power the same way, quietly and without a great stir. Had it not been for his fateful decision to seek an empire by allying himself with Adolf Hitler, his rule might have survived World War II as Generalissimo Franco's did and ended in the transition of fascism to the socialism he said at the end that he had always believed in. Sic transit gloria mundi.

Bibliography

Documents
Records of United States relations with Italy, 1910–1943, State Department Archives, U.S. National Archives, Washington.

Newspapers
The New York Times; The Times (London)

Unpublished Manuscripts
Hoyt, Edwin P. *Backwater War, The Italian Campaign, 1943–1945.*

Books
Badoglio, Pietro. *Italy in the Second World War.* Translated by Muriel Currey. London: Oxford, 1948.

Barnett, Corelli. *The Desert Generals.* London: William Kimber, 1960.

Barzini, Luigi. *The Italians.* New York: Athenaeum, 1964.

Battaglia, Roberto. *Story of the Italian Resistance.* London: Odhams Press, 1958.

Bellotti, Felice. *La republica di Mussolini.* Milan: Zagara, 1947.

Bond, Johd. *Mussolini the Wild Man of Europe.* Washington: Independent Publishers, 1929.

Borgese, G. A. *Goliath: The March of Fascism.* New York: Viking, 1938.

Buckley, Christopher. *The Road to Rome.* London: Hodder & Stoughton, 1945.

Campanelli, Paolo. *Mussolini.* London: Pallas, 1939.

Chabod, Federico. *A History of Italian Fascism.* London: Weidenfeld & Nicolson, 1963.

Ciano, Galeazzo. *Diaries, 1939–43.* Edited by Hugh Gibson. Garden City, NY: Doubleday, 1946.

Collier, Richard. *Duce!* New York: Viking, 1971.

Deakin, F. W. *The Brutal Friendship.* London: Weidenfeld & Nicolson, 1962.

De Fiori, Vittorio. *Mussolini, Man of Destiny.* London: J. M. Dent, 1928.

Dombrowski, Roman. *Mussolini: Twilight and Fall.* London: Heinemann, 1956.

Dulles, Allen. *The Secret Surrender.* New York: Harper & Row, 1966.

Ebenstein, William. *Fascist Italy.* London: Martin Hopkinson, 1939.

Fermi, Laura. *Mussolini.* Chicago: University of Chicago Press, 1961.

Finer, Herman. *Mussolini's Italy.* London: Victor Gollancz, 1935.

Fusti, Carofiglio. *Vita di Mussolini e storia del Fascismo.* Turin: So-
    cieta Editrice Torinese, 1950.
Goebbels, Joseph. *The Goebbels Diaries.* Edited and translated by Louis
    P. Lochner. Garden City, NY: Doubleday, 1948.
Gorlitz, Walter, ed. *The Memoirs of Field Marshal Keitel.* Translated
    by David Irving. New York: Stein & Day, 1966.
Hitler, Adolf. *Mein Kampf.* New York: Reynal & Hitchcock, 1939.
———. *My New Order.* New York: Reynal & Hitchcock, 1941.
Hoyt, Edwin P. *Hitler's War.* New York: McGraw-Hill, 1988.
Jackson, W. G. F. *The Battle for Rome.* New York: Charles Scribner's
    Sons, 1969.
Kirkpatrick, Ivone. *Mussolini.* London: Odhams Press, 1964.
Koon, T. H. *Believe, Obey, Fight. Political Socialization of Youth in
    Fascist Italy, 1922–43.* Chapel Hill: University of North Carolina
    Press, 1985.
Kurzman, Dan. *The Race for Rome.* Garden City, NY: Doubleday,
    1965.
Ludwig, Emil. *Talks with Mussolini.* Translated from the German by
    Eden and Cedar Paul. Boston: Little, Brown, 1933.
Lussu, Emilio. *Enter Mussolini.* London: Methuen, 1936.
Mammarelli, Giuseppi. *Italy after Fascism.* South Bend: University of
    Notre Dame Press, 1966.
Matthews, Herbert L. *The Fruits of Fascism.* New York: Harcourt
    Brace, 1943.
Monelli, Paolo. *Mussolini: An Intimate Life.* London: Thames & Hud-
    son, 1953.
Mussolini, Benito. *The Fall of Mussolini, His Own Story.* Translated
    by Frances Frenaye. New York: Farrar Straus, 1945.
———. *My Autobiography.* Translated by Richard Washburn Child. New
    York: Charles Scribner's Sons, 1928.
Mussolini, Rachele. *La mia vita con Benito.* Milan: Mondadori, 1948.
Nolte, Ernest. *Three Faces of Fascism.* London: Weidenfeld & Nicol-
    son, 1965.
Owen, Frank. *Three Dictators.* London: Allen & Unwin, 1941.
Packard, Reynolds and Eleanor. *Balcony Empire.* London: Oxford, 1942.
Patti, Ercole. *Roman Chronicle.* London: Chatto & Windus, 1965.
Robertson, Angus. *Mussolini and the New Italy.* London: Allenson,
    1929.
Saporiti, Piero. *Empty Balcony.* London: Victor Gollancz, 1947.
Seldes, George. *Sawdust Caesar.* New York: Harper and Bros., 1935.

Shirer, William. *The End of a Berlin Diary*. New York: Popular Library, 1947.

———. *The Rise and Fall of the Third Reich*. New York: Simon & Schuster, 1960.

Skorzeny, Otto. *Secret Missions*. Translated by Jacques Le Clerq. New York: E. P. Dutton & Co., 1950.

Slocombe, George. *A Mirror to Geneva*. London: Jonathan Cape, 1937.

Smith, Bradley F., and Elena Agarossi. *Operation Sunrise*. New York: Basic Books, 1979.

Smith, Dennis Mack. *Mussolini's Roman Empire*. New York: Viking, 1976.

Snowden, Frank. *The Fascist Revolution in Tuscany, 1919–22*. Cambridge: Cambridge University Press, 1989.

Steiner, H. A. *Government in Fascist Italy*. New York: McGraw-Hill, 1938.

Taylor, A. J. P. *The Origins of the Second World War*. London: Hamish Hamilton, 1961.

Tompkins, Peter. *Italy Betrayed*. New York: Simon & Schuster, 1966.

Treves, Paolo. *What Mussolini Did to Us*. London: Victor Gollancz, 1940.

Villari, Luigi. *Italian Foreign Policy under Mussolini*. Appleton, WI: Nelson, 1956.

Von Ribbentrop, Joachim. *Memoirs*. Translated by Oliver Watson. London: Weidenfeld & Nicolson, 1954.

Notes

Chapter 1

For the initial chapter in the life of Mussolini, I used all the standard biographies published in English and Mussolini's *My Autobiography*. I relied heavily on Ivone Kirkpatrick's *Mussolini* and Rachele's *My Life with Mussolini*. It was apparent, even when Mussolini was a child, that his ambitions transcended ordinary politics. One day his mother heard mutterings from his room and went up to discover him practicing a speech. "That is the speech I am going to make when I am master of all Italy," he said. His mother thought he was a little bit crazy but she recognized in the boy something unusual. She was his greatest inspiration to succeed, although she gave him much pain at the time because of her insistence that he and his brother and sister practice the rituals of the Roman Catholic church. He said he did not believe in God, but later he decided he did believe, and at the end he was studying theology.

Chapter 2

Mussolini's *My Autobiography* was central to this chapter, but Kirkpatrick provided some insights, including glimpses of Mussolini's life as revealed in letters to friends of the period. Also, biographer Richard Collier had the privilege of long interviews with Rachele Mussolini in the autumn of her life, and I relied on this study for some material about the Mussolini household in this period. Rachele's own book was very useful. The U. S. Department of State Archives had a complete account of the attempt on the life of the King, and a good deal of information about political affairs in Italy at this period, which provided background information.

Chapter 3

Kirkpatrick, *My Autobiography*, Collier, and Laura Fermi's biography were the bases for this chapter. Mussolini was still not important enough to warrant notice by the American embassy in Rome, but several of the political events in which he participated were reported in detail. Richard Washburn Child, American ambassador in the early years, was so taken by Mussolini that he translated his autobiography into English. Ambassador Page's discussion of the Italians reads like a political primer for Americans at home who knew nothing of European affairs, which, of course, was pretty generally the case in the second decade of the twentieth century.

Chapter 4

The American embassy political reports were primary sources for the situation in Italy in the immediate postwar period. For Mussolini's activities, I relied on the autobiography, Kirkpatrick, Collier, Fermi, and a strange book published in America by one of Mussolini's enemies, called *Mussolini, The Wild Man of Europe*. It is laced with scandal, much of which was obviously true, for Mussolini was ever the satyr, but its political viciousness makes some of the material seem suspect. It is true that Mussolini loved the ladies, perhaps too well, but the same can be said of John F. Kennedy, and only the salacious of mind have allowed Kennedy's sexual adventures to color political judgments.

Chapter 5

I used the consular report of Archie Clifton from the American embassy papers to illustrate the rise of fascism in Trieste. The material about the elections in Italy is from American embassy sources. The account of the troubles in Venice comes from embassy reports and the Kirkpatrick biography, which in large part was based on British embassy documents over the years.

Chapter 6

For Mussolini's adventures in this period, I relied on Kirkpatrick and Collier and My Autobiography. The American embassy papers were invaluable. This was the period in which the embassy began to understand that Mussolini was not just a clown or a radical adventurer, but a strong force in Italian political life. It had taken them a long time. The British were much quicker to accept his importance and to begin to pay attention to him.

Chapter 7

The sources for this chapter were the American embassy papers and the Kirkpatrick and Collier biographies and the Fermi biography. The Fermi biography contains the text of the Fascist Quadrumvirate's proclamation on the eve of the March on Rome. The American embassy's report gives the flavor of the Italian situation at the moment.

Chapter 8

Kirkpatrick has an excellent description of the processes by which Mussolini took power in 1922. The March on Rome was planned by the Fascists to be violent, but Mussolini did not want violence and subverted his own followers by using the threat of violence to secure the prime ministry. The reactions to his entry are described very well by the American embassy reports on the situation in Italy.

The story of the Lausanne conference was given to me by my friend Imre Kelen, of the team of Derso and Kelen, who were unofficial caricaturists to the League of Nations in the 1920s and 1930s. Kelen was at Lausanne at the time.

Chapter 9

The Borgese book is important to give a personal glimpse of Mussolini at this point in his life. Borgese's interview gives an insight into Mussolini's methods. He liked to talk to everyone and get their opinions, whereupon he would do precisely as he chose. But that does not mean that he was immune to advice. In a sense, he took Borgese's advice at this period, although he would never admit that.

The Matteotti case developed into a cause célèbre, which Mussolini had never foreseen, and it changed the course of his regime. He had been heading for democratization of his government. Secure in power, he felt that he could carry out the reforms he wished much better with the participation of the Socialists and Republicans. And as a reformer, Mussolini's record is clear. But his program was scotched by the Fascists, whom he had a great deal of difficulty controlling. The Matteotti case became an international scandal because of the international press, which squeezed every bit of juice out of the affair. What is remarkable is how much accurate information was disclosed, and how Mussolini allowed himself to be excoriated without fighting back. In this, as in his treatment of his enemies all through the regime, there is a distinct difference in behavior between Mussolini and Hitler and Stalin. Mussolini was oppressive, but very few people were killed in Italy, particularly as compared to Germany and Russia. Perhaps it was the Italian disposition, to whom violence is a personal and temporary phenomenon, compared to the Germanic and Slav temperaments, to whom violence comes more easily and lasts longer.

As Mussolini almost immediately recognized, the Matteotti affair was the turning point in his government, and the killing was most certainly the result of some ill-considered words spoken to Giovanni Marinelli, who took them literally and acted on them.

Chapter 10

Mussolini's autobiography was the key to this chapter. The material from the London *Times* comes from the records of the American embassy, as does the very extensive report on Italy in the London *Daily Mail*. As my friend Reynolds Packard, correspondent for United Press Associations in Rome in the 1930s observed, Mussolini spent enormous amounts of money cajoling the international press.

Chapter 11

As a journalist himself, Mussolini understood the press of the world and its motivations. He had very little use for the press except as he controlled it for his own purposes. His encounter with the British press was typical of his relations with the international press. He considered most reporters to be Socialists and thus in league with his enemies.

Chapter 12

Most interesting about the Mussolini relationship with the world was his acceptance in the 1920s, when he was lionized worldwide for his accomplishments in bringing Italy out of chaos. His "War of the Wheat" was a fine success, and he used it to build Italy in the eyes of the world. Even Winston Churchill came to visit him and remarked candidly that if he had been an Italian he would have become a Fascist. All of this was quickly forgotten when Mussolini invaded Ethiopia. Then when he sided with Franco in Spain, he turned the whole liberal press of the world against him. This process is as revealing about the press as it is about Mussolini and his fascist regime.

Chapter 13

Mussolini's satyriasis made a field day for the press, which continued all his life. Richard Collier delves into it with gusto. I found it to be no more important to his political life than a common cold. His wife Rachele never came to his office when he was a newspaper editor nor did she interfere in his political life. His other great love, Clara Petacci, was interested only in her personal relations with him. John Bond, in his biographical study, makes much of the "marriage" between Mussolini and Giovanna D' Alsier of Trento. A book about Margherita Sarfatti was published in America in 1993, going into great detail about her love life with Mussolini. But to me, all this is no more than incidental music, no more important in Mussolini's life than Marilyn Monroe was in the life of John F. Kennedy. In fact, in a biography of Marilyn that I wrote twenty years ago, my research indicated a brief affair between Marilyn and Bobby Kennedy, but no relationship at all with John. This leads me to suspect that the Kennedy-Monroe relationship is the figment of the journalistic imagination. In the same tenor, I could find no relationship between Mussolini's political activities and his sexual life, and so, generally speaking, I eschewed the discussion as diverting from the main point. Even at the end, Mussolini felt completely alone, although shortly before his encounter with the partisans, he tried to save both Rachele and Clara. Rachele did his bidding and was saved. Clara insisted on following him and was destroyed. Her last words, as they stood up against the wall, about to be shot down, were "Aren't you glad I followed you to the end?" There is no record that Mussolini answered the question.

Chapter 14

Had international affairs gone differently, Mussolini would have gone down in history as the defender of the peace in the 1930s. That is what he was. His failure at that time is largely to be laid at the door of France and England, who emasculated his four-power peace pact at a time when Hitler could have been brought into it. Had the British and French not stuck stubbornly to the restrictions of Versailles, World War II might have been avoided. The breakup of Germany in 1920 contained all the elements that brought on the war; the establishment of the "bastard" state of Czechoslovakia, the partition of Germany; and the allocation of Danzig and the Polish Corridor to Poland. Hitler's designs on Austria were a natural outcome of the breakup of the Hapsburg Empire, but Italy alone resisted them in 1934, and as long as possible, in the face of the growing might of Germany. In fact, one might attribute most of the sins that brought on World War II to Versailles, including the Pacific War, which primarily was the result of the refusal of the Western powers to grant equality to the Japanese and Chinese. The proof of the pudding is in the eating. And in 1993, three-quarters of a century after Versailles, the changes made in the world map there all have vanished. Historically speaking, Versailles was one of the great disasters of the world, prompted entirely by hatred and greed on the part of the Western European allies, and it was seen as a disaster at the time by the Americans, who refused to participate in the world of Britain and France's making. The Italians were not heard, their hopes for empire were ignored, and the basis for the overrunning of Ethiopia was also set at Versailles. Mussolini learned that he could not trust the British, whom he once admired, and they threw him into alliance with Hitler, whom secretly he detested.

Chapter 15

In the 1930s the Americans obviously did not know what to think about Mussolini. They were impressed by his anticommunism and confused by his anti-socialism, and as yet naziism offered no threats. Mussolini tried hard to assure the peace of Europe, and when he failed, he chose to go it alone and build his own empire. The British, who encouraged his colonial efforts at first as a buffer against France, turned against him, prompted by public opinion, which made the breach between Britain and Italy irreparable. But the British did not have the moral courage to go all the way and impose economic sanctions against Italy in a way that would have hurt—an oil embargo. Barring that, Mussolini triumphed in Africa. And his course of empire was set.

Chapter 16

The beginning of the Spanish Civil War posed a difficult problem for the liberal regimes of the world. The Americans did not know how to react. When Americans enlisted in the International Brigade to fight for the Spanish government against Franco, Adolf Berle, the undersecretary of State, described their activities as "prematurely anti-Fascist." That was because the United States was having difficulties expunging the favorable image of Mussolini at home. But by 1937, the Western powers had completely alienated Mussolini and thrown him into the arms of the Germans. Literally, he had no place else to go. This change was indicated in the American embassy's reporting of Italian affairs. Suddenly in 1937 the embassy began looking for evidence of fascist wrongdoing.

Chapter 17

William L. Shirer's *Rise and Fall of the Third Reich* tells a great deal about the movement toward a German–Italian alliance, and Joseph Goebbels's diaries tell more. Mussolini dragged his heels all the way, but by 1938 there was no hope of assistance from a flatulent Britain and a paralyzed France. Hitler had his way in Austria. Then Mussolini intervened with him to stop an attack on Czechoslovakia, and the Western powers gave up and let Hitler have his way. There was no turning back then. War was inevitable. All that remained to be seen was how far the Western powers would let Hitler push them before they would turn, like a besieged water buffalo, and fight. Hitler's visit to Rome was a great success for the Italians, because the German dictator was impressed by Mussolini's apparently effortless command of his country. The course of Mussolini's anti-Semitism and imperial ambitions is traced in Dennis Mack Smith's *Mussolini's Roman Empire*. None of the Western writers who have dealt with Munich have given Mussolini proper credit for managing those negotiations, so bemused have they been with the German success and the Western failures. Munich, in a way, was Mussolini's high point as a diplomatist, and his linguistic skills made it possible, for he was the only one at the conference who spoke German, French, and English.

Chapter 18

Beginning with 1939, the diaries of Count Ciano, Mussolini's son-in-law and foreign minister, become very valuable in tracing the story of the dictator and his empire. Ciano was a shrewd observer, and he saw after a few months that Hitler was determined to pursue his course, without reference to the needs of his Italian ally. He began to advocate an arm's-length relationship, and he did his best to keep Italy out of the war he knew would be disastrous. But by this time, 1940, Mussolini was convinced that Hitler would conquer all of Europe, and Benito yearned to have some of the spoils for his own empire. He was totally bedazzled. When he got nothing from the Hitler table, after the fall of France, he determined again that he would go it alone, and extend his empire by conquering Greece.

As is described by several writers who were there, including Reynolds Packard, the Greek campaign was a fiasco, and proof positive that whatever else he had done Mussolini had not created a fighting army for Italy.

Chapter 20

Ciano is the witness to the fact that Hitler still revered Mussolini and would never forget Mussolini's act in permitting without opposition the *Anschluss* with Austria. This leads to the inference that if Mussolini had sent troops to the border in 1938 as he did in 1934, Hitler would again have backed down. This further indicates that much of the power Hitler had until 1939 was based on hyperbole and his flourishing of the sword while the Western powers were paralyzed. Even Mussolini did not suspect that Hitler was about half as strong as he painted himself to be. But by 1941, all that had changed, and with Mussolini's failure in Greece, he became very definitely second fiddle in the Axis partnership.

With the coming of war, the American reporting from Rome stopped. The reporting of Italian events continued from Switzerland and Portugal, but it was not the same. The reports depended on traveler's tales, and these were always suspect, either of being old and outdated, or of being highly fictionalized. But one mystery that has always existed in American folklore was resolved, as reported by Ciano. Why did Hitler join Japan in declaring war on America? The answer is because the Japanese government so requested, and the Rome-Berlin-Tokyo Pact was invoked. There was honor among thieves. That is why Mussolini declared war on the United States and obviously, it is why Hitler did as well.

Chapter 21

The story of the Swiss-Italian couple in Milan is from an American embassy report from Bern on conditions in Italy. The material about Ciano's trip to Germany is from his diary. The story of the Klessheim trip of Mussolini is from Ciano and the Goebbels diaries. The discussion of the Italians fighting in Africa is from the Rommel papers. The material about Hitler in the east is from *The Memoirs of Field Marshal Keitel*. The material about the Treviso meeting is from Ciano.

Chapter 22

Ciano is the source for much of the material about the Germans. Richard Collier is the source for the material about Rachele in the crisis. The detail of the meeting of the Grand Council of Fascists is from an interview with Dino Grandi conducted in London after he fled the country that year.

The story of the conspiracy between the King and Badoglio is told in *Italy Betrayed,* by Peter Tompkins.

Chapter 23

The story of the rescue of Mussolini is from Kirkpatrick and Collier and Max Ascoli's *The Fall of Mussolini.*

Chapter 24

The story of the Republic is from Kirkpatrick, Laura Fermi, and *Italy Betrayed.* Rachele's story is from Collier.

Chapter 25

The story of the end of Ciano is from Kirkpatrick.

Chapter 26

The report of the Polish observer is from the State Department archives. The material about Mussolini's last meeting with Hitler is from Collier and Kirkpatrick and Gorlitz.

Chapter 27

The story of Rachele's confrontation with Clara is from Collier, who got it from Rachele. The story of the German negotiations and the surrender of German forces in Italy is from *Operation Sunrise,* by Smith and Agarossi. The story of Mussolini's last days and hours is from Kirkpatrick and Fermi.

Index

7-1-94   137202

MAY 9 4 Rec'd
BAKER & TAYLOR BOOKS